W0007041

LENIN AND THE MENSHEVIKS

Lenin and the Mensheviks

The Persecution of Socialists under Bolshevism

by

Vera Broido

published by

Gower/Maurice Temple Smith

in 1987 (NEXT: CONTENTS) →

Published by
Gower Publishing Company Limited
Gower House
Croft Road
Aldershot
Hants GU11 3HR
England

British Library Catologuing in Publication Data

Broido, Vera
Lenin and the Mensheviks: the persecution of "socialists" under bolshevism.
1. Rossiĭskia sotsial-demokaticheskaia rabochaia partiia—History Bolshevism 2. Soviet Union—Politics and government—1917–1936
I. Title
947.084'1 PN6598.S64

ISBN 0 566 05203 2

Printed and bound in Great Britain
by Billings & Sons Limited, Worcester.

Contents

Preface

Between October 1917 and the death of Lenin in January 1924 all non-Bolshevik parties of the Left in Russia — Mensheviks, Social Revolutionaries (both Right and Left), Maximalists, Populist Socialists (*Narodnyi Sotsialisty*), Anarchists, the Jewish *Bund*, the Zionist Labour party *Poalei Tsion* and others — were virtually destroyed. Some lucky individuals either escaped abroad or were exiled there; the rest, if not shot, lived out their lives in prisons, camps and remote places of banishment. Only handfuls of 'invincibles' lasted a few years longer in deepest 'underground', while funds and personnel dwindled from year to year.

Although this may be numerically a small issue compared with the wholesale slaughter of the 'bourgeois' parties by the Bolsheviks, it deserves greater attention than it has so far received; for it contributes greatly to a proper understanding of the Russian revolution. General histories of the Russian revolution mention it only as part of the total terror. More specialised books, such as Leonard Schapiro's *The Origin of the Communist Autocracy*,[1] accord it more attention but only as a subsidiary topic, and no work has yet been wholly devoted to the subject. The present work should go some way towards filling that gap.

The material available in archives in Amsterdam, Paris, New York, Stanford and Jerusalem, and in private hands, is so abundant that it proved absolutely necessary to delimit the scope of the book. I have therefore given particular attention to one party, the Mensheviks. In this I was influenced by several considerations. Firstly, the Mensheviks were alone among major Russian socialist parties in repudiating *on principle* all armed resistance or conspiracy against the Bolshevik government, so that their persecution cannot be explained in terms of legitimate self-defence. Secondly, a considerable number of memoirs and monographs had been written by leading Mensheviks to guide me in my work. Above all there is the fact that — to quote L.H. Haimson's Introduction to the book which he edited on the Mensheviks — 'of all the currents in the Russian post-revolutionary emigration ... the Mensheviks had proved by far the hardiest. Through these years of wars and upheavals, and of the enforced migrations that they imposed upon survivors of the Menshevik party — from Russia to Germany, from Germany to France, and eventually to the United States — these survivors had managed, to a remarkable degree, to keep a social community and a political culture in being.'[2]

I was influenced also by a more personal consideration. I come from a Menshevik family: both my parents, Eva and Mark Broido, were prominent members of the party and I shared with them both their Siberian exile under the Tsar and their foreign exile under the Bolsheviks. I feel that I too have inherited some of this culture. This makes me more confident in writing about Mensheviks than about other Russian socialist trends. Moreover, I have in my possession many unpublished letters from Mensheviks in soviet prisons and exile.

But while the main focus of my book is on the persecution of the Mensheviks, much light is also shed on the persecution of other Russian socialists and Anarchists, whose fate was much the same.

I should like to express my very real gratitude to Ellen Dahrendorf, Alec Nove, Boris Sapir, my husband Norman Cohn and my son Nik Cohn, for reading my manuscript. Their corrections and suggestions, factual and stylistic, have been invaluable. My thanks also go to Marina Voikhanskaia for helping me with the Bibliography.

I am much beholden to the Hoover Institution, which, by giving me a grant, enabled me to explore the riches of the archive collected by my late, dear friend Boris Nicolaevsky. I would also like to thank the Hoover Institution Archive for permission to quote from material in the Boris I. Nicolaevsky Collection; and the W. Averell Harriman Institute for Advanced Study of the Soviet Union, successor to the Russian Institute of Columbia University, New York, for permission to quote from the papers in the Inter-University Project on the history of Menshevik Movement.

The system of transliteration adopted here for Russian names of places and persons differs from that of the Library of Congress in two respects: diacritical marks are omitted and the more familiar spelling is retained for such well-known names as Maxim Gorky (not Maksim Gorkii), Trotsky (not Trotskii), Kerensky and Nicolaevsky.

As from 1 February 1918, the Gregorian calendar (new style — NS), in general use in the West, was introduced in Russia, replacing the Julian calendar (Old Style — OS) which ran thirteen days behind. Thus the Bolshevik revolution occurred on 25 October (OS) or on 7 November (NS). All dates before February 1918 are given in Old

Style, all later dates in New Style.

The English equivalent of a *versta* (verst) is two-thirds of a mile or fractionally over one kilometer; that of a *pud* or *pood*, about 36 pounds or 16½ kilograms.

1 Bolshevism versus Menshevism

It is quite outside the scope of the present book to deal in detail with the complexities of Menshevik and Bolshevik ideologies, but for the story to be comprehensible at all, a short survey of the historical background is needed.

Both Bolsheviks and Mensheviks originally belonged to the same party — the marxist Russian Social Democratic Workers' party (abbreviated in Russian to RSDRP, or simply SD). In 1883 a group of Russian expatriates in Geneva — Vera Zasulich, Pavel Axelrod, Georgii Plekhanov and Lev Deich — founded the 'Group for the Liberation of Labour' (*Grupa osvobozhdenia truda*), from which marxist teaching rapidly spread to Russia, giving rise to dozens of marxist groups in industrial and university towns. In 1898 an attempt was made to fuse some of these groups into a party, and a secret congress was convened in Minsk. Unfortunately the tsarist political police arrested almost all the participants even before the constitution of the new party could be properly formulated. Meanwhile in 1895, several marxist groups in St Petersburg had merged into one larger one and formed 'The Militant Union for the Liberation of the Working Class' (*Soiuz borby za osvobozhdenie rabochevo klassa*), which together with the Geneva group laid the foundations of the future RSDRP.[1]

Marxism was but one of several currents within the Russian revolutionary movement of the nineteenth century. The writings of Marx and Engels became available in Russian translation in 1872, but the prevailing revolutionary trend at that time was populism, which invested its revolutionary hopes mainly in the peasants. However, the populists, the *Narodniki*, had failed to rouse the peasants and had been devastated by the tsarist police in spite of all their conspiratorial skills. Many young Russian revolutionaries became disillusioned with populism and were looking for a new faith. Axelrod, Zasulich, Deich and Plekhanov — all four prominent populists in the past — found that faith in marxism. Georgii Plekhanov became 'the father of Russian marxism' when he popularised it in 1882, 1883, and 1884.

The effect was revivifying. Here was a new socialist theory which claimed to be scientific and to follow universal laws of history; it opened up new fields of activity among the workers; and it allowed the young Russian movement to join the mighty stream of European socialism.[2]

Was marxism relevant to Russia? Not really. Marx's predictions presupposed an established bourgeois society with a legal order and with political freedoms; and a 'class-conscious' proletariat engaged in a 'class war' with the bourgeoisie. Russia was an absolutist monarchy without political freedoms; it had not yet experienced a bourgeois revolution; and its bourgeoisie and working class were in their infancy. Moreover, much of Russian industry being state owned, there was no clear conflict between capitalists and workers. As Pavel Axelrod rightly said in 1881, there was no real class war in Russia, only a conflict between tsarism and a revolutionary intelligentsia supported by dissatisfied individuals of all classes.[3] A long way to go, it would seem, before any of Marx's 'laws of history' could begin to operate; and a long time before a socialist revolution could take place. This meant postponing the realisation of one of the most cherished hopes of Russian radicals. As the Social Revolutionary* Steinberg said: 'Russia at the dawn of the twentieth century knew no more magic word than "revolution". The idea of the revolution was ... loved and revered by all who dreamt of liberty ... there was enchantment in the very sound of the word....'[4]

What gave Russian marxists courage was the fact that both sides in the class war were developing very fast in Russia.** Furthermore, the working class was showing itself to be receptive to revolutionary propaganda. When the early populists tried to carry revolutionary propaganda to the peasants they were met with incomprehension and even hostility in the villages, but when the same populists went among urban workers they found them more approachable. They even stimulated the formation of the first two working-class associations

*The Social Revolutionary party (SR) was formed by veteran populists at the turn of the century. It was not marxist and continued in many ways the *Narodniki* tradition. Thus it was mainly oriented towards the peasants and had a terrorist wing.

**The number of workers in industrial enterprises employing over a hundred workers grew from 706,000 in 1865 to 1,432,000 in 1890. And as their numbers grew, workers became more self assertive: there were 29 strikes between 1878 and 1880, involving 35,000 workers, in support of demands for higher wages and shorter hours of work. The strikes were not always successful but they did lead to the introduction of labour laws. The factory law of 1882, the first ever to be issued in Russia, prohibited work by children under twelve years of age and restricted to eight hours the work of those between twelve and fifteen years. The second act, of 1885, prohibited, in some industries, night work by women and adolescents below the age of seventeen. But for the rest the average working day remained twelve and a half hours, and in the textile industry up to fifteen hours.[5]

—the South-Russian Union of Workers formed in Odessa in 1875 and the Northern Union of Russian Workers founded in St Petersburg in 1878, each with over two hundred members. Within a year both unions were closed down by the tsarist police and their members arrested, but soon there were workers' groups in Rostov-on-Don, Saratov, Kiev and Kharkov.[6] These were hopeful signs, certainly, but only a strong dose of wishful thinking could have blinded the enthusiastic marxists to the inappropriateness of their marxism. In the event, all Russian marxists eventually modified their marxism in one way or another, or shed it altogether.

The St Petersburg *Soiuz borby* included some very exceptional people — Alexander Potresov, Liubov and Stepan Radchenko (both participated in the First Congress at Minsk), Krzhizhanovskii, Gurvich (better known as Fedor Dan), Vladimir Ulianov (better known as Lenin) and Iulii Tsederbaum (better known as Martov). All were in their twenties and some, for instance Martov,* had already experienced prison and exile. The group at once began organising secret workers' groups in the factories and producing and distributing propaganda broadsheets, leaflets and brochures. It was difficult and dangerous work, as police spies and *agents provocateurs* tracked the propagandists to the very gates of the factories; even trams going to factory districts 'were infested with police spies'.[8] Often the most promising workers' groups were ferreted out by the police, and soon the central group itself was decimated: in December 1895, Lenin and several other members of the group along with many of the most promising workers were arrested; in January 1896 it was the turn of Martov and many more workers, so that the total number of arrests amounted to a hundred. And though Fedor Dan, Alexander Potresov, Martov's younger brother Sergei (Ezhov) and several others moved up to fill their places, they too were arrested in the course of 1896.[9]

A whole year passed before the members of the group were sentenced (without trial, by administrative order) to three years each in Siberian exile. Martov and several others were sent to unhealthy and isolated parts of arctic Siberia, where they were cut off from all contact with the outer world for nine months each year.[10] Lenin was among the lucky ones — he was exiled to a village in the Minussinsk district, blessed with a temperate climate and great natural beauty.**

*At the age of eighteen, when a student in St Petersburg, Martov was arrested and after some time in prison exiled to the Polish-Lithuanian town of Vilno. There, however, he continued his revolutionary work. In 1894 he helped to compose the handbook *On Agitation* by A. Kremer and S. Gozhanskii, which was later used by the St Petersburg group in their work.[7]

**I speak from experience: as a child I spent several years in Minussinsk — the first summer in Kuragino, just such a village as Lenin's Shushenskoie — when my mother, Eva Broido, was in exile there.

Married to Nadezhda Kurpskaia and having both her and her mother to minister to his comforts, he went on hunting trips with fellow exiles and kept up a regular correspondence with family and comrades at home and fellow exiles in Siberia. He received newspapers and books, even from abroad, and seems to have done a prodigious amount of reading.

Meanwhile marxist influence had spread in European Russia and local committees of the *Soiuz borby* had been formed in Moscow, Kiev, Ekaterinoslavl, Poltava, Nizhnii Novgorod, Kharkov, Vilno and Minsk.[11] What was urgently needed was a centre which would provide theoretical guidelines to all these organisations. When Lenin, Potresov and Martov returned from Siberia, they met together and decided that this need would best be served by a newspaper, to be published abroad and then smuggled into Russia. Accordingly, the three men —the 'triple alliance', as they called themselves — left Russia and founded the newspaper *Iskra* (The Spark — that would light the flame) and the journal *Zaria* (The Dawn) in Munich in the winter of 1900–1901 (the publication was later transferred to London and then to Geneva). Pavel Axelrod, Vera Zasulich and Georgii Plekhanov (Lev Deich had been arrested when on a secret journey into Russia) joined the editorial board so that the two component parts of the party were brought together.[12]

It is more than probable that already greater ideological differences existed within the *Iskra* group than its members were aware of. During the four years of prison and exile Lenin had almost certainly started on his separate course. But the excitement over their joint venture made for harmony and at first all went well; in particular, the friendship between Martov and Lenin had never seemed warmer. At the *Iskra* editorial office everybody admired Lenin's enormous energy and his organisational talents — Martov called him *primus inter pares*. But soon misgivings arose among Lenin's co-editors. He was found to be intolerant and often rude towards comrades in Russia whenever they disagreed with the line taken by the *Iskra*, and did not scruple to use underhand methods in dealing with party committees in Russia; he was enrolling and training some unsavoury characters as distributors of *Iskra*; he was intriguing against and undermining his opponents by every means at his disposal, fair or foul. Honesty among comrades was such an integral part of revolutionary ethics that his co-editors were slow to see what was happening and they completely failed to recognise that Lenin was secretly building up his empire and selecting his troops.

It was inevitable that a conflict would develop between Lenin and the rest of the *Iskra* group. It came to a head at the so-called Second Congress* of the party, which met in July–August 1903, first at

*The First Congress had been the ill-fated gathering at Minsk in 1898.

Brussels and then in London. Among the items for discussion was that of membership. Lenin proposed that only those who were prepared to become 'professional revolutionaries', that is full-time conspirators, should qualify for membership of the party. Opposition came from Martov, who agreed that under Russian conditions a strictly conspiratorial core was essential, but insisted that it should be embedded in a wide party. He argued that Lenin's proposal would exclude many *bona fide* adherents of the party who, for one reason or another, could not become full-time conspirators. He therefore proposed a less narrow membership clause. It would seem that most of those present failed to see the implications of Lenin's proposal and it was passed, though with only a small majority. This majority was reversed within three months but Lenin seized the opportunity to name his followers Bolsheviks (majority men) and his opponents Mensheviks (minority men).[13]*

It soon became evident that the party was divided not just on the issue of membership but on the very nature and aims of a socialist party in Russia.[14] And in fact, the two sections became all but in name two separate parties.** The Menshevik party was broadly democratic (Martov's 'wide' party), allowing both intellectuals and workers to join and to acquire influence. Its leadership was collective rather than individual — Martov, for instance, was often in the minority and never laid claim to exclusive leadership. When serious differences of opinion arose, as over the support of the 1914 war, *** they were not allowed to split the party. Ideologically, the Mensheviks came to see their commitment to marxism as a kind of sacred trust on behalf of the workers. In the words of Pavel Axelrod (who, together with Vera Zasulich, Alexander Potresov and eventually Plekhanov, had sided with Martov), the 'essence of menshevism' consisted in creating an independent, politically conscious working class. Pavel Axelrod, who

*One might wonder at the apparently 'meek' acceptance of this nickname by Martov and his followers. The fact is that at first they simply disregarded Lenin's jibe as an attempt to divide the party where they were hoping for an agreement. In any case they regained the majority by November 1903 and did not bother, or probably thought it undignified, to repudiate the name Lenin had bestowed on them. Later on, when the name had become established, they might even have taken a certain pride in it — Martov said that it was sometimes one's moral duty to be in a minority.

**For many years both used the name RSDRP — RSDRP (b) and RDSRP (m). When the Bolsheviks changed their name to Communists in 1918, the Mensheviks still kept the old name RSDRP or SDs. But to most Russians they remained Bolsheviks and Mensheviks.

***The so-called 'defensists' supported the war effort because they considered the war to be a defensive war. The 'internationalists' opposed it on principle. Both Martov and Lenin participated in the international socialist anti-war conference at Zimmerwald, but Martov did not share Lenin's 'defeatism' — Lenin believed that only a military defeat would bring tsarism down and therefore desired it.

became the great old man of menshevism, much beloved and respected by all its factions, was typical of the essential moral rectitude and humanity that was also part of the 'essence of menshevism'.[15]

Mensheviks working inside Russia, the so-called *praktiki*, had to display as much personal courage and 'professionalism' as the Bolsheviks, but they refused to make a virtue out of conspiracy and used legal methods when they were possible — as they became, at least partially, after 1905. They concentrated on organising literacy classes for workers,* as well as more advanced ones for the study of marxism and the history of the European working-class movement. So generations of literate and 'politically conscious' (*soznatelnyi*) workers were raised. The Mensheviks also initiated working-class organisations such as trade unions, cooperatives, mutual help funds, workers' libraries and clubs. In all these organisations they encouraged workers to develop their own initiative (*samodeiatelnost*). During strikes they helped to formulate economic demands as well as broader, political ones. Mensheviks had arrived at the conclusion that no socialist revolution would take place until the working class was strong enough to carry it out. Maxim Gorky (a Russian writer who was a personal friend of Lenin's, but often critical of him) shared their view when he said in January 1918: 'A social revolution without a proletariat is an absurdity, a senseless utopia.'[16] Social revolution was still the ultimate aim, but it had to be postponed for the time being.

The Bolshevik party developed into a hierarchical, centralist party (Lenin's 'monolithic' party). Lenin was preoccupied above all with the idea of revolution and with the seizure of power. For this purpose he was training cadres as troops of the future revolution, while the party leadership was to be its General Staff. Workers who were prepared to become whole-time professionals were accepted into the party, but the working class as such figured very little in Lenin's immediate plans, only as a 'revolutionary force' and the 'vanguard' of the remote revolution. Lenin had very little confidence in the ability of workers to acquire political consciousness and he ridiculed Menshevik activities among the workers as 'trade unionism' (which did not prevent him from trying to dominate them). Inside his party, discipline was strict and dissent was not encouraged. In 1921, he was to forbid all opposition within the party on threat of expulsion.[17] In effect Lenin almost always got his way by the sheer force of personality. But it is an interesting fact that, in spite of the strictest party discipline and conspiracy, the Bolshevik party was much more

*For instance, my mother, Eva Broido, at one time taught the future President of the Soviet Union, Mikhail Kalinin, reading and writing. He was then a worker recently come from the village.

often penetrated by police spies and *agents provocateurs* than the Mensheviks.

The rift between the two parties went deep, yet on both sides there were many who deplored it. Repeatedly, and even after the October coup, many leading Bolsheviks wanted to heal the breach. Fedor Dan quotes from an open letter of the Bolshevik Central Committee: 'Disunion oppresses us, surely no less than it oppresses you. Could we not make it up?' After analysing the differences, it goes on to ask: 'are they so serious that for their sake the social-democratic party should be split into two parties? . . . Everything leads to the same conclusion: that there are no substantial and serious obstacles to a reunion.'[18] Trotsky, in 1907, affirmed that 'the differences of opinion between our factions are so insignificant, so uncertain, so minute, that they seem like chance wrinkles on the great brow of the revolution.'[19] The Mensheviks on their side never lost the hope of reunion. In 1907 Maxim Gorky heard Martov address the party congress in London: 'that astonishingly attractive man spoke with youthful passion, and it seemed that he felt particularly deeply the tragedy of the split, the pain of misunderstanding.' He heard Martov plead: 'the split must be overcome, the party is too weak to be broken in two.'[20] But Lenin remained stubbornly opposed to all attempts at reunification. When he felt strong enough he convened a party congress in 1912, proclaimed his group to be the true social democratic party of Russia and solemnly expelled Mensheviks from it. He could not accept anything short of total capitulation. It would indeed seem that, in the words of Leonard Schapiro, 'the Mensheviks were the first of the many socialist victims of the illusion . . . that genuine co-operation with communists was possible on any terms other than complete surrender.'[21] By 1918 Martov saw it clearly enough when he wrote to Alexander Stein in Berlin: 'no bridge is possible [with Bolshevism] except outright surrender, since Bolshevism does not admit the idea of an opposition party. . . .'[22]

Lenin never forgave the Mensheviks for not having 'surrendered' to him in 1903. He constantly raged against them and, according to his wife, often cursed them in his sleep.[23] His biographer, Louis Fischer, quotes from the story told by a young woman who visited Lenin in Geneva and who on one occasion went for a climb with him. Arriving at the top of the mountain they were confronted by a magnificent panorama and she impulsively turned to her companion to share her delight with him — and there he was, sitting on a boulder, staring gloomily at the ground and muttering: 'Ah! these Mensheviks — how they mess everything up!'[24] It is difficult to interpret Lenin's pathological hatred for the Mensheviks. Was it because they had been his closest comrades and his closest opponents? Because they were the first to challenge his idea of himself as the only true interpreter of the will of history? Or because they were a reminder of a shared past which he had forsaken? For a man not generally given to doubts or regrets, he allowed the Mensheviks to irritate and annoy him beyond reasonable measure. Towards Mortov personally, Lenin's feelings were ambivalent — he had every reason to hate him, yet he seemed to have kept a sentimental attachment to him to the end of his life. Maxim Gorky remembered Lenin saying to him: 'I wish I could have Martov with me — he was such a splendid comrade!'[25]

Lenin's character, his beliefs, and his motives remain something of a mystery to the present day.[26] A secretive man, he kept his own counsel. It is however comparatively easy to discard the many trappings of the Lenin legend that had been built up around him by his worshippers inside and outside Russia. What, then, was he really like? He was undoubtedly a man of great will power; a man of iron self-discipline which made him give up chess and smoking because they took up too much time, and forego listening to music because it made him soft. His intellect was quick and sharp, but more shrewd than subtle. He had the mind of a chess player — always playing for advantage and watching for openings. He had a biting tongue, but he was not a brilliant orator or writer. He was, however, a prolific writer: he is said to have written some ten million words in the thirty years between 1893 and 1923.

In his early days in St Petersburg, Lenin seems to have been less masterful than he was to become later. He was 'ready to learn' from the older Russian marxists abroad — he considered himself their 'pupil'. When he visited them in Switzerland in the spring of 1895, he sat at their feet and Axelrod described him as 'serious, businesslike and modest'.[27] But when Martov met him in St Petersburg later in the same year, he already observed in him 'contempt and distrust of people', and 'rudeness' in polemics.[28] Gradually Martov began to distrust him thoroughly. It became impossible to argue with Lenin. He branded anybody as traitor who did not share his opinions and he flew into violent rages at those who opposed him (though usually these rages were witnessed only by his wife). In its obituary of Lenin, the Menshevik paper *Sotsialisticheskii Vestnik* (Socialist Courier) described him as a 'typical leader of a sect', 'aflame with his idea', convinced that 'the party — is me! the working class — is me! communism — is me! the proletarian state — is me!'[29]

Lenin held his ideas to be sacrosanct, but he changed them easily and often. Not for lack of decisiveness — he despised wobblers — but because strategy or tactics demanded it; and these too he changed according to particular situations. His changes of ideas were often so drastic that his own comrades could not at first believe it. Repeatedly he adopted the very ideas that he had previously attacked in his opponents.* His changes of tactics were always accompanied by abuse and derision: he had inexhaustible reserves of invective and many quite ordinary and inoffensive nouns acquired a pejorative flavour when he used them. But whichever was Lenin's dominant idea of the moment, he hammered it home in word after word and page after page in a repetitive, hypnotic manner — like driving in a nail,[30] said Victor Serge, or like a village schoolmaster drilling into his pupils the basic principles of his subject,[31] said Angelica Balabanova. He was a bit of a pedant, with his orderliness and punctuality, which he practised himself and demanded of others. But there was also a streak of recklessness in him and he was fond of quoting Napoleon's 'On s'engage et puis on voit'.[32]

Lenin could never bear to be anything but first in any situation: first at school (gold medallist),[33] first at the *Iskra*, first in the party and eventually first in Soviet Russia. Not because he was ambitious for himself, but because he believed that he was the best — for the party and for the country. He did not seek popularity and did not want to be worshipped — Angelica Balabanova called him 'an impersonal dictator'[34] and Louis Fischer described him as one in whom 'political fanaticism combined with sobriety'.[35] A fanatic he certainly was — not of the heart but of the brain.[36] Bertrand Russell who had a long talk with Lenin in 1920 found him 'without a trace of hauteur', 'entirely destitute of self-importance'; but also rather inhuman: '... an embodied theory', one who 'despised a great many people' and had 'little psychological imagination'.[37] This lack of psychological imagination was perhaps his greatest failing — he neither understood nor allowed for human limitations. He 'never confused feelings with politics', says his biographer Louis Fischer. He was puritanical in his private life.[38] Even at the height of his power he was modest in his appearance and in his personal tastes and needs, and even kindly. We are told that he was kind to children. He also loved cats, perhaps because he felt an affinity to them — Vera Zasulich used to call him 'cat' or even 'wicked cat' in the *Iskra* days.[39]

Lenin was quite amoral in his politics. Like the nineteenth-century Russian Jacobin and Anarchist Peter Zaichnevskii, in many ways his model, he held that enemies should be exterminated by any method and was quite ruthless and merciless in his dealings with them. He also authorised bank robberies and sham marriages with heiresses to replenish party funds. He was quite unaware of the corrupting effect of such methods on personalities less stable than his own. Angelica

*In 1917 he cribbed his agricultural policy from the SRs and in 1921 his New Economic Policy from the Mensheviks.

Balabanova observed that Lenin's Bolshevik party seemed to harbour a germ of corruption within it, which increased with power and, spreading outwards, bred and attracted careerists and opportunists.[40]

Lenin undoubtedly believed himself to be the bearer of a historical mission. Hence his unlimited faith in himself, his intolerance towards rivals, real or potential, and his readiness to 'use' (one of his favourite terms) individuals or even whole classes for his own political ends. These are also the characteristics of megalomania, though he showed no outward signs of it. He was a secret megalomaniac, as there are secret drinkers.

Lenin's preoccupation with the problem of armed uprising and seizure of power became over the years a true obsession. In his mind he was forever planning and preparing for it. He worked out the last technical details of the uprising. In a brochure written in 1906, he proposed the formation of 'battle units' of ten, five, or even three persons, preferably consisting of close and trusted associates from the same factory or the same neighbourhood, which would train secretly in preparation for the armed uprising. Such a rising, he said, would be best carried out 'towards the end of summer or the beginning of autumn'. He also perfected the system of secret cells, later so effectively applied in Russian as well as international Communist practice.[41] All this stood him in good stead during the summer and autumn of 1917.

2 *The February Revolution and the October Coup*

The 1917 revolution had a sort of rehearsal in 1905/6. It was sparked off by the shooting down of a peaceful crowd in front of the Winter Palace on the 'bloody' Sunday, 22 January 1905. This 'unprovoked butchery', as the London *Times* of 24 January called it,[1] ended the age-old devotion of the Russian people to the Little Father Tsar and led to a mini-revolution. It was suppressed by the tsarist government but not before the workers and their socialist mentors had shown their strength by conducting several impressive strikes and by instituting (on Menshevik initiative)[2] the soviets which were to play such a crucial role in later developments. The liberal bourgeoisie took the important step of forming its first political party — the party of Constitutional Democrats (*Ka-De-ty*, or Kadets). On his side the tsar yielded some ground by proclaiming a (moderate) constitution and allowing a (modest) parliament, the Duma, to be elected. But since he made the Duma unworkable by constantly dissolving and then reconvening it (there were to be four Dumas altogether), and by allowing his police almost as much scope as before (in fact all social-democratic deputies of the second Duma were arrested and sent to Siberia), this exercise in semi-legal democracy hardly enabled Russian 'parliamentarians' to learn the technique of government or statesmanship. As the perceptive historian W.H. Chamberlin has said: 'the heavy hand of repression on the middle class denied the opposition the opportunity to develop administrative experience and responsibility and imparted to the political life of pre-war Russia the unreality of a debating club.'[3] So that when tsarism fell early in 1917, there was only a bunch of half-baked Duma politicians to take over the government.

As for the socialist parties, none of them had expected the revolution to break out when it did. Discouraged by the failure of 1905, they expected nothing for a long time — not perhaps in their lifetime,[4] said Lenin. And indeed but for the war, which undermined the autocracy and fed popular discontent, he might have been right. The revolution broke out with elemental force, entirely spontaneously, not masterminded or directed by any socialist party.[5] It began inconspicuously on Women's Day, 25 February (old style) — Women's Day like May Day being one of the days that the socialists had taught the workers to celebrate. After mass meetings and speeches in some of the factories, crowds of women workers poured into the streets of Petrograd * demanding bigger bread rations, food shortages being the cause of much discontent among workers. The women's demonstration passed off peacefully on the whole; but next day the workers of one of the biggest Petrograd factories, the Putilov Works, joined the demonstration. On that day, 26 February, there were 197,000 workers on strike in Petrograd, out of a total of 400,000, and mass meetings and demonstrations now spilled over into the centre of the city. Police were guarding the bridges of the Neva, but the demonstrators crossed over on the ice of the frozen river, shouting cheerfully to policemen and onlookers. By 27 February the strike was general and students joined in. Surprisingly, the Cossacks stood by without attacking the marchers.

The tsar, from his distant Army Headquarters, ordered suppression of all disorders. Some hundred ringleaders from among the workers were arrested and so were some of the mutinous soldiers; and some 'loyal troops' did fire on the crowds on Sunday 28 February killing about four hundred and wounding another forty. But after that these troops seemed to melt away. By 29 February some regiments of the garrison mutinied and there was general fraternisation. In just *four* days all was over. The last action by the jubilant crowd was the burning down of the District Court in Shpalernaia Street and the famous prison (colloquially known as *Predvarilka*) next door to it. Many other prisons were forced and political and criminal prisoners set free. Tsarist ministers were arrested and police officials queued up to be taken into custody, which they very sensibly preferred to the chance of being lynched in the street. On 1 March the whole country was already in a state of revolution, with on the whole very little bloodshed.

The bemused tsar was forced to abdicate and the almost equally bemused Duma formed a Provisional Government on 2 March — 'provisional' until a Constituent Assembly could be elected to decide on the future form of government. Everybody urged the Duma to assume power, as this seemed the most legitimate measure, but in fact, again on Menshevik initiative,[6] a Soviet of Workers' and Soldiers' Deputies, about 250 strong, had already assembled at the Tauride Palace in Petrograd on 29 February and it was the Soviet that

*St Petersburg, because of its German-sounding name, was renamed Petrograd during the war.

immediately assumed control of the situation. The Soviet distributed food and fuel supplies, while its 'workers' militia' was keeping order in the capital. Being very close to the masses the Soviet enjoyed more genuine authority than the Duma.

Elections to similar soviets, all based on the experience of 1905, were held with lightning speed all over the country, so that at the All-Russian Congress of Soviets held on 11 April there were 479 delegates present, representing 138 local soviets, seven armies and 39 smaller military units.[7] The Petrograd Soviet, having grown very large and incorporating representatives of provincial soviets, was declared the All-Russian Soviet. At its head was the Central Executive Committee, known as VTsIK, and the Praesidium of the VTsIK.

Thus began the troubled history of the dual power (or 'dual impotence' as Trotsky called it)[8] in which the Provisional Government was by far the weaker partner. The Constituent Assembly, to be elected by general, direct, equal and secret ballot, was to decide on the new constitution and the government, and was also expected to introduce land reform and other urgent reforms. In the meantime, the Provisional Government introduced a truly democratic order.[9] Lenin, who arrived in Russia from abroad in April 1917, described it later as 'the freest country in the world'.[10] But the Provisional Government was beset on all sides by mostly insoluble problems, partly bequeathed by the old order and the war, partly arising from the overwhelming desire of the Russian people to end the war and return to normal conditions. The country was starving, the army was demoralised by repeated defeats and the criminal ineptitude of its command, and the Russian empire was falling apart — Finland and Poland and the Ukraine were all clamouring for independence. Nor was the peasantry prepared to wait for land reform.

The Provisional Government was composed mainly of members of the Kadet party, including one industrialist, one manufacturer, and one *zemstvo** liberal. It thus represented a cross section of the Russian middle class, which had been mildly 'forward-looking' and even 'revolutionary' under absolutism, but was becoming frightened by the rapidly growing power of the revolutionary masses. The liberal bourgeoisie, weak and uncertain of its aims, now backed away from the revolution, so that by mid-summer of 1917 Martov observed 'certain segments of the bourgeoisie rapidly going over to the camp of reaction. ... the Russian bourgeoisie is no longer a revolutionary factor.'[11]

Tsarist tyranny, which had so fatally devitalised the bourgeois

*A *zemstvo* was an organ of local self government in provincial and rural districts, introduced by Tsar Alexander II.

intellingentsia, had had a very different effect on the masses. It had generated a constant ferment and a suppressed energy which erupted in the revolution; and the success of the revolution proved intoxicating. The Petrograd Soviet, in its early days, was in a fever of jubilation and celebration. Small delegations from factories and army units were constantly arriving with 'fraternal greetings', to be received with tumultuous cheers. Each prominent socialist returning from Siberian exile or from abroad was given a festive reception and immediately co-opted into an already enormous VTsIK.* The VTsIK was in almost permanent session and its indefatigable chairman, the Menshevik Chkheidze, hardly ever returned home to sleep but simply took short naps on the floor in one of the many rooms of the Tauride Palace. No one who had witnessed it could ever forget the ebullience, the excitement of those crowded sessions.** And not only in the Tauride Palace, everywhere in the working class districts of the capital there was a sense of triumph. On the Obvodnyi Kanal (where my family lived at the time) spontaneous meetings sprang up almost hourly on street corners and were addressed by local workers, often incoherent with excitement, by students or by orators specially summoned from the Soviet. The mood of the masses was optimistic and confident and there were no limits to their expectations.

The Mensheviks proved unable to harness this revolutionary potential to any practical purpose. They were blinded by their rigid marxist formula of 'bourgeois revolution first, socialist revolution later' and tried to restrain the masses. They preached self-abnegation and patience to them, told them to stand aside until such times as the bourgeoisie had built a solid capitalist system. This made no sense to workers and peasants — why should they renounce the power that was in their hands already? They did not trust their former oppressors, the capitalists and the landlords, and they did not trust the Kadets. Practical politics clashed with socialist theory and the Mensheviks were paralysed by indecision. They felt strongly that to plunge backward Russia into a socialist experiment was to court disaster. On the other hand to preach abstract marxism to the masses at that particular moment was obviously sheer folly. Their indecision cost the Mensheviks their political future. In early 1917 they were at

*The festive reception given to Lenin at the Finland station in Petrograd has been falsely portrayed by soviet cinema and writers as a unique occasion. In fact, whenever a well-known socialist leader, of whatever party, was expected in Petrograd it was a routine procedure to give him a hero's welcome at the station.

**Something of the atmosphere survives in the memoirs of N. Sukhanov and in *The Russian Revolution* by Raphail Abramovitch. My own recollections are mainly second-hand, from accounts by my father, Mark Broido, who was a member of the VTsIK and head of the Secretariat of the Petrograd Soviet at the time.

the height of their popularity; together with the Social Revolutionaries* they dominated the soviets, and the masses trusted them. But their fatal 'self-restricting dogma'[12] led them from one mistake to another: from merely supporting the Provisional Government to actually joining it, thus shouldering all its heavy responsibilities and sharing all the blame. Indeed, Fedor Dan admitted in 1946 that the Menshevik concept of the bourgeois revolution rested on 'illusions'.[13]

In addition, the majority of the Mensheviks in the soviets, the so-called 'defensists', were in favour of continuing the war until a general and just peace could be assured. In this they were, at first, in harmony with most workers and soldiers, who were mostly 'patriotic'. Only when the war dragged on beyond endurance did the people begin to long for 'peace at all costs'. The Mensheviks did not take this change of popular mood into account quickly enough. The small group of anti-war Mensheviks led by Martov — the 'internationalists' — were more aware of the people's mood, but they had very little influence in the party at that time. They did not even have a paper of their own: together with several other non-Menshevik Internationalists, Martov contributed to Maxim Gorky's journal *Novaia Zhisn* (New Life), until he and his group started their own, *Iskra*, on 26 September.[14]

In the course of the summer of 1917 the Menshevik party underwent a painful process of reorientation. Between May, when Martov returned to Russia, and October, there was a significant shift to the left, which expressed itself in Martov's rise to leadership. Soon many majority Mensheviks, among them Fedor Dan and the Central Committee, were following his line. Martov advocated the transfer of power to an all-socialist government which must act with determination. As another majority Menshevik, Boris Bogdanov, was now moved to say: 'one must either forego power altogether or have the courage to assume full responsibility'.[15] But it was too late — the Mensheviks had lost the ear of the masses, who now listened with approval to the extravagant and utterly irresponsible propaganda of the Bolsheviks. The swing in popular feeling was complete: in September 1917 both the Petrograd and the Moscow soviets of workers' and soldiers' deputies declared their support for the Bolsheviks.

Lenin proved to be much more flexible than the majority of the Mensheviks. He, too, had originally believed in the inevitability of the 'bourgeois stage' of the revolution, ** but he was quick to see that it

*The Social Revolutionaries (SRs) had a large following, mainly among the peasants.

**In 1905, Lenin wrote in *The Two Tactics of the Social Democracy in a Democratic Revolution*: 'we, the marxists, must understand that there is not, and cannot be, any path toward true freedom for the proletariat and the peasantry other than the path of bourgeois freedom and bourgeois progress.'[16]

was simply not applicable in Russia — neither the bourgeoisie nor the proletariat was playing its 'historical role' according to marxist theory. So why not bypass the bourgeois stage altogether? This was entirely in keeping with his essentially pragmatic temperament. Pavel Axelrod was to say in 1919 that 'Bolshevism is ... nothing but a savage and pernicious throwback to Bakuninism, Nechaevism and Blanquism.'*[17] But it is possible that Lenin believed he was following Marx's dicta to the letter when he plunged Russia into a socialist revolution. Marx had said in 1850 that the business of revolutionary leaders was to pre-empt the revolutionary process, to drive it artificially to a crisis and to make a revolution even if the preconditions for it did not exist. Lenin did exactly that.

Martov was acutely aware of the dangers of Lenin's course. As his close associate at the time, Raphail Abramovitch, recalled: 'Our situation was especially difficult. Like the Bolsheviks we were basically hostile to Kerensky's government. We felt that it was not doing anything to save the revolution, to conclude peace, to put through the land reform.... But an *armed* uprising against Kerensky's government, an uprising that would trigger a fratricidal war among the partisans of the revolution, an uprising that would make it impossible for the socialist parties to agree and unite — this we regarded as a crime.'[18]

Lenin was not afraid to start a fratricidal carnage: in his view civil war was one of the essential ingredients of the revolution. When he returned to Russia in April 1917 he was already full of plans for an armed uprising. A two-hour speech which he delivered within a few hours of his arrival, before he could possibly have acquainted himself with the actual situation in the country, stunned his party comrades. To those of them who had been in Russia throughout the war or had returned there before him, his speech seemed utterly divorced from Russian reality. They tried to enlighten, to dissuade him, but in vain; in the end they yielded to his single-minded determination.[19] The objective situation might not be ripe yet, but he was determined to 'give history a push'.** And events soon played into his hands, as the Provisional Government proved unable to cope, as dissatisfaction among workers and soldiers grew, and as the political parties in the soviets failed to give a clear lead.

*In the middle of the nineteenth century several Russian revolutionaries preached 'the use of the axe' — they advocated physical destruction of tsarist officialdom, landlords and other 'exploiters'. Foremost among them were Michael Bakunin, Peter Zaichnevskii and Peter Tkachev (A.L. Weeks called his political biography of Tkachev *The First Bolshevik*). Nechaev was a devious and dishonest conspirator; Auguste Blanqui (1805–1881) was a fiery French revolutionary, organiser of the 1870 uprising.

**Words attributed to Andrei Zheliabov, one of the conspirators hanged for the assassination of Alexander II.

Such an atmosphere was ideal for Bolshevik demagogy, utterly unrealistic though most of its promises were. The first to respond were soldiers and sailors; the workers were not so easily roused. Contemporary observers all agree that the prevailing mood among factory workers was apathy. War-weary and hungry, the Russian people had lost much of the enthusiasm of the February days. In that vacuum, Bolshevik propaganda, with its appeal to class hatred and its incitement to violence, had a strong attraction. And that vicious propaganda was allowed full scope in the 'freest country in the world'. Only after the abortive Bolshevik attempt at an uprising in July 1917 did the government briefly imprison a few Bolshevik leaders, while Lenin himself took refuge in Finland.

In the meantime secret military preparations were carried out under the direction of Lev Trotsky, whom Lenin was lucky to win over to his side. Trotsky had tended to steer his own course hitherto, but in July he joined the Bolshevik party and became a wholehearted supporter of Lenin. He was probably one of the few to understand and to share Lenin's plans. On 23 September he was elected chairman of the Petrograd Soviet, a post he had occupied, at the age of 26, in 1905. Under the impact of General Kornilov's failed attempt to seize power,* and helped by Bolshevik-inspired rumours that the government was preparing to surrender Petrograd to the Germans, the VTsIK of the Petrograd Soviet established a Military-Revolutionary Committee (MRC) for the defence of the revolution. Trotsky was appointed chairman, and he entirely subordinated the Committee to Bolshevik aims. Except for fourteen Left SRs and four Anarchists, all other members were Bolshevik.[21]

This arrangement suited Lenin's plans admirably: they could now mature under the auspices of the Soviet — and this was most useful, since many soldiers and workers responded only to calls from the Soviet and not from the Bolshevik party. At the same time Lenin's and Trotsky's real intentions were kept secret both from the Soviet and from the rank and file Bolsheviks. The participation of the Left SRs, who were soon to split from the SR party and join the Bolshevik government, only helped to maintain the camouflage. Under the energetic leadership of Trotsky, the MRC posted hundreds of commissars in most of the military and naval units in the Petrograd area; it also directed the activities of the Bolshevik paramilitary force, the Red Guard, which had been recruited from among Petrograd

*The conspiracy of the commander-in-chief, General Kornilov, against the Provisional Government that had appointed him 'effectively destroyed the masses' trust in the officer corps and contributed to the success of Bolshevik propaganda. The Kadet party was clearly implicated in the plot although some of its members were in the government'.[20]

factories and trained and supplied with rifles and machine guns by the Bolshevik party's Military Organisation.*

As Lenin had figured out long ago, autumn proved the most auspicious time. The MRC struck in October, and Lenin came out of hiding.

Soviet historians and above all Soviet cinema like to portray the October coup as a prolonged burst of mass heroism, but nothing could be further from the truth. The 'heroic storming' of the Winter Palace, seat of the Provisional Government, by the Red Guard and sailors was in reality a puny affair as the defending force consisted of a small contingent of officer cadets and a small part of a women's battalion. The MRC having occupied the telegraph exchange and other key buildings in the city, and the greater part of the Petrograd workers and garrison waiting passively for the outcome, Kerensky's government was ousted before it knew what hit it. The tsarist government had been toppled in four days, the Provisional Government in only two —both collapsing of their own inner weakness.[23]

On the morning of 25 October (old style) the MRC announced that it had taken over the state power. The same evening Lenin and Zinoviev appeared in the Petrograd Soviet to welcome 'the victorious revolution of the proletariat and garrison of Petrograd'.**[24] The Bolshevik coup had been timed to coincide with the Second Congress of Soviets which opened on the evening of 25 October. The theatrical effect it produced before such a large audience was prodigious. The Congress promptly elected a VTsIK of 62 Bolsheviks, 29 Left SRs and 10 others, and a Workers' and Peasants' government or Council of People's Commissars (Sovnarkom) composed entirely of Bolsheviks. The new VTsIK gave the new government an enthusiastic welcome, thus conferring a kind of legitimacy upon it.

The Bolsheviks had come to power under the slogans 'Dictatorship of workers and peasants' and 'All power to the soviets!'. Both turned out to be camouflage for the Bolshevik party, which established its own dictatorship and grabbed all power for itself. But the Bolsheviks

*Both the Military Organisation and the Red Guard were created shortly after the February revolution. By July 1917 the former was said to number 26,000 men and the latter some 20,000.[22]

**Whereupon the three Menshevik members of the Praesidium of the VTsIK (Mark Broido, S. Weinstein and Mark Liber) resigned and all Menshevik delegates left the Soviet, together with the Right SRs and other socialist groups and parties. This gesture was, no doubt, intended to 'shame' the Bolsheviks, but to Lenin it can only have been welcome. The last to go was Martov and his group after Trotsky had confined them to the 'dustbin of history'. Earlier Martov pleaded for the street fighting to stop: a peaceful solution must be found and a united democratic government formed. His speech was greeted with a tumult of applause and his proposal was carried unanimously,[25] showing clearly that even the Bolsheviks and the Left SRs present were in favour of it.

were in too weak a position to act alone, so they manoeuvred, taking the Left SRs into the government, though only for a short time and pretending to tolerate free soviets and trade unions while making sure that they were under Bolshevik control.

All these manoeuvres bought Lenin a little time, but other Bolshevik slogans called for immediate realisation. The slogan 'land and peace' was aimed at soldiers, most of whom were peasants in uniform, and indeed it proved very effective in the October rising, which succeeded largely owing to the soldiers. A decree on land temporarily satisfied the peasants, though soon afterwards the treatment meted out to them turned them into the most bitter enemies of the Bolsheviks. With regard to 'peace' Lenin realised that his only possible course lay in negotiations with the Germans, and he began them at once. It was none too soon. The Russian army was falling apart so fast that a military defeat was inevitable. A peace treaty seemed certainly preferable. Lenin was almost alone at this moment in seeing it so clearly. Many Russians, including many soldiers, many socialists and even many Bolsheviks, still harboured some patriotic scruples; and they were also afraid of the extent of territorial losses that Germany was certain to inflict on Russia. Even Trotsky, who led the Bolshevik delegation at the peace negotiations at Brest-Litovsk, had a moment of hesitation when the Germans stated their exorbitant demands. But Lenin stood firm and, as always, swung his party after him. He risked much. Had the war ended with German victory, Russia would have been dismembered and Lenin's government overthrown — even perhaps the Romanovs reinstated. The German offensives on the western front between February and July 1918 did almost succeed, but when Germany lost the war the Brest-Litovsk treaty was cancelled and the occupied territories were restored to Russia. Nothing could have raised Lenin's prestige in the country and in his own party higher. The outbreak of a revolution in Germany added to Lenin's optimism: the road towards world revolution seemed clear.

Yet when the German revolution collapsed, Lenin's courage must have faltered. It was the hope that the Russian example would spark off similar revolutions in other countries, and eventually in the whole world, that in his own eyes justified the risk of starting his 'irresponsible adventure', as the Mensheviks called the October coup. He knew well enough that without material and technical help from fraternal foreign countries his regime had little chance of surviving.

Having boldly seized power, Lenin was faced with the job of actually administering the country. Like most Russian intellectuals, he had little experience of practical politics, and during the long years of his foreign exile he must, to some degree, have lost touch with

Russian life and people. Nor could his marxist or jacobin mentors offer him any guidance. His own inclination seems to have been to follow the words of the Internationale (or the teaching of Bakunin) and to destroy the old world to its foundations before building a new one on its ruins. But life allowed him no time for such extravagant action — people had to be fed and factories and trains run. The Provisional Government had dismally failed to cope with the economic crisis, but now Lenin did worse. There was a terrible feeling of unreality in the flood of decrees 'of a declarative rather than practical nature', as Chamberlin so aptly described them.[26] The Sovnarkom literally deluged the country with them. These decrees, usually drafted and always signed by Lenin as head of the government, gave a spurious impression of energy and determination but did little to create order in the existing chaos. In the course of time most of the early decrees were, in fact, reversed — at least those that were reversible. But in many cases, the damage done was irremediable.

The country was also deluged with propaganda: floods of hatred and incitement to violence against the 'enemies of the people' were poured out until the whole country was driven to the verge of paranoia. Huge wall posters and strips of red cloth strung across streets repeated *ad nauseam* the same slogans as those printed right across the pages of Bolshevik publications. One needs only to look at the early numbers of *Pravda* or *Izvestiia* to see that a whole new language had been created, a jargon of hyperbole, from which Russia has not recovered. It was a mixture of indiscriminate abuse, familiar from Lenin's own polemical writings, and deliberate illiteracy — 'talking down' to the common man, as it were. The high priest of this Bolshevik journalese was the 'poet' Demian Bednyi (pseudonym meaning Poor Jack), whose daily jingle either glorified the latest government pronouncement or vilified its enemies. Lenin himself seemed at times nauseated by it; he warned that at some future day it might be said that the revolutionary phrase has killed the revolution.[27]

All this created an unbearable sense of tension which precluded a return to normality. There were wine riots in Petrograd when wine shops and cellars were broken open. In the provinces the excesses were more serious. The Red Guards went about sacking, looting, arresting and shooting anybody they liked, including workers and peasants. Their activities in the countryside were particularly devastating and roused bitter hostility against the new regime. The Sorcerer's Apprentice had set loose forces he could not control.

3 *The Mensheviks after the October Coup*

The Mensheviks had denounced the Bolshevik coup as an irresponsible folly and had predicted that the destruction of the existing capitalist structure of industry and trade at that particularly critical moment would plunge the country's economy into complete chaos. They advocated a gradual transition to socialism, with, for the time being, a mixed economy and considerable concessions to private enterprise. In 1917, and even in 1919, when these ideas were more fully set out in the Menshevik party programme 'What's to be done?',[1] Lenin did not heed them; he was forced to retreat in 1921, but by then the national economy lay in ruins and the bourgeoisie (big and small), the technical intelligentsia and the peasants had been thoroughly antagonised and the workers demoralised.

But though, in 1917, the Mensheviks deplored Bolshevik folly, they feared the reactionary right much more. It has always been, and still is, an article of faith in leftist circles that the threat to a democratic society comes from the right and not the left. The Mensheviks were no exception.* This explains to a large extent their passivity towards Bolshevik intrigues during the summer and autumn of 1917: they were restrained by fear of playing into the hands of the reactionaries and the Germans. Other socialists were equally apprehensive. S.P. Melgunov, a member of the Central Committee of the Populist Socialists (NS), wrote that there was only one possible outcome to 'the illusory victory of the Bolsheviks ... an inevitable triumph of the bourgeoisie and, who knows, perhaps even the restoration of the tsarist regime'.[2] Swayed by fears of such an outcome, the Mensheviks for a brief moment, between 26 and 29 October, joined the SRs, the NSs and some other groupings in the Committee to Save the Country and the Revolution (*Kometet spassenia rodiny i revolutsii*) with the view of stopping the Bolsheviks. Politically this Committee was a non-starter — there were too many conflicting currents within it. It fell

*Though according to Sukhanov (p. 531), Martov warned in September 1917 that the Revolution was threatened 'not by the Right but by the Left'.

apart almost at once after a lamentable attempt had been made, on 29 October, to stage an armed uprising — an attempt planned and carried out by a group within the Committee without the knowledge of other members.[3] The only result of the uprising was that some more wretched officer cadets were killed or arrested.

Thereafter the Menshevik party dissociated itself from all armed conspiracies against the Bolsheviks, and this became one of its most firmly held policies. A marxist party had no right to weaken the working class by in-fighting; Mensheviks and Bolsheviks were two wings of the same party and should therefore not fight each other. That was why Mensheviks had so desperately striven for unity since 1903. Eventually they would fight side by side with the Bolsheviks against the Whites.[4] There was also another reason which tied their hands: by the end of 1917 the overwhelming majority of the working class was supporting the Bolsheviks. Three weeks after the Bolshevik coup, Martov was writing to Pavel Axelrod that 'almost the entire proletariat stands behind Lenin'.[5] This was enough: the Mensheviks, a workers' party, could not fight workers, even if the workers had been led astray. Nevertheless, they felt it to be their duty to warn that the Bolshevik regime would be resisted by the peasants and by the greater part of the urban population. Only by 'blood and iron' would the Bolshevik government be able to stay in power; it would 'inevitably turn into a worst kind of dictatorship, a minority government relying on bayonets and repressing the free will of the people'.[6] Inevitably there would be civil war, and to forestall this and to reintroduce some order into the situation, the Mensheviks proposed the formation of a government of all democratic and socialist groups and parties.

The proposal was taken up by the powerful Vikzhel[7] (the All-Russian Executive Committee of the Railwaymen's Union) which threatened a railway strike unless a government of 'all socialist parties from the Bolsheviks to the NSs' was formed. Since the Vikzhel controlled the only means of transport and had the unlimited use of railway telegraph lines, it was a force that could not be ignored. Between 29 October and 2 November negotiations were conducted under the auspices of Vikzhel between the representatives of all socialist parties including the Bolsheviks. The presence of the Bolsheviks was significant: there were many moderate men in the Bolshevik Central Committee who had thought the October coup premature and who were keen on enlisting the support of other socialists. There was an immediate enthusiastic response from factories and army units, many of which had supported the coup only half heartedly. A wave of resolutions welcomed the Vikzhel initiative.[8] Even the Bolshevik sailors of the destroyer *Oleg* broadcast from their ship on 30 October their joy at 'the glad tidings' of negotiations among 'all socialist parties who are trying to form a bloc'.[9] The idea of an all-socialist government was very popular among Moscow Bolsheviks, both in their party organisation and in the Military Revolutionary Committee. This so alarmed Lenin that he sent an urgent order to the Petrograd party committee: 'The Moscow people are demanding agreement with Mensheviks and SRs. Must rebuff.... Immediately pass a resolution against agreement.'[10]

The negotiations reached a stage when mutually acceptable ministers of the future government were nominated: it was to include three Mensheviks and two Bolsheviks, with the leader of the Right SRs, Victor Chernov, as premier. Lenin was not on the list and Trotsky was removed from it — with the agreement, be it noted, of the moderate Bolshevik negotiators, who were opposed to Lenin's and Trotsky's extremism. But on the morning of 4 November it transpired that Lenin had once again prevailed in the Bolshevik Central Committee and that the Bolshevik negotiators had been reprimanded. There had been apparently a fierce struggle over the issue, as a result of which five members of the Central Committee and eight members of the Sovnarkom had resigned, declaring that a large part of the proletariat had supported the negotiations and warning that the only alternative to a broad socialist government was a Bolshevik government based on political terror, which they abominated.[11]

After the failure of the Vikzhel negotiations, the Mensheviks reviewed their position at the Extraordinary Congress of their party on 4 December, 1917. Fedor Dan, one of the leaders of the majority in the Petrograd Soviet, admitted that the policies of the democratic parties in the Soviet had been built on mistaken premises and had played into Bolshevik hands: 'the masses were too exhausted' and 'no longer able to wait' for peace, and land should be transferred immediately to land committees. Dan stressed the deep dissatisfaction of the broad masses caused by the war, the economic havoc and the indecisive policy of the Provisional Government.[12] Even the arch-coalitionist Iraklii Tsereteli, until recently a minister in Kerensky's government, recognised that it had been impossible to organise an acceptable people's government because most of the democratic elements were 'in a state of passivity' while the more active ones supported the Bolsheviks.[13] Only Alexander Potresov remained unshaken in his belief that cooperation with bourgeois parties was essential in order to save the country. For him the only threat to the revolution came from the Bolsheviks; bolshevism, he maintained, *was* counter-revolution and should be resisted, if necessary by force of arms. Such views were not acceptable to the rest of the party and indeed Potresov and his group left it formally in 1918.[14] Georgii Plekhanov, hovering between bolshevism and menshevism and worried, about the course the revolution was taking, died in 1918.[15]

The Extraordinary Congress of the Mensheviks elected a new Central Committee, which had an internationalist majority: Axelrod, Abramovitch, Astrov, Akhmatov, Ber, Eva Broido, Gorev, Gogua, Dan, Ezhov, Martov, Martynov, Maiskii, Pinkevich, Semkovskii, Cherevanin, Erlikh and Iugov.[16] In May 1918 Georgii Kuchin and Mark Liber joined the Central Committee as representatives of the right wing.[17] Martov was now acknowledged to be the chief, though not the only, leader of the party: it was not a Menshevik custom to foster *vozhdism* (the cult of a leader). Martov 'was an intellectual, not a single-minded commander,' wrote David Dallin. 'His authority rested on intellect and devotion to the cause, but he needed a leader at his side to direct the actual work.'[18] And he had in fact several able men and women to assist him, including Fedor Dan who had married his sister Lidia.

Martov, whom Gorky described as a strikingly attractive personality[19] and Nikolai Sukhanov as the most intelligent man he ever met,[20] was at first sight anything but impressive. His physique had been undermined from early infancy — his nurse had dropped him as a baby, breaking his leg and causing a slight limp. Arrested by the tsarist police at the age of eighteen and a half he underwent the nerve-wrecking experience of a year in solitary confinement followed by three years of exile in Vilno only to find himself back in prison a few months after his return to St Petersburg. Exiled again, this time to the mosquito-ridden, swampy Turukhansk, he probably contracted there the tuberculosis of the throat which destroyed his vocal cords and eventually killed him. A slight, limping and stooping figure, with thick glasses and a cracked voice he was hardly the image of a passionate revolutionary, yet this was precisely what he was. He had the genuine revolutionary temperament and great moral courage. He was quite fearless in denouncing injustice or wrong wherever he saw them. The writer Konstantin Paustovskii observed him closely and repeatedly in the Soviet during 1918, and this is how he described him: 'Tall, scraggy and irascible, a ragged scarf wound around his sinewy neck, he would jump up frequently to interrupt the speakers and shout words of indignation in a hoarse, breaking voice. An instigator of many a stormy incident, he would not calm down until he had been deprived of the right to speak, or had been debarred for a few sessions.' His hoarse voice could still shake the walls; he boiled with rage and shook his clenched fist, leaving the rostrum only after the chairman had called the militia.[21] How often, one wonders, did he expect to find himself in a Bolshevik prison. In the event, he was the only Menshevik leader to escape arrest altogether, though he was for a short time subjected to house arrest.* It is a safe guess that his protector was Lenin himself.

Martov was a passionate socialist, but he was also a democrat through and through, for whom 'the means must be such that they do not contradict the ends'.[22] He took his commitment to the working class seriously and he abominated Lenin's cold-blooded manipulation of workers and of people generally. Martov was a man of unimpeachable integrity and honesty — 'an absolutely sincere man',[23] Lenin said of him to Maxim Gorky in early 1918. He was highly intelligent, with that razor-sharp, over-subtle mind that is a politician's worst enemy, always ready to see his opponent's point of view and unlike Lenin, to acknowledge his own errors. 'We are an intelligent superfluity,' he said to his fellow Mensheviks after the October coup.[24] Yet he was no wobbler. While admitting that the October revolution was 'historically necessary', and that the Brest-Litovsk peace negotiations were 'a strikingly audacious and revolutionary act', he utterly repudiated Lenin's and Trotsky's methods of government.[25] In a letter to a personal friend, written in December 1917, Martov said: 'To me, socialism has always meant, not negation of personal freedom and individuality, but on the contrary, their supreme realisation.' He found that Bolshevik society was reducing everybody to a common level and that the 'quasi-socialism' that the Bolsheviks were implanting 'in Asiatic soil' was resulting 'in such a stink that one can hardly stand it'.[26]

Meanwhile, the Menshevik party had pitifully shrunk in size. In August 1917 it still had just over 200,000 members, as many as the Bolsheviks; yet by the end of the year their Petrograd branch of 10,000 was reduced almost to zero and in the nation-wide elections to the Constituent Assembly, which began in November 1917, the Mensheviks received a mere three per cent of the total vote.**[27]

The Constituent Assembly opened on 5 January 1918, only to be dissolved by the Bolshevik government on the following day. It might strike one as incongruous that the Bolsheviks had allowed the Assembly to open at all, or even allowed the elections to it to take place. But the idea of an All-Russian Constituent Assembly was immensely popular with all parties, including the rank and file of the ruling party, and in both town and country, and the government was at first afraid to arouse too much resentment. Only after the overwhelming electoral victory of the Right SRs did it decide to

*Lenin's other old comrade, Alexander Potresov, was arrested in September, 1919. He fell very seriously ill in prison and was released by the end of the year. Eventually he went abroad.

**The SRs obtained 15,848,000 votes, the Bolsheviks 9,844,000 and the Mensheviks 1,364,826.

disband the Assembly. Without a Bolshevik majority it was no use to Lenin. But it was done clumsily: a peaceful demonstration in support of the Assembly that took place on the eve of the opening day was dispersed by the Red Guard and several workers were killed. This turned the workers against the Bolsheviks.

When some of the victims were buried on 9 January scores of thousands marched in the funeral procession and dense crowds lined the ten-mile long route. A banner carried by the workers of the Semiennikov factory, one of the largest in Petrograd, read: 'Eternal memory to the victims of the violence of the Smolnyi* autocrats!' At a huge meeting of protest held at the factory, Menshevik speakers were warmly received.[28] This showed how unstable workers' support of the Bolsheviks was, and how easily it could be withdrawn. These were early symptoms of a turn of the tide.

Nevertheless the Menshevik party, defeated and disorientated, had reached a very low ebb. A conference held in Moscow on 21–27 May 1918 showed just how weak the party was. Party organisations often lacked funds for the most essential expenses, including railway fares; contact with provincial branches was often broken for long periods. Those delegates who managed to come to the conference in Moscow were tired from overwork and from the harsh conditions of life. They were dispirited by persecution, by the closing of their newspapers, the ban on their meetings, the arrests (and in some cases, not yet numerous, executions). Some Mensheviks decided to retire into private life, while others, activated either by a sincere desire to do useful work for the country or by the ambition of playing a role in the ruling party, went over to the Bolsheviks. But there remained a sound core which was determined to carry on the fight. They might have lost the battle for the kind of revolution they wanted, yet they would try to save what could be saved, by becoming an honourable and loyal opposition to the Bolshevik government, fighting it 'politically, not by military conspiracies',[29] by criticising wrong policies while offering alternate policies where possible. Above all they would attack the indiscriminate terror that the Bolsheviks were practising in the name of the proletariat. The accredited Bolshevik 'wit' Karl Radek ridiculed the Menshevik Central Committee as 'the central committee of the party of the dead'[30] (in an article entitled "A voice from the Tomb", *Pravda* of 15 October, 1918); though if it was dead, it was certainly not lying down.

The Mensheviks did not repudiate on principle the notion of a dictatorship of the proletariat; they considered it to be a legitimate

*The former Smolnyi Institute, a finishing school for the daughters of the nobility, had been Lenin's headquarters since his seizure of power.

state between the bourgeois and the socialist revolutions and even recognised that during that stage terror might be temporarily unavoidable. But they abominated and denounced Bolshevik terror because it was wielded by a small minority which claimed that it represented the proletariat, and because it was becoming a permanent institution. From October 1917 to 1922, when its voice was effectively silenced in Russia, the Menshevik Central Committee constantly protested, both at home and abroad, against Bolshevik terror.

It was Martov, in particular, who voiced this protest most eloquently. He wrote and spoke against the terror as a matter of principle, long before his own party began to suffer seriously under it. The execution of Captain Shchastnyi of the Baltic Fleet* in June 1918 drew from Martov his brilliant pamphlet *Away with the Death Penalty*.[31] Martov exposed in it the hypocrisy of the Bolsheviks who had officially abolished the death penalty in October 1917 (and incorporated this abolition in the Soviet Constitution of March 1918) yet practised it daily, with or without trial. In February 1919 Martov protested against the shooting of the four grand dukes, including the historian Nikolai Mikhailovich who had never taken any interest in politics; he protested against the shooting of Veniamin, the Metropolitan bishop of Petrograd, and other priests.[32] In November 1920 he was roused to fury by Trotsky's system of taking hostages (mothers, wives, children) to ensure the loyalty of his officers (see p. 46 below): 'One must have the narrow mind of a policeman to believe that the threat to massacre the innocent would deter ... a fanatic or a White-guard conspirator....'[33] But the Bolsheviks were shooting not only the Whites, the bourgeois, the former industrialists or landlords — they were shooting workers and peasants and socialists.

*Captain (sometimes referred to as Admiral) Shchastnyi, an officer so popular with the sailors that they protested against his arrest, was accused of plotting against the Bolshevik government. He denied his guilt and asked for witnesses to be heard. His request was not granted; he was shot within ten hours of the verdict.

28

(page bleep)

Is blank

4 *The Terror*

It could be argued that none of the savage Bolshevik terror was necessary to the success of the revolution. Some violence is unavoidable in revolutionary situations, yet the February revolution had claimed a comparatively small number of victims. The exact number of victims under Bolshevik rule will remain for ever unknown, but it certainly went into many thousands during Lenin's life and into many millions later. The argument that the terror was in self-defence against the Whites is not valid, as it started long before and continued long after the Civil War. To confuse the two issues —the terror and the Civil War — is to misunderstand the very nature of the Bolshevik regime. A later chapter will deal with the Civil War; but as for terror, it is essential that its special significance in the context of bolshevism should be grasped at this point. Extreme violence, far in excess of what was required, was in fact deliberately built into the very structure of the Bolshevik state — as the Mensheviks (and for that matter many moderate Bolsheviks) had feared.

Shortly before his seizure of power Lenin vehemently rejected such 'instruments of state coercion as a standing army, a police force and officialdom'; the proletarian state, he said, would arm 'the entire people', 'all the poor', 'all adult citizens of both sexes', who would take 'the organs of state power directly into their own hands', destroy the bourgeois order and 'crush the resistance of the exploiters'. For this, Lenin argued, no special apparatus, 'almost no machine', was needed, only 'the armed masses ... transformed into a universal people's militia'. The 'smashing' and 'crushing' of the bourgeois minority by an overwhelming majority of the population was not expected to take long, after which the state would become altogether superfluous and 'wither away'.[1]

It is difficult to assess the degree of sincerity in these utterances of the consummate demogogue Lenin, but in any case they very soon became immaterial. His was not an 'overwhelming majority' and, faced with resistance not only from former exploiters but from wide sections of the population, including trade unions, Lenin completely changed his tone. The anarchic violence of an 'armed people' proved in any case uncontrollable and what he now wanted was a very special organ of *controlled* terror. This special organ was the VCHK (pronounced Vecheka).[2]

The Vecheka (*Vserossiiskaia Chrezvychainaia Komissiia po borbe s kontrrevoliutsiei i sabotazhem*) — All-Russian Extraordinary Commission for combating counter-revolution, speculation and sabotage,* colloquially known as Chrezvychaika or Cheka — was undoubtedly given that cumbersome title to distinguish it from the hated tsarist political police, the Okhrana, as well as to emphasise, through the inclusion of the word 'extraordinary', its temporary nature. However, the Russian people were not duped and equated in their minds the Cheka with the Okhrana. Both institutions were hated, the Cheka eventually even more than its tsarist predecessor. Only during the rule of the Provisional Government had Russia been free from the sinister grip of a political police. During its short rule order was maintained by a militia of modest size with elected officers, subordinated to local councils.[3] The Provisional Government, with the support of the Petrograd Soviet, abolished the death penalty and proclaimed an immediate amnesty for political prisoners, freedom of speech, press, assembly, and the right to strike. Thus, for that short period of time Russia knew freedom as it had never known it before. But come October and 'Russia' — in the words of the novelist Vassilii Grossman — 'chose Lenin'. And Lenin's Russia 'was built on unfreedom'.[4]

The Vecheka was a direct descendant of the Military Revolutionary Committee, the MRC, which had organised the Bolshevik coup. For a short time after the coup the MRC exercised supreme state power and after the formation of the Sovnarkom it continued to be responsible for the security of the new regime. The MRC sprouted many provincial MRCs, which carried out security work in the provinces, towns and villages, and also various sub-committees, one of which occupied the premises at 2 Gorokhovaia Street which were to become the headquarters of the Vecheka and later of the Petrograd Cheka.

It was Felix Dzerzhinskii, a member of the Bolshevik Central Committee and of the MRC, who proposed, on 7 December 1917, the immediate setting up of a special organ to be called Vecheka 'for the revolutionary settlement of accounts with the counter-revolutionaries.... Do not think that I seek forms of revoultionary justice; we are not now in need of justice.'[5] Lenin was in complete agreement with this line of thought and the Sovnarkom, with Lenin in

*At first the title also included 'abuse of authority', but this matter was later shifted to a sub-committee of the Vecheka.

the chair, approved both the setting up of a special commission and its proposed name.[6] The new 'extraordinary' organ was to be directly responsible to the Sovnarkom, and thus to its chairman Lenin. In this manner the aims and the activities of the Vecheka could be kept secret from the VTsIk* or even from the Bolshevik Central Committee, which would probably have objected to some of them.

And who was to be the chairman of the Vecheka? 'We must find a staunch proletarian Jacobin,'[7] said Lenin, and 'surely we shall not fail to find our own Fouquier Tinville.'** — while Trotsky gloated over 'that remarkable invention of the French revolution which makes man shorter by one head'.[8] Lenin found his Fouquier Tinville in Felix Dzerzhinskii himself, who became and remained the head of the Vecheka until his death in 1926. Like Lenin, Dzerzhinskii was no proletarian; both came from small landed gentry.

So the Vecheka was born in the spirit of the French revolution as an organ of revolutionary vigilance and a guardian of revolutionary virtue. The resemblance went very deep. There is a striking parallel between Lenin and Dzerzhinskii on one side and Robespierre, St Just and Tinville on the other: all were fanatics who combined a vision of a purified world with a readiness to kill. Robespierre had written: 'the basis of the people's government in the revolution is both virtue and terror; virtue without which terror is fatal; terror without which virtue is powerless'[9] (my translation). A decree of the Committee of Public Safety of 1794 reads: 'You must entirely refashion a people whom you wish to make free; destroy its prejudices, alter its habits, limit necessities, root up its vices, purify its desires.'[10] As for Dzerzhinskii: 'Proletarian coercion [*prinuzhdenie*] in all its forms, beginning with shootings, is a method of shaping the Communist Man.'[11] From this it followed that it was the duty of every Bolshevik to work for the Cheka; members of the Bolshevik party and the Bolshevik youth, the Komsomol, were urged to join it: 'every Communist must be a chekist;'[12] the Cheka, generally described as the shield and the sword of the revolution, was the best that the party has created; it was 'the pride and joy of the Communist party'.[13] For Lenin 'a good Communist is ... a good chekist'.[14] And on the tenth anniversary of the Vecheka, Bukharin was still heaping extravagant praise on the Cheka.[15] The public was expected to help the Cheka by observing and reporting the least signs of counter-revolutionary activity. This universal spying and informing turned out in the long run to be the most corrupting aspect of life under Bolshevik rule.

*The MRC had been nominally responsible to the VTsIK, but Lenin might have felt that the VTsIK still contained too many non-Bolshevik elements.

**During the French Revolution, Fouquier Tinville was public prosecutor in Robespierre's Revolutionary Tribunal and kept the guillotine busy.

Bolshevik terror was designed to consolidate a controversial minority rule. Its mechanics were simple — all those who did not accept the official ideology or conform to the official models of 'true proletarian', 'good Communist' and the like, were cast into the role of 'enemies of the people'. By constantly inventing and enlarging categories of 'enemies' the regime frightened the populace into complete, cowed conformity. The terror was both punitive and preventive, directed equally against actual opponents and potential deviants and dissenters.

The Bolsheviks proved to be masters of this kind of terror. Lenin set the tone in early December 1917 when he called for the Russian land to be purged 'of all vermin'.[16] By debasing and vilifying their enemies the Bolsheviks made mass persecution and even shootings psychologically acceptable — to themselves, at least. They created an atmosphere of hatred and fear and established vast numbers of categories of enemies, such as 'counter-revolutionaries',* 'speculators', 'social bandits', 'saboteurs' and 'wreckers'. All these terms were applied in the loosest possible manner.** Equally they introduced into the long-suffering Russian language a host of ambiguous and even utterly misleading terms such as 'revolutionary justice', 'revolutionary legality' and 'revolutionary conscience'.

Nobody would deny that there were real counter-revolutionaries. There were also great numbers of criminals freed from prison during the February revolution, and there were many homeless deserters from the Army who were a real threat to law and order. Ordinary militia or a re-organised police force could have dealt with all these. But they would not have known how to deal with imaginary or exaggerated crimes used by the Bolshevik government as a means of terrorising the population. For instance it was an open secret that in the spring of 1918 almost the entire Russian population, including members of the ruling party, was to some extent engaged in 'speculation' — not on the Stock Exchange which had been abolished, but by bartering or selling worn clothes or household articles or other urban goods for bread and other agricultural produce in the street markets. These markets had been declared illegal by the government but continued to function nevertheless, sellers and buyers always

*Even socialists were included in this category. This is how a Soviet dictionary defines a Menshevik: *Menshevik* — member of the anti-marxist, opportunist party which is an agency of the bourgeoisie inside the workers' movement and which had become, after the victory of the socialist revolution in Russia, the stronghold of bourgeois counter-revolutionaries, a band of wreckers, spies and diversionists, enemies of the people.[17]

**Already in 1909 Pavel Axelrod had accused the Bolsheviks of using words of abuse as readily as the Black Hundreds (an ultra-reactionary, pogromist organisation) who used to brand their enemies as 'enemies of the people' and 'enemies of the state'.[18]

ready to scamper at the first sign of a Cheka raid. Those caught landed in prison, but this did not discourage the rest. After all this was the only way to survive in starving Russia, since the government failed to organise food supplies for the cities. Bertrand Russell who visited Russia in May–June 1920 found the situation still much the same: 'The rations are not sufficient.... the attempt to suppress private commerce has resulted in an amount of unprofessional buying and selling which far exceeds what happens in capitalist countries ... [and] being illegal, it places practically the whole population of Moscow at the mercy of the police.'[19] A well known non-Bolshevik writer, N.V. Ustrialov, had this to say: 'The entire country, including the Communists themselves, live in violation of the Communist decrees; all of Russia is engaged in speculation.'[20]

Universal though these practices were, it was always possible, when it suited the authorities, to label those who indulged in them as counter-revolutionaries. Moreover, workers who went on strike or peasants who expressed their dissatisfaction were accused of 'sabotage' and 'banditism'; while technical and administrative personnel could always, when convenient, be accused of 'wrecking' or of 'economic crime'. And the Vecheka was given authority to deal with all these offences, as well as with petty crime and mere barter.

Felix Dzerzhinskii, the head of the Vecheka, was a Polish revolutionary with many years of tsarist prison in his past, though a Bolshevik only since 1917. He earned for himself such names as 'The Saint of the Revolution', 'The Soviet Savanarola', 'The Grand Inquisitor of Bolshevism' and also 'Iron Felix'. He worked sixteen to eighteen hours a day, seven days a week, and ate, slept and worked at his office.[21] An ascetic, personally incorruptible — Trotsky spoke of him as 'a man of high moral purpose' — he saw himself and his chekists as men with 'cool heads, warm hearts, and clean hands',[22] and was quick to punish his subordinates for any infringement of the strict regulations that he repeatedly issued. Despite all this, bribery and extortion soon became routine practices among the chekists. It was quite possible for a rich man to buy his freedom for jewels or big money. More than any other Bolshevik institution the Vecheka attracted careerists, criminals, psychopaths and sadists, and the atrocities committed in its prisons and camps were to surpass anything previously known in Russia. It also grew to monstrous proportions, the central Vecheka giving birth to provincial chekas, urban and rural (by August 1918 there were already 40 provincial and 365 district chekas)[23] and to Cheka departments in the Army, Navy, industry and so on. Eventually there were also special Cheka troops with their own heavy weapons. Instead of bringing order and justice into the land, the Cheka became an utterly lawless, arbitrary instrument of injustice (and so were its successors, the GPU, the NKVD, the MVD, and the KGB of today). The Vecheka became a power unto itself, defying the verdicts of the Revolutionary Tribunals (created a month before the Vecheka, they preserved at least the trappings of legality), ignoring the Commissar of Justice, and arresting, sentencing and shooting people as it liked. Characteristically, most of its activities took place in the dead of night, in interrogation offices and cellars.

Lenin was to define 'dictatorship' (in October 1920) as 'power without limit, resting directly upon force, restrained by no laws, absolutely unrestricted by rules'.[24] True, he had also said that only 'an insignificant minority of the population, the landowners and capitalists', needed to be destroyed; 'a handful of men ... they will disappear in a matter of weeks'.[25] When he found himself in reality confronted by massive opposition, he intensified the terror and proclaimed that it was 'absolutely indispensable'.[26]

Many prominent Bolsheviks and even members of the Central Committee were revolted by the all-pervading and arbitrary terror that had somehow come to rule the country, but few dared to criticise it openly. An honourable exception was the veteran Bolshevik Mikhail Olminskii, who was one of the editors of *Pravda*: in several signed articles he exposed the excesses of what he called 'criminal' terror and called for fundamental reform of the Vecheka.[27] But Dzerzhinskii, though from time to time he had some chekists imprisoned or shot for corruption and similar offences, took no notice of such basic criticism, whether it came from Bolshevik, Menshevik or other sources.

In general, the chekas were allowed every licence in their dealings with 'counter-revolutionaries'. It did not matter whether they were perfectly peaceful citizens or active plotters against the government, they were imprisoned and often shot on the basis of social origins alone. Once, when Lenin was reproached for carrying out 'social extermination', he replied with evident pleasure: 'Well put ... that is exactly what we should do ... but we cannot say that!'[28] The top chekist Martyn Latsis gave the following advice to cheka interrogators: 'Do not seek ... proof of whether the prisoner has rebelled against the Soviets with arms or in speech. First you must ask him to what class he belongs, what his social origin is, what his education was and his profession. The answers must determine the fate of the accused.'[29] If you were born or had moved into the nobility or the middle class, if you had been an army officer or a cleric, a merchant or an industrialist, you were a 'class enemy' and therefore outside the law. This was, of course, patently absurd, quite apart from the preposterous basic assumption. Many of the revolutionaries, including Lenin, Trotsky and Dzerzhinskii, came from the nobility or small gentry or the merchant class, while many of the war-time officers were neither of the nobility nor hostile to the revolution. As for the professional middle class the majority was very much in sympathy with the revolution, provided only that it guaranteed freedom of intellectual and artistic expression. In fact, the terrorisation of professional men and women by the Bolsheviks was a stupid blunder; soon the Bolsheviks were appealing for help to scientists, technicians and specialists of all kinds, but by then collaboration was not willingly given.

The attempt on Lenin's life on 30 August 1918 unleashed a wave of terror — officially styled Red Terror — to which all the rest had been only a prelude. The unsuccessful attempt on Lenin (made by Fanny Kaplan, originally an Anarchist, later an SR) followed closely upon the assassination of Uritskii, Head of the Petrograd Cheka, and both were interpreted as an all-out attack on Bolshevik leadership. The reprisals claimed many thousands of lives, and countless hostages were shot all over Russia.[30] In Petrograd it was officially reported that 500 hostages were shot, including four former tsarist ministers,[31] and 800 persons executed during the first six weeks of Red Terror; in addition 400 were shot in a single night in Kronstadt.[32] Even in quite small towns batches of 150, 50, 30 people perished. Nor were the chekas the only agents of destruction: local soviets, army units, in short all and every branch of Bolshevik power was called upon to wreak vengeance.

On 5 September 1918 the Sovnarkom issued the famous 'Decree on the Red Terror'; it was pale in comparison with Lenin's earlier incitement to summary justice in his 'Socialist Fatherland in Danger!' (21 February), but it strengthened the Vecheka's hand by formally conferring on it the right to carry out executions on the spot — something which it had hitherto been doing without legal sanction.[33] The Commissar for Internal Affairs, Petrovskii, who had signed the decree on the Red Terror, exhorted all local soviets to meet the least opposition with 'wholesale executions.... Show no wavering or indecisiveness in carrying out mass terror.'[34] On 3 September the Vecheka published a proclamation calling upon the working class to 'crush the hydra of counter-revolution.'[35] The first number of the *Vecheka Weekly** insisted: 'It is time ... to introduce in deeds not words, the most merciless, highly organised mass terror. In bringing death to thousands of people with hands unsoiled by work [*beloruchki*] ... we shall save the socialist revolution.... We have drawn the sword and will not sheath it as long as one single foe remains.' And the Bolshevik press truly 'undammed the sea of blood' as Zinoviev's paper

*Six issues of this periodical 'for the instruction and ideal guidance' of provincial chekas appeared between 22 September and 27 October 1918.[36]

Krasnaia Gazeta claimed (on 21 August 1918): 'Without mercy or pity we shall strike down our enemies by the tens, the hundreds. Let their numbers reach thousands. Let them drown in their own blood.... SRs and Mensheviks everywhere are carrying out the bloody orders of their masters.... There shall be no mercy for them.... Let the blood of the bourgeoisie and its servants flow — more blood.' And: 'Tomorrow we shall make thousands of their wives put on mourning.'[38]

The reference to SRs and Mansheviks is disingenuous. The attempt on Lenin's life was made by the SR woman, Fanny Kaplan, *on her own initiative* and not by orders of her party; and Mensheviks, of course, eschewed all forms of terrorism. The purpose of describing these two parties as servants of the bourgeoisie was simply to discredit them in the eyes of the workers.

As the wave of terror spread through the country it enveloped workers and peasants as well as the rest of the Russian people. Finding themselves at the receiving end of Bolshevik violence and seeing no improvement in the food and fuel situation, workers and peasants realised that both politically and materially they were no better off — and in many ways worse off — than before the Bolshevik coup. The fruits of 'their' revolution had been snatched from their hands by the very government that claimed to be 'their' government. Strikes and protests began before the year 1917 was out. And in the same measure in which the Bolsheviks were losing their popular support, the Mensheviks and the SRs were winning it back. At the Tenth Congress of the Communist Party in March 1921 — that is after three and a half years in power — Zinoviev had to admit that if a congress of industrial workers were convened, ninety-nine per cent of them would turn out to belong to no political party or to the SRs and the Mensheviks. And though Trotsky ridiculed this statement as a 'monstrous exaggeration' he had to concede that there was some truth in it.[39]

No wonder that the SRs and the Mensheviks were a thorn in Lenin's side. Not only were they rivals for support amongst workers and peasants but they had the experience and knowledge that qualified them to expose the weaknesses in his policies. And yet he could not at that stage silence or exterminate them as he was prepared to do the bourgeois parties; they had to be handled carefully so as not to antagonise substantial numbers of workers and peasants who were in sympathy with them. Also they were known and trusted abroad, among European socialists, for whose support and material help the Bolsheviks were bidding. For all these reasons the Vecheka was instructed to tread softly; members of socialist parties were repeatedly arrested (usually on the eve of important elections) but soon released; party clubs and journals were allowed to function though they were constantly raided and often banned. And socialists were even tolerated in the soviets. It was harassment rather than outright persecution. The Mensheviks were themselves amazed at the comparatively mild treatment they received. This cat and mouse game lasted until 1921 when the cat at last pounced. But that lay several years ahead.

5 *Anti-Bolshevik Revolts and the Civil War*

Much of the summer of 1918 was occupied by small anti-Bolshevik revolts, easily crushed, which the Bolsheviks blamed indiscriminately on socialist parties. For the record the role of the Mensheviks in these revolts should be made clear. As was pointed out earlier, the Mensheviks were against armed revolts on principle; and the Menshevik Central Committee expelled all party members who disobeyed that ruling.[1] Unfortunately rail and postal services being utterly disorganised throughout 1918, this ruling sometimes remained unknown in the provinces. Most of the local party branches seem to have arrived at the same point of view as the Central Committee of their own accord, but some individual Mensheviks decided to take part in the revolts. These few cases are well documented and easy to trace.

The first major insurrection in which some Mensheviks were involved took place in Iaroslavl in July 1918. It had been planned by the legendary conspirator Boris Savinkov, formerly an SR but expelled from his party for being involved in the Kornilov affair (see p. 17). Savinkov was the organiser of several secret anti-Bolshevik societies, from *Donskoi Grazhdanskii Soviet* (Citizen's Council of the Don region) to *Soiuz Zaschity Rodiny i Svobody* (Union for the Defence of Motherland and Freedom). Some of these societies were entirely composed of tsarist generals and officers, others had attracted some individual SRs, NSs, Kadets, and even Mensheviks (mainly from Plekhanov's and Potresov's groups). In Iaroslavl the Mensheviks had been influential among the workers (see p. 81) but their prospects were not good: a local cheka had just been formed, Menshevik papers were banned, it was tempting to support an uprising that promised to recall the Constituent Assembly and to restore democracy. Even so, the local Menshevik committee kept aloof from Savinkov; he was able to enlist the help of only a few right wingers. Those Mensheviks who had joined the staff of the insurrection were told by the local committee to resign; most of them submitted, but two refused (I.T. Savinov and E. Diushen) and were promptly expelled from the party. When the news reached Moscow the Central Committee endorsed the expulsion, and so did the special conference of the Moscow regional committee, which ruled that 'in the present political circumstances any armed action against the Bolshevik government is sheer adventurism benefitting only the counter-revolution.'[2]

The Iaroslavl revolt, which had spread to Murom and Rybinsk, was put down by Cheka troops. The reprisals that followed included the execution of first 57 and then another 350 captured insurgents; it would seem that prominent in these reprisals was N.A. Bulganin, the future marshal and leading member of the Bolshevik government, who served in the Cheka during 1918.[3]

A much bigger 'adventure' was enacted by the SRs in the wake of the Czech legion's progress from the Volga to the Urals and Siberia.[4] It involved not one or two isolated cities but a vast territory with a population of millions of peasants who were beginning to turn against the Bolsheviks. The Czech legion or corps had been formed mainly from prisoners-of-war of Czech origin. They had been fighting with the Austrian army, but surrendered *en masse* to the Russians, since they felt no allegiance to the Hapsburg empire and were hoping to establish an independent Czech state after the War. The Czech legion, 30,000 to 40,000 strong, had its own officers and arms, was well disciplined and trained and was moving in an orderly manner, with Bolshevik permission, towards Vladivostok, where it planned to embark for France. The ultimate objective of the legion was to join the Allied armies fighting on the western front; they were represented in Paris by the Czech National Council under Masaryk and Beneš and were considered to be part of the Czech Army in France. The majority of the Czechs were democratic and many were socialist. In so far as the Bolsheviks had concluded a separate peace with Germany and Austria and were undemocratic, the Czechs were anti-Bolshevik; but they wanted no armed conflict with the Bolsheviks. That was provoked by the Bolsheviks themselves: in mid-May, 1918, Trotsky issued an order to disarm the legion, to shoot on the spot any legionary carrying arms and to intern entire trainloads if even one armed man was found inside. This Bolshevik order was possibly given under German pressure, since the Germans certainly did not want any armed troops to reach the Allies.[5] The Czechs, however, refused to give up their weapons and, intent only on ensuring their own safe progress, advanced on Bolshevik-held towns — from Penza to Samara, Kazan, Simbirsk, Orenburg and so to the Urals. Bolshevik forces being at that time still very weak in Siberia, the Czechs soon held the whole Trans-Siberian Railway to Vladivostok.

To some of the Right SRs this situation seemed to offer a good opportunity for an anti-Bolshevik revolt, especially since the democratic Czechs seemed to be the right kind of allies. Hoping for Czech protection and even active help, the SR-inspired 'Committee of the Constituent Assembly' (KOMUCH) formed a rival government in Samara; and then a provisional government, the Directory, in Ufa.[6] By then the SRs had been joined by some Kadets, some NSs, some Plekhanovites, and even some Mensheviks. The regional Menshevik committee, acting in ignorance of the decision of their Central Committee, declared full support for the Samara government in August 1918. In their paper *Vechernaia Zaria* they appealed to 'all those who are struggling. . .for democracy, to come to the defence of Samara. Some other Menshevik groups along the Volga, in Kazan, Ufa, Orenburg, also felt it to be 'unthinkable to stand aside'. Obviously many local Mensheviks were strongly tempted to join the Right SRs in their revolt, but there were also many who called for a stop to the internecine struggle.[7]

Meanwhile, having found that the Czechs would not actively embroil themselves in internal Russian conflicts, the SRs had to look elsewhere for military support. They invited some Russian military personalities to join their government: first General Boldyrev and then Admiral Kolchak. This was their undoing: rightist and outright reactionary elements quickly gathered around them. Admiral Kolchak was one of the military figures closely connected with the White armies which were being formed in southern Russia. On 18 November 1918, he was declared Supreme Ruler — in effect commander-in-chief of the White armies — and on the same day he overthrew the Directory and had several SRs and other democrats arrested.[8] His rule lasted for about a year, after which he was arrested at Irkutsk by the Political Centre (a predominantly Menshevik and SR body), tried by a special commission of two SRs, one Menshevik and one Bolshevik and shot on 6 February 1920, after the Bolshevik forces had entered the town.[9] By then the Czechs had completed their evacuation via Vladivostok.

A similar sequence of events took place in the north where American and British troops landed in August 1918. A Provisional Administration of the Northern Region was optimistically set up by SRs, NSs and Kadets under the leadership of the old Populist (later NS) Nikolai Chaikovskii.[10] At first local Mensheviks supported the Administration; but soon it began to move to the right. When the Kadet N.A. Startsev was appointed chief of civilian affairs, he promptly ordered the arrest of several Menshevik and SR leaders and had the Menshevik bureau at Archangel closed down. And in January 1919 the White General Miller became head of the northern government and recognised Kolchak as Supreme Ruler. Thus ended all attempts to restore democracy in Russia. Thereafter the SRs, too, foreswore all armed resistance to the Bolsheviks.

Local Menshevik organisations which had been involved in 'rival' governments usually recanted quite sincerely. There was only one member of the Menshevik Central Committee to join the Samara venture and that was Ivan Maiskii. This latter-day Bolshevik and soviet diplomat — he was to become soviet Ambassador in London —had joined the Samara government without informing his Central Committee and in full knowledge of its decision against cooperation with that government. As soon as his behaviour became known, he was expelled from the party, along with a few other, minor figures. The Menshevik Central Committee felt that its stand had been vindicated: the logic of events invariably led to a shift to the right that rendered democratic risings 'totally negative'.[11]

By August 1918 foreign intervention had become a serious problem: the British had landed in Murmansk in March (ostensibly to prevent their stores from falling into German hands) and the Japanese in the Far East in April; in July more British and French missions arrived, and later Americans. Their aim was primarily to prevent the eastern front from collapsing altogether, thus releasing German forces for the western front; but when the Bolsheviks concluded the peace treaty of Brest-Litovsk with the Germans, they became a definite target for Allied hostility. In the Civil War Allied missions supported the Whites against the Bolsheviks and Allied governments proclaimed a blockade of Russia which was not lifted until January 1920.[12] In the event, Allied help to the Whites proved too slight and too unreliable to influence the outcome decisively and the treaty of Versailles (1919), by restoring to Russia the territories lost to Germany, substantially helped the Bolsheviks. Nevertheless, the blockade and the presence of Allied military missions had a great nuisance value and helped to confuse an already confused situation. The Mensheviks condemned foreign intervention as firmly as they did anti-Bolshevik revolts, and they tried to influence western socialists to dissuade their respective governments from taking part in it.[13]

There was one non-military kind of intervention which proved most beneficial to Russia and which had the enthusiastic support of all democratic Russians. When famine broke out in 1921 in the whole of southern Russia, America, represented by the American Relief Administration (ARA), founded in 1919 by the future President Herbert Hoover to assist war-stricken countries,[14] came to the help of the hard-pressed Bolshevik government by sending massive supplies of food. With them came a team of three hundred Americans, and a further 11,700 Russians were recruited by them in Russia to help with the distribution. In Russia itself a Famine Relief Organisation had already been formed by the liberal intelligentsia, some of them very close to the Mensheviks; it had the support of Maxim Gorky, and through him the tentative approval of Lenin. Characteristically the Vecheka was highly suspicious of that 'nest of liberals' and Dzerzhinskii recommended the arrest of its members. Lenin, in spite of what he had promised Gorky, agreed, and on the very day that the first contingent of ARA personnel arrived in Moscow, the Russian Famine Relief Organisation was dissolved and almost all its non-Communist members arrested. Later in the same year both the Vecheka and Lenin himself admitted that these people had committed no crime: they had been arrested for purely political reasons. The probable reason for their arrest was in fact the usual Bolshevik fear of allowing any contact between soviet citizens and foreigners. Only the intervention of Hoover and Nansen saved the lives of the leaders of this humanitarian group. Throughout their work in Russia the Americans and the Russians working for the ARA were closely screened and watched by a large network of Vecheka agents. To the present day the ARA itself has been portrayed by soviet propaganda as permeated by US intelligence agents whose vile purposes were foiled by Vecheka vigilance; and as if to disinfect the country from foreign infection, many of the ARA's Russian workers were arrested after the winding up of the American mission in the summer of 1923.[15]

The Civil War proper, fought out between the Red Army and several White armies led by former Imperial generals and officers, began in late 1918 and was over by the end of 1920. It was accompanied by monstrous losses of life and devastation of land. The Bolshevik L. Kritsman gave the number of civilian dead as over seven million for the period 1 January 1918 to 1 July 1920 (in the territories in which registration was carried out); there were over five million typhus cases during 1919 and 1920.[16] One would arrive at a much higher figure for the entire population of the whole territory under soviet rule. No statistics exist of atrocities and massacres committed by both sides. For many years after, enormous numbers of homeless and orphaned children roamed the country.[17]

Quite early in 1918, however, long before the Civil War began, the Bolsheviks became involved in a territorial war with the Ukraine. This fertile and ancient land, with its own language and its own culture, had a long-standing separatist tradition. In the nineteenth century the separatist movement was persecuted and its leaders, including the poet Shevchenko, imprisoned. After the February revolution, the newly established democratic Central Rada (National Council) renewed the demands for Ukrainian autonomy. Socialist ministers of the Provisional Government were ready to make concessions to these demands and went specially to Kiev to negotiate a settlement.[18] But as usual the Provisional Government procrastinated; the Rada would wait no longer and it unilaterally declared the Ukraine independent.

In principle the Bolsheviks, who had seized power meanwhile, did not oppose national self-determination. But for anyone in power in Russia there was a snag: the Ukraine was the richest grain-producing region of Russia and, together with the adjacent Don territory (which had also declared its independence), the richest industrial and coal producing region. These considerations naturally overruled all else; the Bolsheviks attacked the Ukraine and the Don territory in January 1918 and with lightning speed occupied several key towns.

The peace treaty of Brest-Litovsk was signed on 3 March and ratified on 15 March, and in mid-April the Germans, who had already occupied the whole of the Ukraine, ousted all Bolshevik forces from it, deposed the Central Rada and installed General Skoropadskii as the new Hetman (ruler). Since the Germans had stripped the country bare of food and raw materials, while their puppet Skoropadskii tried to reinstate former landlords, they were soon heartily hated by the population.

However, the German occupation of the Ukraine served as a buffer between the Red Army which was then being formed and the White armies which had begun to assemble in southern Ukraine, the Don and elsewhere, but which withdrew further to the south before the German advance. Both gained time to regroup and retrain and it was not until the Germans were defeated by the Western Allies and left Russia altogether that the two came face to face.

Confronting the Bolsheviks was a formidable array: Kolchak in Siberia, Miller in Archangelsk, Iudenich at the gates of Petrograd and, above all, Denikin and Wrangel at the head of the so-called Volunteer Army in southern Russia; and behind them all the material and moral support provided by the Allied missions.

The White armies were passionately anti-Bolshevik and anti-revolutionary, but they were not united by any common policy or purpose. Some were monarchist, yet not enamoured of Nicholas Romanov. Others did not even want to bring back the old order: this was the case with the commander-in-chief, General Denikin, who says as much in his valuable chronicle of the Civil War.[19] The White armies were led by professional soldiers, as many generals of the Imperial Army and hundreds of officers rallied to them; yet no amount of professionalism was capable of stemming the moral rot that soon replaced the early enthusiasm. For one thing the White armies were followed wherever they went by a huge train of officers' families, dispossessed merchants, industrialists and landlords, also with their families, all bent on vengeance but meanwhile causing unspeakable confusion. For another, the officers were in an unsteady and defeatist mood, over-reacting to reversals and defeats. Their invariable reaction to both victory and defeat consisted of wild orgies and indiscriminate looting, from Allied stores or the local population. They were copied in both respects by the other ranks and the innumerable petty crooks who swarmed round the army. As Denikin says in his book, his forces left behind them 'a residue of violence, looting and anti-Jewish pogroms'.[20] He describes the return to base of the famous Mamontov cavalry unit which had just carried out a brilliant raid against the Bolshevik rear: columns of carts, miles long and heavily loaded with loot, moved towards the base guarded by long lines of combat personnel.[21] And General Wrangel, reporting to Denikin on 9 December 1919, puts it more strongly still: 'The war is becoming a means of growing rich, requisitioning has degenerated into pillage and speculation. What cannot be used on the spot is sent to the interior and sold at a profit.... The army is completely demoralised and is rapidly turning into a bunch of tradesmen and profiteers.'[22]

Potentially more dangerous for the fortunes of the White 'crusade' was the fact that they had forfeited whatever mass support they might have enjoyed. At first the peasants, disillusioned with the Bolsheviks, welcomed the Whites. Denikin, in his book, quotes from a booklet by the Menshevik Kuchin-Oranskii: 'the Volunteer Army's advance was supported by peasant unrest, which prepared the ground for them.' But the Whites committed the error of allowing former landlords to re-establish themselves, usually by force, with the help of the military. In some places these landlords, after settling old scores, increased the rents for holdings in an outrageous manner.[23] No wonder that the peasants who had been deserting from the Red Army now began to desert from the Whites.

On the other side, the Bolsheviks had no army to speak of at the onset of the Civil War. Their own demagogy had caused disarray and confusion in the army. Before their seizure of power, Bolshevik propaganda had urged soldiers to insult and disobey their officers and to desert. Now they had to attract soldiers back into the army, as well as to find officers to lead them. An untrained and ill-equipped mass of unwilling and often hostile peasants and workers — such was the unpromising material out of which Lev Trotsky, chairman of the Revolutionary War Council and Commissar for War shaped an effective and ultimately victorious Red Army. A vain but superhumanly energetic and able man, he raced in his special train along the front lines, making rousing speeches, bullying as well as encouraging his commanders and soldiers. He proved himself an organiser and a military leader of genius and his prestige and popularity among the troops was immense. He did not scruple to employ former officers of the Imperial Army — as many as 30,000 of them, including General Shorin, Colonel Sergei Kamenev (who was put in command of Soviet forces facing Kolchak) and the future Marshal Michael Tukhachevskii[24] — but he took their families hostage to make sure that they did not desert or sabotage the war effort. He appointed political commissars to every army unit to watch over its morale and behaviour; if a unit disobeyed orders or retreated he ordered the political commissar, the commanding officer and every tenth man to be shot. He also allowed his troops and the special detachments of the Vecheka attached to the armies to commit atrocities comparable to those committed by the Whites.

Trotsky's vindictiveness showed itself particularly clearly in his treatment of the peasant army of Makhno.[25] This army was centred on the village of Gulai Pole in the Ukraine where Nestor Makhno,* a native of the village and a convinced anarchist, had set up several communes, a farm workers' union and a peasants' soviet. There he organised periodic congresses where the peasants could discuss their problems. This rural democracy suited the peasants admirably and made *batko* (little father) Makhno greatly loved. When central authorities — Russian or Ukrainian or even German — tried to stamp out his little domain, he had no difficulty in raising an army of irregulars. His Revolutionary Insurgent Army grew first to 20,000, later to 40,000 men, and many of the smaller local peasant bands joined him. His army, flying the black Anarchist flag, suffered from chronic shortage of arms but made up for it by fast riding, lightning raids and clever ambushes; it could disperse, hide and reassemble with incredible speed. It had the sympathy of villagers over a large territory and this was a great help. Sometimes when, exhausted by fierce fighting, the insurgents arrived at a friendly village, they would pass on their arms to the villagers; these would then mount fresh horses and take their place in the battle. At first the insurgents made limited punitive raids, killing, secretly and quickly, landlords who were known to be gross exploiters, German officers (but not other ranks) and Bolshevik commissars.

In 1918 Makhno's army fought the Germans in the Ukraine, and their Ukrainian puppet, Hetman Skoropadskii; later and well into 1920, it fought now the Bolsheviks (for their War Communism) and now the Whites (for their plans of reinstating landlords). When

*Born of a poor peasant family, Makhno was arrested in 1908 at the age of nineteen and condemned to death for involvement in an anarchist murder of a policeman; his sentence being commuted to life imprisonment, he spent nine years in the Butyrki prison in Moscow, where he mixed with fellow revolutionaries. When he left, in 1917, he was a more convinced anarchist than ever.[26]

Makhno made common cause with the Red Army his help was considerable, as his irregular troops could harass the rear of the White armies more effectively than any regular army unit. On two important occasions Makhno played a significant part in Red victories: when Denikin advanced on Orel and threatened Moscow in the summer of 1919, Makhno's army cut Denikin's supply lines, which forced him to retreat; and in October–November 1920 Makhno helped the Red Army to rout Wrangel, a victory which signalled the end of the Civil War. But throughout Makhno insisted on full autonomy for his army and this did not suit the Red Command. Trotsky ordered the massacre of Makhno's insurgents as soon as he was sure of Denikin's defeat. The Red Army attacked in force, killing thousands of Makhno's followers, torturing and then killing their families and destroying their houses. After several months of fierce fighting only about 250 men remained alive and Makhno escaped with them over the border into Romania.

The outcome of the Civil War was often in question. At the height of the White offensive in June 1919, Lenin is reported by Lev Kamenev to have said: 'Only a miracle can save us.'[27] But slowly the Bolsheviks gained ground. Helped by local partisans they regained Siberia, entering Irkutsk in January 1920 and capturing the State Gold Reserve which Kolchak had seized earlier.[28] The title of Supreme Ruler passed from Kolchak to Denikin on 4 January 1920, but the Whites, hard pressed by then, had to abandon the attempt to rescue Kolchak (and the State Gold Reserve) and withdrew from Siberia. The Civil War ended with the utter defeat of the Whites on all fronts.

In the event, it was not a miracle that saved the Bolsheviks but the fact that Russian peasants and workers, on balance, found them the lesser evil: however disgusted they were with Bolshevik rule, they hated the Whites even more. This became ever clearer as the war developed. At first the peasants found little to choose between the two sides: the Whites and the Reds looted and pillaged and massacred with equal brutality and peasants groaned under both. Peasants fought sometimes on one, at other times on the other side, but never with much enthusiasm, and always ready to desert and return to their villages. Only when they were defending their own neighbourhood — usually under a local leader — did they display real fighting spirit; then they could be truly heroic. But in the end they came to prefer, if only by a small margin, the Reds who had originally given them their land, dispossessed the landlords and were 'of the people' to the Whites who were taking away land, reinstating the former landlords, and themselves behaving like *bare* (masters).

Workers and revolutionary intellectuals were even less inclined to support the Whites, however much they were suffering under the Bolsheviks. As the Menshevik Raphail Abramovitch explained: 'they were altogether incapable, psychologically and politically, of making common cause with the Whites.' Besides, they still harboured 'a vague hope that once the Civil War was won, the internal family quarrel with the Bolsheviks could somehow be settled.'[29] In a letter sent to party organisations, the Menshevik Central Committee said in August 1919: 'Of the two regimes locked in implacable struggle we must choose the one that ... alone holds a possibility of developing into democracy ... of saving the revolution and protecting the interests of toilers.... How can one refuse to defend — arms in hand, if necessary — a regime that, despite everything still contains some possibilities of revolutionary development ...?' The letter concludes with the lame hope that 'the transformation of the soviet regime is at least conceivable, no matter how small the actual chances of reforming it from within'.[30] Such were the illusions which the Mensheviks still harboured at that time.

Quite consistently, the Menshevik Central Committee ordered a mobilisation of party members and conducted a recruiting campaign for the Red Army. In doing so they exposed themselves to a double persecution: by the Whites who considered them as bad as the Bolsheviks, and by the Reds. They did not endear themselves to Lenin by supporting him in the Civil War: he hated nothing so much as being supported by Mensheviks, and continued to bracket them together with the SRs as counter-revolutionaries and as accomplices of the Whites, the landlords and the capitalists. In an address to all party members of 9 July 1919 entitled 'All out against Denikin', the Bolshevik Central Committee openly encouraged indiscriminate terror, urging comrades 'to seek out and imprison and sometimes even to shoot hundreds of traitors among the Kadets, the politically neutral, the Mensheviks and Social Revolutionaries, who act (some with arms, some conspiring, others agitating against mobilisation, like the printers and the railwaymen among the Mensheviks) *against* the Soviet government, i.e. *for Denikin*.'[31] When, at the Seventh Congress of Soviets in December 1919, Martov protested against 'the monstrous growth of terror', Lenin once again asserted that 'both terror and the chekas are absolutely indispensable.' 'Nor,' he declared, 'do we conceal who it is that we deprive of rights ... it is the group of Mensheviks and SRs.'[32]

Towards the end of the Civil War, the Soviet government turned its attention to all those countries and regions populated by national minorities which had declared their independence in 1917–1918. These countries and regions had their own, often very ancient, languages and cultures and had suffered much under the ruthless russification policy of the tsars. The Mensheviks recognised the validity of the national aspirations of these peoples and acknowledged the right of national minorities to self-determination. In a wider context they declared in 1920: 'Aggressive revolutionary wars as a method of carrying social revolution into foreign countries are unacceptable to social democracy.'[33] As for Lenin, he had no such reservations. He was guided by considerations of political power when he ordered the Red Army to invade independent territories, depose their governments and replace their institutions with soviet replicas. Thus the Ukraine became the Ukrainian soviet Republic with a Ukrainian soviet government, Ukrainian soviets and a Ukrainian counterpart to Vecheka, the Vucheka, the last named going down in history as particularly bloodthirsty.[34] In short, the Bolsheviks continued in essence the policy of the tsars — under a certain amount of camouflage.

One example of Bolshevik territorial policy fits particularly well into the framework of this book because the country in question had a Menshevik government; this country was Georgia, a small country in the Caucasus. The three major ethnic groups in the Caucasus (or Trans-Caucasus to give it its official name) were the Georgians, the Armenians and the Azerbaijan Tartars. The Muslim Tartars, who naturally looked to Turkey for support, were traditional enemies of the Christian Armenians and frequently massacred them; the Armenians, in turn, looked to Russia for protection. The only thing that united the whole region was hatred of the tsarist regime, and that made a disproportionate number of their educated élite join the revolutionary movement.

The Georgian revolutionary movement had a strong contingent of highly politically conscious workers. It was well organised though it suffered much from the bitter rivalries between Bolsheviks and Mensheviks. Georgian Mensheviks had always been very close to Russian Mensheviks, and individual Georgians — Tsereteli, Chkheidze and others — had played a leading role in the Russian party. But the Georgian Menshevik party on the whole came to oppose the participation of socialists in the Provisional Government and wanted the soviets to take over. In Georgia Mensheviks took over the government with the support of the workers' soviets, and formed a national guard for its defence.

Georgia was content to remain part of Russia as long as Russia had a democratic government which would not interfere with its culture and inner life. But after the seizure of power by the Bolsheviks and after the conclusion of the Brest-Litovsk treaty which ceded parts of Georgia to the Turks, it became obvious that Georgia had to fend for itself. An attempt to form a united Trans-Caucasian Republic in partnership with Azerbaijan and Armenia failed, and on 26 May 1918 Georgia proclaimed its independence under a Menshevik government, with the Menshevik leader Noah Zhordania as both premier and president of the Soviet.[35]

The new country was beset on all sides by hostile forces, but its worst enemy proved to be within: Georgian Bolsheviks recognised only one fatherland and one government and that was Lenin's Russia. These Bolsheviks fomented discontent and rebellion among disbanded soldiers and other unstable elements. In November 1919 they staged an abortive coup, after which almost a thousand of them were imprisoned by the Georgian government. Like their Russian counterparts, the Georgian Mensheviks had scruples about using violence against their opponents; they did not shoot the prisoners.

And so the inevitable happened and independent little Georgia was swallowed by its 'big brother'. The year 1920 saw a typical Lenin manoeuvre: he offered to recognise Georgia's independence in return for the legalisation of its Bolshevik party.[36] The Georgians agreed. The agreement was signed on 7 May 1920, and all local Bolsheviks were released from prison. Meanwhile the Red Army occupied Azerbaijan and Armenia, while inside Georgia Bolsheviks were once again, and more openly this time, preparing a rebellion. The order to begin the rebellion was finally given by Moscow in January 1921, and the Red Army ordered to come to its aid — Lenin wanted the overthrow of the Menshevik government to look like an internal uprising.[37] On 16 February units of the Eleventh Red Army, and a few days later the Red cavalry under its famous commander Budennyi, crossed into Georgia; soviet forces were approximately 100,000 strong, with heavy artillery, while the Georgians were no more than 50,000 men, armed with light weapons only.[38] The Georgians defended themselves bravely and desperately and held out much longer than their neighbours in Armenia or Azerbaijan had done, but their position was an impossible one; and on 18 March 1921 the government capitulated. Soviet Russian occupation was fiercely resented and hated by Georgians and they rose against the oppressors in 1924: the rebellion was put down with much bloodshed. At sessions of the Socialist International, Russian Mensheviks repeatedly protested against Bolshevik conquest and subsequent persecutions and so made the story of Georgia known abroad.

6 The Harassment of Socialists

Doctrinal differences apart, most Bolsheviks harboured no hatred against fellow revolutionaries with whom they had shared tsarist prison and exile: they were certainly reluctant to see them persecuted. Martov's sister, Lydia Dan, remembered many occasions when she was warned over the phone, by some anonymous caller or by a close personal friend among top Bolsheviks, when to expect a house search.[1] If the socialists were nevertheless persecuted it was entirely due to Lenin, supported by Trotsky and Dzerzhinskii. He was determined to keep them in prison and even to 'shoot them if they showed their noses' (according to his notes scribbled during the Eleventh Communist party Congress in 1922).[2]

The first socialists to be repressed were the SRs — understandably, in view of the great popularity they enjoyed among the masses, particularly among peasants. The Right SRs had received the largest number of votes of any party in the elections to the Constituent Assembly and presented a serious problem for the government. But the involvement of the Right SRs in anti-Bolshevik revolts and governments, in Samara and elsewhere, soon gave the Bolsheviks ample excuses for persecuting them.

Both the Right and the Left SRs were heirs to the individualist tradition of the *Narodniki*, from whom they also inherited the propensity to use terrorism when other, more democratic, policies failed. And both were more loosely organised and more difficult to control than the two marxist parties. Hence there were terrorist acts, including the attempt on Lenin's life, and armed conspiracies undertaken by various members of the two factions with or without the agreement or even the knowledge of their respective central committees.

The Left SRs more or less eliminated themselves politically by first joining Lenin's government, in November 1917, and then leaving it soon after. It goes without saying that this short-lived alliance was a tactical move on Lenin's part.[3] The Left SRs had left the government mainly because they thought the terms of the Brest-Litovsk peace treaty humiliating. Their indignation found expression in the assassination of the German Ambassador, von Mirbach, and an abortive rising in Moscow in July 1918. After that all members of their Central Committee were arrested; a prominent member of the party, Alexandrovich, and several sailors were shot; and the Left SR press was shut down. This was followed by mass arrests in the provinces. Finally, the party was wiped out after the Kronstadt rising of 1921, in which the Left SRs, together with the Anarchists, had been active. The Left SR losses up to 1921 are said to have been twenty-six leading party members shot, with four others dying in prison.[4] In April 1920 it was estimated that Left SRs formed the largest contingent in the main Moscow prison, Butyrki.

The Anarchists, like the Left SRs, had actively supported the Bolshevik coup, but became disillusioned almost at once. They valued individual freedom above all and objected violently to the suppression of free press and free speech. They began to talk of the need for yet another revolution — a 'third revolution' — an idea that found an echo among the Kronstadt sailors in 1921 and among anti-Bolshevik peasants during the Civil War. The Cheka soon found a reason to round them up. During the October days the Anarchists, like the Bolsheviks, had attracted many outright criminal elements; these continued to loot and kill in spite of warnings by the Anarchist Federation. Under the pretext of routing 'criminal riff-raff', armed Cheka units surrounded twenty-six Anarchist strongholds in Moscow in the night of 11/12 April 1918 and after a fierce battle — ten to twelve chekists were killed and thirty to forty Anarchists killed or wounded — over five hundred were taken prisoner.[5] However, when the Cheka raided Anarchist centres in Petrograd on 23 April, there was no bloodshed and genuine Anarchists were soon released.[6] In later years the Bolsheviks displayed no such leniency. According to Anarchist sources in Berlin, by 1922 180 prominent Anarchists had been arrested, of whom 38 had been shot and 70 died in prison or in exile; all the rest had either died or fled abroad.[7] These figures do not take into account the large numbers of peasants in Makhno's army which fought under the Anarchist flag, who had been treacherously murdered on Trotsky's orders (see p. 47), nor Anarchist sympathisers in the Kronstadt rising.

The Bolshevik press and the Cheka persistently described all socialists and Anarchists as counter-revolutionaries. Indeed, from early on Lenin had equated 'counter-revolution' with 'counter-bolshevism', thus creating confusion and uncertainty in the minds of simple people. This was one of those 'big lies' which, as Hitler also knew, never fail. Lenin knew perfectly well that Russian revolutionaries could not possibly make common cause with real counter-revolutionaries; he simply needed to denigrate them so as to make their persecution more acceptable.

Bolshevik restrictions on the freedom of the press affected all opposition parties alike, even though Kadet and other 'bourgeois' papers were the first to suffer. A government decree on the press dated 27 October 1917 (old style) sanctioned the closure of papers hostile to the government or guilty of distortion of facts; and already on 25 October the Petrograd MRC had closed the liberal paper *Obshcheie delo* (Common Cause) and arrested its editor, the former *Narodnik* Vladimir Burtsev — a man who had been famous for exposing Okhrana agents inside the revolutionary movement.[8] Then, on 6 November, the MRC resolved that all Moscow papers 'regardless of orientation' could appear freely, and on 17 November the VTsIK promised to allocate paper to all shades of public opinion.[9] Yet on 19 November the MRC established a Supervisory Commission for the press and on 18 December a Revolutionary Tribunal on the press was set up by the government with powers to close or fine publications found guilty of 'crimes against the people' — meaning criticism of the Bolshevik government. Both were eventually superseded by the Vecheka which also conducted searches, carried out arrests and closed premises. Censorship was introduced officially in March 1918: all newspapers were required to send three copies of each issue to the Vecheka, on pain of being closed down. Similar measures were carried out in the provinces by local chekas. Allocation of paper and printing facilities were put under government control. The central organ of the Menshevik Central Committee, *Rabochaia Gazeta* (Workers' Journal), was closed down in December 1917; and during May–June 1918 its successors *Novyi Luch* (The New Ray) and *Vpered* (Forward) as well as several SR and other socialist papers were closed. On 16 July the independent *Novaia Zhisn* (New Life), edited by Maxim Gorky, suffered the same fate. Closures and fines were also imposed in the provinces. So throughout 1918 and 1919 socialist papers were allowed to appear only very intermittently.

This state of affairs caused great indignation among workers. In November 1917 the trade union of printing workers formed a 'Committee for the freedom of the press' and invited Menshevik and SR central committees and the Petrograd Town Council to send representatives. The appeal issued by the Committee made the point that 'freedom of the press has become the privilege of one party — the Bolshevik party. The revolution has been deprived of the word.' In December 1917, the All-Russian Congress of printers' unions in Moscow followed this up with a resolution (endorsed by almost all votes, though the prominent Bolshevik Bukharin spoke against it) protesting that 'the persecution of the press by the Sovnarkom ...

deprives the people of the last possibility of obtaining information about the activities of the government and places this government entirely beyond all control or accountability'.[10] The Petrograd paper *Rabochii Internatsional* (Labour International) described a meeting of some sixteen thousand workers at the Putilov Works; the meeting had carried a resolution which demanded that all newspapers be allowed to resume publication and all arrested socialists be freed.[11]

In June 1918, Mensheviks, SRs and other oppositionists were expelled from the VTsIK and from local soviets (see p. 82); and almost all their papers were closed down. This was a great blow to the Mensheviks' precarious 'legal status'. They were partially reinstated in the soviets in November 1918, and the SRs in February 1919, but neither expulsion nor reinstatement made much practical difference as both parties were harassed by the Cheka throughout the whole period.

The Cheka needed no particular excuse for arresting socialists, but from time to time a government decree provided a convenient cover for its work. One such was the decree of July 1918. Ostensibly it was a decree for the mobilisation of the bourgeoisie for work in the rear —part of Trotsky's plan for compulsory labour. This decree of 20 July 1918, followed by a similar but more strongly worded decree of 5 October, was meant to apply to those who lived on income not derived from manual labour, such as former directors of joint stock companies, merchants or brokers, but also to professional men and women, lawyers, former army officers,[12] bourgeois journalists, priests, monks and peasants who employed hired labour.[13] It was widely used as a pretext for street raids, when men and women were picked up by the Cheka simply because they looked middle class; it was enough that their clothing, however shabby, was not that of manual workers or peasants. Sometimes, when the chekists were given a quota of arrests to make, they arrested just anybody. Under these umbrella decrees many socialists, too, were arrested, at random and for no reason.

At that time Peters was at the head of the Vecheka — Dzerzhinskii having temporarily resigned — and this is what he said about the arrested Mensheviks: '... we divide them into active and passive ones. The latter will be freed, but there will be no mercy for the former.'[14] Although the persecution of Mensheviks remained comparatively mild throughout the first two years of Bolshevik rule, it was not negligible. In the course of recurrent arrests Mensheviks could savour to the full the bitter realisation that barely a year after the downfall of tsarism, they were once again in prison, protesting against bad prison conditions (these were worse than in tsarist times); while their relatives queued for hours to hand in their *peredacha* (parcels for prisoners) with a few items of underclothing and a little food.

The persecution of Mensheviks by Lenin's government was, in fact, conducted on two levels. Menshevik leaders were treated comparatively tolerantly. On the second, much less publicised level, the persecution of Menshevik rank and file and working-class followers was severe. Here the true face of leninism showed itself most clearly. Dzerzhinskii denounced the SRs and the Mensheviks as causing industrial unrest and he urged the Cheka to suppress that unrest.[15] Cheka troops, and often the army, were ordered to break up strikes and to arrest all strikers, and to disperse and shoot down workers' meetings and demonstrations. In the Bolshevik press Menshevik and SRs were commonly blamed for strikes — and in terms that made them appear as outside agencies, pernicious groups of intellectuals poisoning the pure minds of the workers. This deliberately overlooked the fact that many workers were members of one or other of these two parties and had, in fact, suffered for their convictions under the tsarist regime. They were soon to suffer for them under Bolshevik rule as well.

7 *The Bolshevik Government Against Workers and Peasants*

Lenin's policy towards the workers was at all times ambiguous and his pronouncements before and after his seizure of power were contradictory. Did he consider himself a champion of the workers or did he simply use them as a convenient lever by which to hoist himself into power? His professed intention was to use his power for their good, yet he had no understanding of workers as human beings and little real sympathy with them. He said that workers would run the factories and eventually the state, but when they proved too backward, too ignorant and too undisciplined to run the factories, let alone the state, he felt no compunction about sending them to concentration camps. He certainly had no use for any manifestation of the 'creativity of the masses' that he professed to admire. Perhaps as Bertrand Russell remarked (see p. 9 above), Lenin simply lacked psychological imagination. People had to be fitted, willy-nilly, into his plans for a remote and perhaps unrealisable future. When individuals, groups, even whole classes of people did not fit in, he applied one of three methods: first he flattered and tried to seduce them, then he tried to outmanoeuvre them, and finally he coerced them. Sometimes he applied two of these methods, or even all three, at the same time, but he really preferred the third method, that of coercion, as being the quickest and the most efficient.

His policy towards the workers is a case in point. Before and after the October coup workers were flattered into thinking that they were the rulers of the country, the chosen class; and they were urged to enter the administration. This proved, in fact, partially successful; workers who belonged to the small semi-educated elite often showed great administrative ability. Unfortunately they were then swallowed up by the governmental machine and were lost to the working class. As Fedor Dan put it, the fact that the Bolsheviks survived the first months of their rule at all was largely due to the devoted work of the cadres of gifted worker-organisers whom the Mensheviks had been so patiently training in *samodeiatelnost* (self-reliance and initiative).[1] On the other hand the broader influx of less educated workers into the administration was an outright disaster. It was one thing to absorb individual workers into the administration, or even into the party, and quite another to absorb and control large numbers of them. To allocate to the largely illiterate Russian workers as a class the responsibility of running industry or state was simply absurd.

This emerged clearly from the second of Lenin's experiments in flattering the workers — the short lived 'workers' control of industry.'* In a number of articles and brochures written during the summer and autumn of 1917, Lenin had expressed his belief that the transition from a capitalist to a socialist economy would be 'gradual, peaceful and tranquil'. Capitalism, he wrote, had created large-scale production, and 'the great majority of functions ... have become so simplified and can be reduced to such elementary operations of registration, book-keeping and checking, that they will be fully within the reach of all literate people, and it will be quite possible to perform these functions for any ordinary "workman's wage"'. The economy would thus be controlled by workers and peasants 'who would *learn quickly* by their own experience, how to divide the land, production and bread'. Furthermore, Lenin argued, 'workers' control is *capable* of becoming universal in scope, all-embracing, omnipresent, and the most accurate and conscientious *accounting* of production and distribution ... Therein lies the essence of the proletarian, i.e., the socialist, revolution.'[2]

Though much of what Lenin said during the summer of 1917 was pure demagogy, he seems to have believed in this naive vision of the future. In any case he actually instituted workers' control of industry through a decree promulgated on 27 November 1917. The whole structure rested on a bureaucratic machine capped by an All-Russian Council of Workers' Control which was supposed to work out the rules and issue instructions, form and send out commissions of trained instructors and settle disputes between workers and factory owners. But in effect, this clumsy superstructure was never called upon to control the Control; it was never convened and soon disappeared from the scene altogether.[3] Nor were the trade unions put in charge of the undertaking, as the Mensheviks suggested; though the trade unions were eventually blamed for its collapse.

Thus it was left largely to the workers themselves to implement the decree. They found themselves authorised to supervise production, the purchase of raw materials and the sale of the industrial output, and to examine all the business correspondence and account books of their respective factories. This was accompanied by torrents of hate propaganda against 'blood-sucking capitalists', and assurances to

*The Russian word *kontrol* is more correctly translated as 'supervision'

workers, soldiers and peasants that 'all grain, factories, tools, products and transport' were from now on wholly theirs.[4]

The results were predictable. *Izvestiia* reported that there was 'chaos in the minds of a number of people. The ideas of socialism are quite often interpreted . . . as an opportunity to divide property . . . and the workers are now carrying away the machines . . . from the plants . . . thinking that these objects belong to them.'[5] Worse still, many workers expected to find lots of money in factory office safes, waiting to be 'expropriated'. Obviously, in the absence of trade union leadership, the most uneducated, raw workers went on the rampage. According to Maxim Gorky's paper *Novaia Zhisn*, workers interfered with the work of the administration, annulled the orders of the managers and upset the economic plans of enterprises.[6] The technical and managerial personnel, prevented from exercising any authority or initiative, became sullen and often hostile; and factory owners, though not at first officially dispossessed, ceased to take part in the work of the factories. By mid-1918 industrial production had practically come to a standstill.[7]

The situation was considerably worsened by the state of the railways. Shliapnikov, who as Commissar for Labour had, together with Lenin, signed the decree on workers' control, reported to the VTsIK in March 1918 that there was 'complete disorganisation of the railways' and that it was getting worse. 'New locomotives and rolling stock were not produced and the existing ones not replaced, while workers in repair shops were engaged in fitting railway cars for the use of fellow workers and their families; train crews often refused to take trains out; and the workers being guaranteed their pay, blatantly neglected work.' He warned that labour discipline on the railways needed to be rigorously re-established 'at any cost and before all else.'[8] Tomskii, chairman of the Central Committee of the Council of Trade Unions, pointed out that 'the decline in labour productivity has reached catastrophic proportions and industrial production is threatened with complete collapse'.[9] Moderate Bolsheviks tried to get to the root of the trouble. Thus Rykov argued that 'workers have less experience than specialists, so that every effort to replace specialists by workers makes the situation so much the worse'.[10] But in general the Bolsheviks were more inclined to blame or threaten the workers than to admit that they themselves had largely created the situation. The Bolshevik Gastev said in May 1918: 'What we really have is sabotage on a nation-wide scale, by the whole people, by the proletariat.'[11] And sabotage was of course a matter for the Cheka.

What Lenin himself felt about the collapse of his illusions remains unrecorded. In his public pronouncements he continued to extol the 'creativity of the masses'. In January 1918 he was insisting that it was 'only an old bourgeois prejudice that ... the ordinary worker and peasant are incapable of managing the affairs of state;'[12] and in March 1918 he was still talking of 'the spirit of experiment and independent initiative of the proletarian masses'.[13] But by January 1919 he was talking in a very different vein. The workers, he said, had not yet cleansed themselves 'of the filth of the old world.... They continued to stand up to their knees in that filth.' He even conceded that it would be utopian to expect them to change 'all at once'[14] and that the introduction of Workers' Control had been 'a contradictory, an incomplete step'. It had been necessary, he said, so that the workers should learn how to administer industry, but it appeared that 'a long time will be needed before that class can learn'.[15] In this way he shifted the blame from his shoulders on to theirs.

Workers' control was in fact an economic catastrophe and had to be abolished. In December 1917 the Supreme Council of National Economy was established under the chairmanship of Felix Dzerzhinskii, and it was supposed to work out an overall plan for industrial production. But in the event it proved almost as inept as the workers. According to Lozovskii, a Bolshevik critic, this body created 'both in the centre and locally, a number of entangled and cumbersome control organisations interfering with each other's work'.[16] Meanwhile the country's industry was in ruins and much valuable time had been wasted.

After the failure of Workers' Control of Industry (and, for that matter, Workers' Management of Industry, proposed by Lenin as a separate stage in November 1918), exactly opposite methods were introduced: one-man management, with 'bourgeois' specialists reinstated as managers, and the workers subjected to 'iron discipline'. But since Lenin made it clear that the 'bourgeois' specialists would be compelled to fall into line with the proletariat 'no matter how much they resist and fight at every step',[17] while the workers were kept in line by the introduction of disciplinary courts and strict work norms, both sides of industry became uncooperative and dissatisfied. The results were apathy and a further decline of the economy. Periodic official efforts to stimulate enthusiasm for work by means of propaganda inspired few people outside the Komsomol (Communist Youth). Such were the voluntary *subbotniki* which required people after a week's hard work to sacrifice their Saturday rest in order to cut wood or the like — work for which they were often quite unfitted; such were the various 'shock' work programmes — the Stakhanovite movement in the Stalin era or the present day 'work emulation'.[18] All proved unproductive and often outright harmful to the normal functioning of industry as a whole.

Meanwhile the nationalisation of large industrial enterprises followed that of banks; and as railways always had been state-owned, the state was now the largest employer of labour. Labour relations between the Bolshevik state and the workers became worse than between industrialists and workers in pre-revolutionary times. Disciplinary courts, labour books (passports), strict production norms and punishment for absenteeism — now styled 'labour desertion' — and for strikes — now called 'sabotage' — threatened the worker at every step. Nor was this linked with any emergency directly connected with the Civil War. A government decree of 5 April 1921 (that is after the end of the War), signed by Lenin, empowered the disciplinary courts to mete out punishments ranging from public reprimand or reduced pay for three months to compulsory hard labour, or even confinement in a concentration camp, for up to six months.[19] At the same time 'workers' democracy', 'proletarian democracy' and 'production democracy' continued to be stock slogans of official propaganda. Before long not only factories but also the men and women who worked in them became state-owned. Already in 1920 this was spelled out with devastating candour by a high-ranking soviet official: 'Step by step the entire labour force of the country became encompassed by a single leadership and a single principle. . . . [It] was nationalised and having become the property [*sobstvennost*] of the state, was carrying out the orders and the objectives of the state.'[20]

The next logical step was the militarisation of labour, and Lenin and Trotsky had no hesitation in taking that step. The stages that led to its introduction were in themselves significant. After the end of the Civil War Trotsky was summoned to Moscow to deal with the problem of dwindling manpower in industry. It appeared that in the most important branches of industry some 300,000 workers were missing from a total workforce of 1,150,000. It was not difficult to guess where they had gone. Faced with near famine conditions in industrial centres and large cities and 'iron discipline' in the factories, the workers had gone either to villages in search of food or to other regions in search of better conditions of work.[21] Trotsky, flushed with his undoubted success as an organiser of the Red Army, entered, with his usual energy and enthusiasm, into the task of bringing the workers under military discipline. He already had considerable experience in compulsory labour, which he first introduced in 1918. It was then applied to the bourgeoisie, whom 'we want to wipe off the face of the earth,' and Trotsky assigned to them all the most disagreeable and dirty work, such as cleaning barracks, camps, streets etc. 'We must place them in such conditions that they will lose the desire to remain bourgeois. . . . Let every bourgeois house be marked as one in which so many families live who lead a parasitic mode of life and we shall post yellow stickers on these houses.'[22] It is worth recalling that Trotsky himself came from a family of well-to-do merchants.

That was in 1918. In April 1920 Trotsky described, with equal enthusiasm, the compulsory labour laws that he proposed to apply to workers: 'we are organising . . . labour on a new socialist basis . . . for the first time in history, we are attempting to organise labour in the interest of the toiling majority.' But if the workers are to be fitted into a planned and centralised economy, 'labour must be distributed, shifted and ordered in the same way as soldiers are. . . . This is the basis of labour militarisation', and that 'is unthinkable without . . . the introduction of a regime under which every worker feels himself a soldier of labour.' The worker who disobeys orders 'will be a deserter, and punished as such.'[23] The idea was not new to Lenin. At the moment of creation of the Vecheka in early December 1917, Lenin had passed to Dzerzhinskii a hastily scribbled note during a session of the Sovnorkom; in it he outlined a decree that would establish nationwide coercion as 'the first step towards introduction of universal labour service.'[24] In January 1920 Lenin established the Committee of Universal Compulsory Labour, Glavkomtrud, with its infinite number of local sub-committees. Significantly its first chairman was Felix Dzerzhinskii.[25] At the same time, if not earlier, some military units, and indeed whole armies, which were no longer needed for the purposes of war, were converted into labour armies. Thus the entire Third Army with 150,000 men was transformed into one such;[26] Stalin was put in charge of yet another labour army, the Ukrainian.

Lenin endorsed Trotsky's plans at the Ninth Party Congress, held between 29 March and 4 April 1920: 'the proletariat [meaning the Bolshevik party] has the right to resort to compulsion in order to maintain itself at all costs.'[27] At the Third All-Russian Congress of Trade Unions in April 1920, Lenin and Trotsky again defended the principle of labour conscription. Their speeches were attacked and criticised by several Menshevik leaders (Dan, Abramovitch and others) present at the Congress, and to the consternation of the Bolsheviks the Mensheviks were loudly applauded by the audience.

The methods of militarised labour were most forcibly applied by Trotsky to the transport system. Appointed Commissar of Railways in March 1920, he introduced into the work of the railways the principles he had found so effective in the Red Army, namely political commissars as watchdogs over managers and workers. In the transport system the political commissars were subordinated to the Glavpolitput (*Glavnoe politicheskoie upravlenie putei soobstcheniia* — main political administration of transport) which had been established in March 1919. This body had not been very effective at first, so that it had been necessary to mobilise five thousand Communists to strengthen it. Trotsky had furthermore brought with him many political commissars who had worked for him in the Red Army. On behalf of the Glavpolitput he now proceeded to reorganise the entire transport system. He did this without consulting the two trade unions involved, namely that of the railwaymen, Tsekprofsozh (formerly Vikzhel, see page 68) and that of the water transport workers, Tsekvod. When these unions, which were among the largest in the country,[28] protested against the highhanded methods of the Glavpolitput, their central committees were disbanded and replaced by one Central Committee, with Trotsky at the head of a combined trade union, to be called Tsektran (Central Committee of the trade unions of transport workers). Political commissars were attached to railway stations and depots and to ships, ports etc.[29]

The Tsektran became a symbol of oppression of the working class and its actions were bitterly resented, even by many leading Bolshevik trade unionists and particularly by Tomskii, the chairman of the All-Russian Central Council of Trade Unions. Trotsky defended himself at the Fifth All-Russian Conference of Trade Unions in November 1920; and one of his principal assistants at the Tsektran, Goltsman, went so far as to say that 'merciless black-jack discipline' was necessary against the workers and that Tsektran 'will not hesitate to use jail, exile and hard labour'.[30]

In the event the militarisation of labour, as distinct from compulsory labour, did not survive into the era of the New Economic Policy, which was introduced in March 1921. The resumption of free trade and the decentralisation of large industries brought about a certain relaxation of labour relations. The Glavkomtrud was abolished in March 1921, but the system of compulsory labour remained intact.[31]

Bolshevik treatment of the peasants was as bad, if not worse, than Bolshevik treatment of the workers, but the situation was very different. Originally neither Mensheviks nor Bolsheviks were primarily interested in peasants; as marxists, they were more concerned with industrial workers. But in 1917 they found themselves face to face with the peasant problem; they realised that the fate of the proletarian revolution depended on the will of the peasants to feed or to starve the cities. There was already an acute shortage of food in industrial centres, as there was also in the countryside. The 1914 War had depopulated the villages; fields and cattle had been neglected and the surplus grain taken by the army, leaving nothing for the sowing of the next crop. Towards the end of the war soldiers began to desert in ever larger numbers and to drift back to their villages, usually taking their rifles with them. They had long-standing grievances against their landlords and the tsarist government. The decree of 1861 which had abolished serfdom had made them free but had left them materially as badly off as ever. The land allocated to them was not enough for efficient farming and they had been hoping for a more advantageous distribution of arable land and pastures ever since. They were in a desperate and dangerous mood. Lenin recognised the revolutionary (or purely anarchic) potential of this mood and harnessed it to his advantage. By claiming to be the champion of the peasants, he assured himself of their support in October 1917.

However, the conflict of aims between the Bolshevik government and the peasants soon led to serious clashes and eventually to bitter hostility. The requirements of the peasants were reasonable. They wanted enough land to feed themselves, their familes and their cattle; they wanted enough grain for the next year's sowing but also a sizeable surplus of agricultural produce, which could be sold or bartered for tea, sugar, salt, cotton, domestic utensils and agricultural machinery. For this purpose they needed free markets in which they could sell their surplus at a worthwhile price: the official prices fixed by the government were too low. The Mensheviks considered that free markets would win the good will of the peasants while ensuring a steady supply of bread and vegetables for the starving people of the cities, and indeed peasants in their thousands were already trudging to the cities, bringing sacks of food on their backs. Equally, workers from the cities went to the villages in great numbers, also with sacks on their backs — *meshochniki* (sack people) were a familiar sight everywhere —to barter whatever they had (not money, for that was worthless) in exchange for food. But free markets, like free trade and private enterprise generally, were anathema to Lenin and so markets were made illegal. When they continued to spring up here and there they were raided by the Cheka and the unfortunate *meshochniki* were arrested; roadblocks and ambushes were set up on roads, at railway stations and at river ports.

Worst of all, the Bolsheviks deliberately carried the class war into the countryside. This is how Sverdlov, one of the ablest of Lenin's pupils, explained Bolshevik policy to the VTsIK in May 1918: 'two opposite hostile camps' must be created in the villages, 'setting the poorest layers of the population against the *kulak** elements. Only if we are able to split the village into two camps, to arouse there the same class war as in the cities, only then will we achieve in the villages what we have achieved in the cities.'[32] The usual sequence ensued: terror and coercion were followed by disorganisation and resistance. A

**Kulak* — Russian for fist (hard-fisted). This name was applied to well-to-do peasants. Often they were simply more thrifty and hardworking than the listless mass of peasantry, which had been demoralised by centuries of serfdom. Turgenev's *Sportsman's Sketches* provide an excellent introduction to the life of both poor and rich Russian peasants.

decree of 9 May 1918 called on 'all working and property-less peasants to unite immediately for a merciless war on the *kulaks*' and declared all grain-hoarders to be 'enemies of the people', subject to no less than ten years' imprisonment, exile, and confiscation of all property. The decree authorised the Food Commissariat to extract from the peasants all grain in excess of official quotas (these barely covered the needs of a peasant family), and at official prices.[33] This was in spite of the protests from the peasants that the quotas and the prices were too low. The Food Commissariat formed provisioning detachments, to which especially indoctrinated workers were assigned, to carry out the forcible requisition of grain (so-called *prodrazverstka*) and also 'to organise the labouring peasantry against the *kulaks*' (decree of 27 May 1918).[34] There were over 10,000 workers in these detachments at the end of July 1918, and approximately 45,000 in 1920.[35] One can imagine what hatred of the workers was generated in the wretched peasants. A decree of 11 June 1918 set up 'Committees of the Poor' (*Komitety bednoty*, abbreviated to kombedy) to help government forces to extract food from their fellow-villagers, both the *kulaks* and the *seredniaki* (middling peasants). Within a few months there were some 80,000 kombedy in existence.[36] Inevitably, private spite and the settling of old scores played a large part in the activities of the kombedy, and often much of the extracted food remained in the possession of the extractors.

This insane policy was called War Communism by the Bolsheviks, implying that it was a response to the stresses and strains of the Civil War and would end with the war. In fact War Communism was intensified rather than relaxed when the outcome of the Civil War was already decided in 1920. Then peasants were compelled not only to surrender their grain but to sow and plant in accordance with high government norms under the supervision of 'sowing committees'. Non-fulfilment of the norms was severely punished.[37] The peasants reacted to War Communism with frequent and violent insurrections, which were repressed with extreme cruelty — peasants were flogged, beaten and shot, and their houses burnt down[38] — and this in turn provoked equally savage retaliations. It was said that locally recruited militiamen refused to take part in this fratricidal war, but the chekas and their special troops had no scruples.[39] According to the leading chekist Latsis, 344 risings (almost certainly by peasants) had been suppressed by mid-1920 in only twenty provinces of the RSFSR.[40]

The best known and perhaps the biggest peasant revolt took place in the province of Tambov, whence it spread to the neighbouring provinces of Penza and Saratov; in all it involved up to 21,000 peasant fighters. The Bolsheviks branded these peasants as 'bandits', but obviously they were no such thing. This emerges clearly from an on-the-spot report sent to Lenin by Tukhachevskii, the Red Army Commander, who had been sent to put down the revolt: 'the causes of the uprising are the same as throughout the entire RSFSR, i.e. dissatisfaction with the policy of food requisitioning and the clumsy and exceptionally harsh enforcement of it.'[41] The revolt started in August 1920 and was finally put down in June–July 1921, but only after Cheka troops and then Red Army units were moved into the province. The soviet forces included 32,000 infantry and 8,000 cavalry, with artillery and machine gunners. Their predictable victory over the peasants was followed by savage atrocities: by July 1921, twenty-five villages were burned to the ground and 250 villagers shot. Five thousand hostages, taken from among the families of the insurgents, were put into concentration camps.[42] The Bolsheviks blamed the revolt on the SRs, but the truth is quite otherwise. The leader of the revolt, Alexander Antonov, a native of the Kirsanov district of the Tambov province, had indeed been first an SR and later a Left SR, but as from August 1918 he had acted entirely on his own. He was not trusted by the SR party, and its Central Committee forbade its local branches and individual members to take part in the revolt. This did not prevent the Tambov Cheka from arresting many local SRs.[43]

Dzerzhinskii's order of 8 January 1921 noted that 'the prisons are packed, chiefly with workers and peasants instead of the bourgeoisie'. Thus history repeats itself: it is said that one half of the victims of the Jacobin terror in the French revolution were workers and peasants.[44]

8 The Destruction of Trade Unions, Cooperatives and Soviets

Lenin lost no time in acquiring complete control over the inner life of the country. The muzzling of the press and of public opinion, the suppression of political parties and the penetration by Bolsheviks of all independent organisations of workers and peasants were virtually completed within the first year of Bolshevik rule. It was never done openly; the pretence that Russia was a 'workers' and peasants' democracy' was never dropped, and elections — to soviets, trade unions and so on — were held publicly. But the results were rigged when the vote went against the Bolsheviks. The destruction of elected bodies was carried out from within in various underhand ways.

Trade Unions

Lenin's instructions to his comrades on how to undermine the trade unions speak for themselves: 'resort to all sorts of schemes and strategems, employ illegal methods and evasions, conceal the truth, in order to penetrate the trade unions.'[1] Once penetrated by the Bolsheviks, the trade unions became obedient tools of the government, though the Bolsheviks continued to talk of them as if they were influential institutions: they were called 'schools of administration', of 'economic management', of 'communism'; they were supposed to be organisations of the ruling class and one of the major institutions of 'socialist democracy'.[2] Congresses of trade unions were invariably opened with great pomp and ceremony and the opening speeches were given by one of the Bolshevik leaders, often Lenin himself. But the president of the All-Russian Trade Union Congress was usually appointed by the government without regard to his experience in trade union work. The sole exception was Mikhail Tomskii, an old Bolshevik trade unionist — and he, indeed, often defended the unions against the government. He was dismissed in 1929.[5]

While the Civil War lasted some of the unions were able to retain some independence.* But with victory in sight, Lenin decided to break them finally. In 1920–1921 all unions still showing an independent spirit — including some of the largest, such as the printers' union, the railwaymen's union and the chemical workers' union — were dissolved and replaced by Bolshevik-dominated unions. A good example of Bolshevik methods of dealing with such unions was the liquidation of the railwaymen's union Vikzhel. A week in advance of the regular (Second) All-Russian Railwaymen's Convention, the Bolsheviks organised a rival conference of railway workers with the view of infiltrating or disrupting the official Convention. This plan failed: the Convention was in a determined anti-Bolshevik mood and even refused to elect Lenin as honorary chairman. Thereupon the Bolshevik minority declared the Convention dissolved and replaced by another consisting of Bolsheviks, Left SRs and a few Internationalists. The name of the union was changed from Vikzhel to Vikzhedor (and then Tsekprofsozh) and all socialist opponents were expelled from it.[5] A similar fate befell the printers' union. The Bolsheviks replaced its Praesidium by another, composed of Bolsheviks, which represented less than half of the union's membership. The old leadership refused to resign and many union members rallied to its support, so for a time the two rival praesidia, with their own followings, existed side by side. It was the old printers' union that gave the great reception to the British Labour and Trade Unions delegation that visited Russia in May–June 1920.[6]

Many large and small delegations from western socialist parties and organisations visited Soviet Russia. Many came ready to find a 'socialist paradise' and were confirmed in their hope after being received by top Bolsheviks, including Lenin, and by leading chekists. Others came with open minds and a desire to learn the truth. All were fêted with lavish hospitality, given banquets — while Moscow starved — housed in the best hotels, whirled from one reception to another, taken on conducted tours of factories, hospitals, schools, even prisons; but always surrounded by a tight cordon of Cheka agents, whose job it was to prevent contact with ordinary Russians, and in the first place with Russian anti-Bolshevik socialists. The Bolsheviks desperately needed to make a favourable impression on these foreigners — and through them on their governments — in order to re-establish normal relations with the rest of the world.

When seven delegates from the British Labour Party and the British Trade Unions (plus two members of the Independent Labour Party and the philosopher Bertrand Russell) arrived in Moscow, they

*For instance, they elected seventy Menshevik delegates to the Third All-Russian Trade Union Congress in April 1920.[4]

were received with particular honours. The British group spent several weeks in Russia, first in Petrograd and then in Moscow; it was taken to several provincial cities and to the Polish front; everywhere it was received with orchestras, welcoming speeches and banquets. Nevertheless, some of the delegates broke out of the routine of unending festivities and searched out the Menshevik Central Committee (Pavel Axelrod had given Dan's address to one of the delegation's secretaries). They were cordially invited to attend two of the Committee's meetings and several members of the Committee visited the British visitors at their hotel. When a festive reception was given by the government for the delegation at the Bolshoi Theatre in Moscow on 18 May, everything was nicely stage-managed: Mensheviks were invited and Abramovitch was allowed to make a welcoming speech. But a much less formal and much more cordial welcome was offered to the British guests at a huge mass meeting organised by the original Central Committee of the printers' union on 21 May. This old Central Committee included outstanding Menshevik workers — Kefali-Kamermakher, Deviatkin, Chistov, Buksin, Romanov. The resolution which was to be proposed at the meeting had been drawn up jointly by the Central Committee of the printers' union and that of the Mensheviks. The meeting was chaired by Deviatkin; the main speaker was the fiery red-headed Kefali. He warned the British visitors that they might be taken to meetings which were bogus and meet delegates whom nobody had elected. Fedor Dan, for the Menshevik Central Committee, spoke of the Menshevik support for democratic socialism and called for an end to foreign intervention in the Russia Civil War. In a democratic spirit the union had also invited several Bolshevik speakers who were listened to politely. The unscheduled appearance of Victor Chernov, the leader of the Right SRs, for whom the Cheka had been hunting high and low for many months, created a sensation. It incensed the Bolsheviks present who shouted for the Cheka to arrest him; the rest of the audience gave him a standing ovation. In the confusion Chernov disappeared as secretly as he had come. The chekists did not find him, though they seized his wife and two teenage daughters.[7]

After the printers' meeting the official press fulminated against the Mensheviks; Dan was arrested and exiled to Ekaterinburg and pressure was put on Abramovitch's constituents to recall him from the Soviet. The brunt of Cheka fury was borne by the printers: eleven members of their board were arrested, together with twenty-nine representatives and members of factory committees, and among those arrested were eleven deputies to the Moscow Soviet. The premises of the old printers' union were raided and closed on 11 June. The meetings of 21 May marked the end of an era — it was the last big oppositional open meeting under Bolshevik rule. As for the British delegation, the memoirs written by one of its members, Mrs Snowden,[8] show that they were saddened by all that they had seen in Soviet Russia and fully understood the nature of the regime. On their return home, however, they were somewhat disingenuous: though they published a full account of the dissolution of the printers' union they did not publish or distribute the illegally printed appeal of forty Right SRs, eighty Left SRs, twenty-eight Maximalists, five Mensheviks and five Anarchists imprisoned in Moscow, nor the Memorandum about conditions in Russia handed to them by the Mensheviks.[9]

The last union to be destroyed was the union of workers in the chemical industry. The Bolsheviks branded it as 'Menshevik', though in fact there were only two Mensheviks in its Praesidium, along with one Right SR (the chairman), one Left SR and one Anarchist. Most of the members belonged to no party, but all were united in the resolve to preserve the independence of their union. Early in 1921 this independence was threatened and tension in the union mounted. During a regional conference in March 1921, when the Bolsheviks proposed that Lenin be elected 'honorary chairman' (this had by then become routine), the majority voted for Martov instead. The Bolsheviks demanded a recount and somehow collected 210 votes for Lenin as against 185 for Martov. The struggle reached a climax at the union's regional congress in October 1921. Instead of the usual hundred delegates, 230 turned up, including a group introduced by the Bolsheviks without being elected. At the first session the tasks of trade unions were discussed; the resolution proposed by the Bolsheviks received 113 votes as against 123 cast for the resolution proposed by the member of the Menshevik Central Committee, I. Rubin. Thereupon the Bolsheviks declared the Menshevik resolution to be subversive of soviet rule, walked out of the building and opened their own 'Congress of Red Chemical Workers'. There, as *Pravda* reported on 9 October, they branded 'all talk of trade union independence from a government of workers and peasants' as shameful. The Red congress elected its own leadership of twenty-one members: twelve Bolsheviks and nine non-party members, the latter chosen from among that group of non-elected participants whom they had introduced illegally. The original congress ended with melancholy good-byes to the old leaders. It was clear to all that this was the end, and many had tears in their eyes. Soon after, most of the leaders were arrested.[10]

The destruction of independent trade unions put an end to the 'workers' creativity' so highly praised by Lenin. Henceforth workers did what they were told to do. Even when they were allotted seemingly responsible tasks, such as fixing wage rates, work norms or production quotas, they had no choice but to endorse decisions already taken by state economic bodies, that is the government. There was no way in which workers could defend their own interests — particularly not in nationalised industries, in which the state proved to be a hard taskmaster, imposing work norms that were higher even than in pre-revolutionary times.

Eventually many Bolsheviks began to doubt whether the party line on trade unions was right. The earliest and most genuine criticism came from the *Rabotchaia Grupa* (Workers' Group). Its leader Miasnikov (fifteen years in the Bolshevik party; seven and a half of imprisonment and hard labour under tsarism)[11] complained that 'our party aims to hit the bourgeois but comes down on the workers.' Lenin replied that freedom of the press and other freedoms would only benefit the servants of the bourgeoisie. Had not the Right SR Chernov and the Menshevik Martov, as well as the Kadet Miliukov, already been hired by 'the world bourgeoisie'?[12] Miasnikov was expelled from the party and he and his followers soon found themselves in prison.[13]

This was by no means the end of the debates within the Bolshevik party. They soon expanded to embrace such fundamental issues as the place of labour under communism and the role of trade unions in the soviet state. Eleven different points of view emerged during preliminary polemics; no wonder Lenin wrote in January 1921 that 'the party is sick, the party is shaking with fever.'[14] However, in the debate on trade unions at the Tenth Party Congress in March 1921, the opposition was represented mainly by the Workers' Opposition, a group led by Alexander Shliapnikov, who had been the first People's Commissar of Labour in the Bolshevik government. The group was supported by many leading trade unionists. Strong words came also from Alexandra Kollontai, who had published a pamphlet entitled *The Workers' Opposition* shortly before the congress. In it she had accused Lenin and Trotsky of betraying the revolution, of distrusting the working class, and of stifling its initiative and creativity.[15] The theses offered to the Congress by Shliapnikov called for a return to the labour democracy of the early days of workers' control, and for giving the trade unions a central role in the economic organisation of the country. There was a trade union crisis, he maintained: 'During the past two years the party and the state organisations ... have reduced the influence of the workers' unions in the soviet state to zero. The role of trade unions ... has been debased to that of an information and recommendation bureau.'[16] His criticism was to the point, but his theses stopped short of calling for free elections and independent trade unions. Also, he failed to make it clear whether democracy was to extend to all workers or only to Bolshevik workers.

At the same Party Congress Trotsky (supported by Bukharin, Dzerzhinskii, five other members of the Bolshevik Central Committee and many other prominent party figures) represented the other extreme. He called for a 'gradual fusion of the trade unions with the soviet apparatus'; explained the 'socialist character of compulsory labour'; and recommended 'methods of proletarian compulsion (mobilisation of thousands of trade union members for service, disciplinary courts, etc.)'. Trotsky, whose brutal methods in the Tsektran (see p. 63) had been fiercely attacked by the Workers' Opposition, called for a transformation of trade unions into 'production unions', that is unions for the achievement of higher production. This was to be accomplished through the re-education of workers by carefully selected leadership and under the general guidance of the party: 'Party leadership within the trade union movement should be greatly increased ... and leading positions occupied by men recommended by the party.'[17] Trotsky attacked those who contrasted 'military methods' (commands, punishment) with trade union methods (persuasion, propaganda, initiative); this was nothing but Kautskyite–Menshevik–SR prejudice, he said. But he too insisted that 'proletarian democracy' should always be strictly adhered to. In fact 'democracy' of every possible and impossible variety was advocated by all speakers. It was as if by then the Bolsheviks had fallen victim to their own demogogic phraseology and quite lost sight of *ordinary* democracy, which presupposes free elections and other civic freedoms. The 'proletarian' or 'socialist' or 'revolutionary' democracy they demanded was meant for Bolsheviks only, not for the rest of the population.

For all its noble championship of trade unions, the Workers' Opposition collapsed like a punctured balloon. The Tenth Party Congress rejected its theses in favour of a compromise resolution proposed by Lenin. This was only a tactical move and it remained abundantly clear that he was not going to change his policies towards the workers. He was, on the other hand, determined to have no more trouble from his own party: at the end of the Congress he introduced a resolution forbidding the formation of oppositional groups under threat of expulsion from the party.[18]

The Cooperatives

The cooperatives were another independent mass movement, this time mainly of peasants (workers participated in it too, but to a smaller degree). It was one of the proudest boasts of the Russian liberal and socialist intelligentsia to have induced peasants — notoriously difficult to organise — to work together in a democratic manner. The Russian cooperatives followed the example of their English prototype created by Robert Owen. They were based on the idea of a 'voluntary cooperation of men for the purpose of the material improvement of life.'[19] Each member took out a small share and this entitled him or her to make suggestions for the better running of the whole, and to elect representatives to cooperative congresses. At the head of the whole system was an elected Soviet of Cooperative Congresses, which coordinated all policies, including cultural ones. The cooperative movement ran consumers' associations, agricultural associations (for dairy produce, grain, etc.), and cottage industries: it also ran credit and savings funds. The movement grew naturally, new branches being founded wherever there was demand for them. It was a movement of which its members were proud; trust was the very basis of it. Among the organisers were SRs, Liberals, Mensheviks, and many non-party people.

In spite of its wide scope and numerous activities the cooperative movement proved very efficient. It grew in popularity and range during the 1914 War: by 1917 it was estimated that it supplied forty-six per cent of the national turnover in food and essential agricultural products (including butter and bread). Its membership increased rapidly, so that by October 1917 it involved — counting the families of the shareholders — almost half of the total population. Proportionately, the number of its various associations also grew: there were by then 24,000 consumers' associations, some 14,000 producers' associations (agricultural, dairy and others) and 16,200 credit and saving associations. There were also 103 periodical publications.[20]

In October 1917, the Bolsheviks were facing a food crisis of colossal dimensions and it would have been sensible to enlist the help of the nationwide, well-organised network of production and distribution cooperatives. But such was not the way of the Bolsheviks: they had to take it over and control it, and they ruined it in the process. Elections were rigged, the leaders were arrested and replaced by Bolsheviks, the Moscow Popular Bank, which was the financial base of the movement, was closed. Finally the very spirit of the movement was perverted by the decree of 20 March 1919. This decree converted the existing cooperatives into uniform 'consumers' communes' and every soviet citizen was compelled to become a member. The decree laid down exact rules of administration; and local as well as central authorities were given the right to introduce their own representatives into it. The old soviets of cooperative congresses were abolished. The new 'consumers' communes' were incorporated into a typical bureaucratic system: a commune at the base, then a district, then a regional union, and finally the Central Union of Cooperatives (Tsentrosoiuz), the latter being nothing more than a department of the Food Commissariat. Robbed of all spiritual content and independent initiative, the cooperative movement lost the loyalty and the trust of the population. To the present day it remains a rather inefficient branch of the state food industry and cooperative shops are in no way different from ordinary state shops.

The *samizdat* journal *Pamiat* (Memory) in its fifth issue (produced in Moscow in 1981 and printed in Paris in 1982) has published an article on the takeover of the cooperatives by the Communist government, mainly on the basis of documents preserved in the family of one of the leaders of the All-Russian Soviet of Cooperative Congresses. Perhaps the most interesting of these documents is the copy of a telegram sent to Lenin by the peasants of two villages of the Tambov region. In it these peasants, who describe themselves as poor, stated that a general meeting of their local cooperative, attended by 9,095 members, had discussed the decree (of March 1919) and unanimously decided to ask Lenin to revoke it. The provisions of that decree, they said, would not improve the food situation but would finally ruin it; and it would also kill people's involvement. Instead of a friendly community of interests, instead of a leadership of freely elected, experienced people who loved their work, there would be rule by commissars and by 'our rural communists' who, they said, 'often work against our people'.[21] Further valuable testimony is contained in a resolution adopted at the regional congress of cooperative representatives at Tver on 2–3 May 1919, in which the congress expressed its disapproval of the decree of March 1919. The dynamism and vitality of the cooperative movement, it pointed out, rested on principles of 'voluntary cooperation' of all members; the compulsory imposition from above of a new administrative system would kill the free development of the movement; interference by officials outside the movement would utterly destroy its living basis, which was rooted in the *samodeiatelnost* (initiative) of local populations and of the elected executive organs responsible to the membership.[22] And that is precisely what happened.

Various smaller workers' organisations were also swept away by the Bolshevik broom. Some were replaced by Bolshevik replicas, while others closed down of their own accord because Bolshevik interference made normal work impossible. For instance, the Union of Hospital Funds* decided to close, at its regional congress in April–May 1919

*This was a system of voluntary health insurance founded by and for the workers in tsarist times. It had medical, statistical and legal departments and issued a periodical journal.[23]

— not without lamenting the destruction of the voluntary health insurance which had been one of the treasured achievements of the Russian working class.

Voluntary workers' organisations had been at the very heart of Menshevik activity before the revolution. Lenin had ridiculed them as 'artisanry', 'syndicalism', 'trade unionism' — all words of abuse in his polemical phraseology — and had accused the Mensheviks of forgetting the far more important work of preparing the revolution. In fact the Mensheviks were training cadres both for the future revolution and for the time after the revolution. Under Menshevik tuition, the working class produced an elite as well as rank and file of exceptional quality. These Menshevik workers were devoted to the interests of the working class and steadfast in the face of persecution, tsarist or Bolshevik.* They put up great resistance to Bolshevik intimidation by voting for resolutions proposed by their Menshevik leaders. This so worried the Bolsheviks that the Vecheka mounted a special campaign to discredit them in the eyes of the workers: local chekas were instructed to proceed against them 'not as Mensheviks but as saboteurs and inciters to strike action.'[25]

The life story of the printer Alexander Fedorovich Deviatkin provides a good illustration of the calibre of the Menshevik workers' elite. Born into a poor and numerous family, he had only two or three years of schooling and was largely self-taught. Early in life he suffered an attack of lung tuberculosis and almost died of it. He became a Menshevik in the early years of the century and remained true to his party for the rest of his life. An active and popular organiser, he rose to be a leader of the printers and chairman of the Executive Committee of the Union of Hospital Funds. He was also an almost constant member of the Moscow Soviet. In 1920 he chaired the famous meeting in honour of the British Labour Party delegation and was arrested together with the entire board of the printers' union. From then on he was in and out of prison, was one of the prisoners beaten up in the Butyrki prison in Moscow (see p. 124) and took part in a hunger strike of twelve days' duration, at the end of which he was too weak to leave the prison when released. For several years he took an active part in Menshevik underground work, dodging the GPU (the successor to the Cheka) at every step. He was again arrested in 1925, imprisoned for three years at Suzdal, and died of typhus in exile in the early 1930s.

*The Menshevik Vera Alexandrova met dozens of these workers when employed at the Union of Hospital Funds in 1918–1919 and she came to respect and love them. It was the contact with these workers that decided her to join the Menshevik party and it was to them that she owed her 'appreciation, intellectually and emotionally, of the historical role and importance of Menshevism'.[24]

It was during her work at the Union of Hospital Funds that Vera Alexandrova got to know him and she left a vivid portrait of him: 'A remarkable speaker, a man of outstanding natural intelligence and extraordinary organisational talents, Deviatkin [combined these qualities] ... with an inbred tact, nobility of heart, a great tolerance towards the opinions of others, and the capacity to catch instantly the meaning of a worker's thought however clumsily expressed. Add to it his attractive looks and voice and one need not wonder at his becoming ... one of the best loved leaders of Menshevik workers.... Wherever he went he was met with affectionate smiles.'[26]

With the defeat of its independent organisations the working class was reduced to the status of a work force — a matter for statistics. But beyond grumbling, holding sporadic protest meetings and occasionally going on strike, workers were hardly in a position to fight back, as unemployment grew, factories were closed and the food situation approached famine. Yet one major attempt was made to defend workers' rights. It was bound to end in failure against the joint might of the Bolshevik government and the Cheka, but that it was made at all speaks clearly of the strength of resentment among the workers.

The attempt was made by a movement which called itself Assemblies of Factory Representatives; it was born at an unofficial workers' conference in January 1918 and was further developed in several conversations between workers and Menshevik and SR intellectuals.*[27] The first to be properly organised was the Petrograd Assembly. It began to function in March 1918 and by 27 March there were 170 delegates from 56 factories. A count made of the first 111 representatives showed that there were 35 Mensheviks, 33 SRs, 1 NS and 48 non-party delegates elected. A worker named Berg, an SR, was elected chairman of the Assembly. At one of the earliest sessions of the Assembly the delegates demanded an end to terror, reintroduction of civil liberties and the recall of the Constituent Assembly. There were two sessions of the Petrograd Assembly in March, four in April, three in May and three in June 1918. At the first of these Kefali-Kamermakher, the printer, Alexander Smirnov, a worker in a cartridge factory, and Glebov, a worker in the Putilov plant were the principal speakers. They surveyed the general situation and the treatment of workers by the Bolsheviks. By May the Assembly made its position clear: 'We, the representatives of Petrograd workers, consider the freedom of unions an inalienable right of the people and one of the most precious conquests of the revolution' — and since the Bolsheviks

*Vladimir Levitskii, Martov's youngest brother, described the movement in a letter to Pavel Axelrod as 'a *true* workers' organisation, uniting the best of the workers' intelligentsia and displaying maximum independence'.[28]

were threatening that freedom, the Assembly urged the workers to go on a general strike against the Bolshevik government. When participation in the official celebrations of May Day was discussed, Glebov spoke against participation: 'We should appeal to all workers to declare the first of May a day of mourning, display black flags and stay at home. Thus we shall demonstrate the whole extent of losses and deprivations that we have suffered.' At the session of 1 June, the Assembly appealed 'to the workers of Petrograd to ... prepare the working masses for a political strike against the present regime, which in the name of the working class shoots it, throws it into prison, strangles freedom of speech, of the press, of the unions, the right to strike, and workers' representation.'* On 29 June, at probably its last session, the Petrograd Assembly passed the following resolution: 'Our press is smashed. Our organisations are destroyed.... Russia has been turned once again into a tsarist dungeon.... To continue living like that is impossible for us.... We, representatives of Petrograd workers, call you out for a one-day political protest strike.... Away with the death penalty! Away with executions and with the civil war! Down with lockouts! Long live the Constituent Assembly! Long live freedom of speech and of the unions! Long live the right to strike!'[30] The one-day general strike was planned for 2 July, but it never took place. The famished masses were too weak to fight on such a scale.

The Assembly movement itself was energetic enough. From Petrograd a delegation went to Moscow in April 1918 and was well received by Moscow workers; during May–June, anti-Bolshevik feeling swept through Moscow factories. The Moscow region too had suffered acute unemployment — 36 textile mills with a total of 130,000 workers and 24 engineering works with 120,000 workers were closed during the period March—April 1918. A second visit to Moscow in June showed that 'the soviets have lost touch with the working masses and are instruments of anti-proletarian and anti-revolution policies.... Newspapers are being closed by the dozen. Meetings are banned. There are arrests among the workers.' The Petrograd delegation was received with ovations in some factories; everywhere they met with sympathy from the workers. Other towns — Briansk and Tula — sent delegates to greet them. In Kolomna, on 25 May, a meeting of some tens of thousands of workers resolved to join the movement; mass arrests followed, whereupon the local factories went on strike.[31]

*How general such feelings were was shown when (also in June) the enormous Obukhov plant, which was being closed down, declared a strike, and the general meeting of its workers passed the following resolution: 'The crimes of the soviet government continue. The prisons are overcrowded. The right to strike has been killed. Strikes are countered by lockouts.... It is not possible to keep silent any longer.'[29]

It seems almost as if the Bolsheviks did not know what to do about the Assemblies. It is possible that they saw in this movement a welcome safety valve for the workers to blow off steam until an improvement in the general situation would reduce their discontent. More probably, they were playing for time in which to win the workers back: certainly some such attempts were made in Petrograd, where the local Bolsheviks tried to join the movement.[32] Meanwhile it was allowed to exist more or less legally and to publish its proclamations openly. Oppositional newspapers, when they did appear, were not prevented from reporting fully on the workers' meetings. But this forbearance did not last long. Soon factory committees were ordered to prevent workers' meetings being held, local soviets were told to ban them. The Bolshevik press described the delegates of the Petrograd Assembly as 'travelling salesmen of social treason'. Several workers from Moscow and two delegates from Petrograd — the workers Krakovskii and Kuzmin — were arrested. When still other delegates from Petrograd were arrested in the small industrial town of Ozery, a crowd of local workers stoned the prison and set them free, and then burned down the building of the local soviet.[33] In March, on orders from the Cheka, six Red guards searched the premises of the Petrograd Assembly and requisitioned all its papers. Then, on 13 June, the entire conference of Moscow factory representatives was arrested at the railwaymen's club of the Alexandrovskii Railways. Altogether fifty-six were detained, including two members of the Menshevik Central Committee, Kuchin and Troianovskii, and among those arrested were several delegates from Petrograd, Briansk and Tula. This led to an indignant protest in Tula, where workers called for a three-day strike and demanded the liberation of the arrested workers.

The Assembly movement had planned to organise an All-Russian Conference of factory representatives and, after that, a large non-party workers' congress. An Organisational Bureau* was elected in Moscow for the specific task of preparing both the conference and the congress. It was intended that the congress should review 'in all its breadth the ... problem of workers' policies'. But it never came to that. The members of the Moscow conference were arrested before they could begin discussions; they had only had time to elect a praesidium and to listen to some local reports. And when the congress opened, on 23 July, all those present were also arrested. The case, officially styled 'the case of the workers' congress', was referred to the Supreme

*The Organisational Bureau was composed of twelve workers representing big trade unions — metal workers, railwaymen, printers — as well as delegates from the central committees of the Mensheviks, the SRs and the Jewish Bund.

Revolutionary Tribunal, but in the event it never came to a trial: the prisoners were simply kept for several months in prison. Meanwhile the Bolshevik press described the Assembly movement as a secret Menshevik conspiracy 'to falsify the will of the working class and to overthrow soviet power'.[34]

Thus ended the gallant attempt to defend the independence of the working class against the 'proletarian' government. For sixty odd years no other such attempt was made — indeed could have been made in Soviet Russia. But the old spirit was not dead. In 1977 a number of workers led by the miner Vladimir Klebanov tried to form a union free from state control. They called it the Association of Free Trade Unions. These workers argued that while the soviet constitution stated clearly that 'in accordance with the aims of building communism citizens of the USSR have the right to associate in public organisations that promote their political activity and initiative and the satisfaction of their various interests', the Soviet authorities always reacted with special brutality to anyone speaking plainly about industry, society or the state. In an appeal to the ILO and western trade unions, these Russian workers complained that 'all our attempts to get justice from government authorities have been in vain' and that their letters to the authorities were not answered. They became the target of arrests and detention in psychiatric hospitals, and by the end of March 1978 the Association of Free Trade Unions was practically harassed out of existence. In October of that year another, similar, workers' organisation sprang up — the Free Inter-professional Association of Workers. Its declared purpose was to defend the workers 'in cases of the violation of their rights in various spheres of their daily activities: economic, social, cultural, spiritual, religious, domestic, and political ... within the framework of the constitution and international agreements signed by the Soviet government'. The fate of the second organisation was no different from that of the first.[35]

The Soviets

The main slogan of the Bolsheviks before and during their coup had been: 'All power to the soviets'; yet within six months this 'parliament of the people' found itself deprived of all real influence in the affairs of state. Though nominally still the highest legislative organ of the country, the VTsIK merely rubber-stamped the decrees submitted to it by the government. As for ordinary deputies, all they were expected to do was to approve resolutions proposed to them and to greet with 'thunderous applause' the appearances and the speeches of Bolshevik leaders.

In April 1918 Martov wrote in *Novaia Zaria* (New Dawn), the newspaper of the Moscow regional committee of the Mensheviks:[36] 'After all that the workers have gone through during the past six months, it should be clear to anyone that "soviet power" is a fairy tale, and not a beautiful one at that. There is no soviet power in Russia, and no proletarian power. Under this label reign armed members of one [Bolshevik] party, who go against both workers and peasants when workers and peasants disagree with them. In reality "soviet power" has turned into an irresponsible, uncontrolled, unjust, tyrannical, and costly power of commissars, committees, staffs, and armed bands.' Such indeed was the real state of affairs — Russian citizens no longer had a forum where they could voice their opinions. Nevertheless, for purposes of propaganda, the very word 'soviet' continued to carry the highest prestige: *Soviet* Russia, *soviet* justice, *soviet* man. Congresses of soviets were made into grand occasions; speeches and resolutions at the sessions were reported at length in the official press. All this window dressing was designed to make a favourable impression on foreign governments and peoples. And for the same purpose a few socialists were allowed to participate.

The destruction of independent soviets was achieved mainly through the manipulation of elections: where the Bolsheviks already had a majority, they did not allow new elections, but where they were in the minority, they ordered elections and then rigged the results. Usually all prominent local opponents were arrested in advance, to prevent their ever being elected; when this did not achieve the desired effect, the newly elected soviet was disbanded and a second election staged.

New elections were in fact desirable, but for quite another reason. In October 1917 the soviets contained an overwhelming number of soldiers of peasant origin, most of whom had since returned to their villages. Many urban soviets had therefore become unrepresentative and a reshuffle was wanted by all. However, the substitution of bogus elections for free ones was another matter, and against that the workers put up quite a fight. In practice this meant resisting Bolshevik intimidation at every level — on the factory and workshop floor, at open electoral meetings in factories, towns, districts and regions, and at the actual casting of votes. Since voting in Russian factories is always by show of hands, 'resisters' were easily identified and could be subjected to special pressures and threats — reductions in food rations, dismissal, blacklisting. And for a blacklisted worker there was no hope of finding another job, and no way of avoiding starvation for himself and his family.

The workers bitterly resented the rigging of elections. They continued to elect considerable numbers of Mensheviks and SRs well into 1918. The Bolshevik I.I. Fokin, sent by the Moscow regional committee of the Bolshevik party to work in Orel, reported that at a meeting of the local soviet, held on 25 November 1917, most of the workers sided with the Mensheviks and most of the soldiers with the Bolsheviks; the workers' division of the soviet elected (to the executive committee) 9 Mensheviks, 3 SRs and 3 non-party delegates as against 5 Bolsheviks. In Tula, according to another Bolshevik observer, 'a considerable part of the workers of the local armament factory and railway junction were still following the Mensheviks and the SRs'.[37] In Briansk, the local soviet of workers' deputies still had a Menshevik majority in late July 1918.[38] In Rybinsk Mensheviks and SRs got seventy-five per cent of votes in the elections to the soviet; in Kolpino's big locomotive works they got fifty per cent; in Briansk and in the Maltsev factories in Bezhitsa, Mensheviks gained a majority, while in the Uzhevsk factory 70 Mensheviks were elected as against 64 Bolsheviks; in Rostov-on-Don 89 Mensheviks and non-party candidates were elected as against 53 Bolsheviks. When the question of re-elections to the local, Bolshevik-dominated, soviet was posed in Sebastopol, 12,000 votes were cast for re-election and 3,442 against; even in the Bolshevik stronghold of Kronstadt only 53 Bolsheviks were re-elected in 1918 as against 131 in 1917. Similar results were reported from many other places,[39] and the Bolsheviks forfeited much of their popular support over the election issue. In Odessa, Kharkov and Kiev, there were demonstrations against Bolshevik violence; in Tula, a conference of workers declared a boycott of the local soviet; and in many places workers refused to recognise the Sovnarkom.

Iaroslavl provided a good example of Bolshevik tactics. In this town, both among rural and urban workers, Mensheviks were very strong (they virtually controlled the trade unions). During the Bolshevik take-over of the town, soldiers obtained a disproportionally large representation in the soviet, and in February 1918 local Mensheviks called for re-elections. The Bolsheviks arrested the leaders of the Menshevik committee and charged them with counter-revolutionary agitation against the Soviet government. This outraged their supporters amongst the workers, who turned the trial into a counter-offensive, delivering pro-Menshevik speeches and demonstrating in the streets. The accused themselves spoke against the anti-popular and anti-proletarian policies of the Bolsheviks. Perhaps because of this overwhelming mass support, they were acquitted and set free. Re-elections to the soviet then took place and Mensheviks and SRs won a clear majority (47 Mensheviks, 13 SRs; 38 Bolsheviks and Left SRs together). At the first session of the new soviet, in April 1918, the Bolsheviks demanded that full votes should be granted to all 23 members of the former executive committee — all Bolsheviks or

Left SRs — and when this demand was voted down, the session was declared closed and the soviet disbanded. When those present refused to accept the closure, Red guards were brought in to disperse them; Menshevik leaders were again arrested and again tried. This second trial excited still greater animosity against the Bolsheviks — declarations of protest were passed at factory meetings, signed by the protesters and taken to the trial by elected delegations; similar delegations came from the trade unions. Preparations were begun for a local general strike. The accused were once more acquitted and released, but the power remained firmly in the hands of the old Bolshevik executive committee and of the local Bolshevik revolutionary committee.[40]

Until about April 1918, Mensheviks were suffered in local and central soviets and even in the VTsIK, where they vigorously denounced Bolshevik terror and economic blunders, along with the destruction of trade unions and of all civil liberties. Then the Bolshevik majorities began to expel Menshevik and SR deputies from provincial soviets; and on 14 June they expelled them from the central soviet in Moscow.[41] We possess an eye witness account of the scene of 14 June in the memoirs of the Bolshevik Elisaveta Drabkina, who was working in the secretariat of the VTsIK at the time. This is what she saw:

> The session of the VTsIK opened at ten o'clock in the evening. The electricity was working badly and ... a kerosene lamp on the chairman's table threw a dim light on Lenin's face and on the lanky, thin figure of Martov crouching in the first row of chairs. The rest of the hall was lost in semi-darkness thus underlining the central role of these two men in the historical drama that was about to unfold.

The chairman Sverdlov put to the vote the proposal to expel from the soviets 'the counter-revolutionary parties of Right SRs and Mensheviks'; after a stormy scene he declared the proposal carried and told the SRs and the Mensheviks to leave the session.

> Martov, hoarse and gasping for breath, snatched up his overcoat and tried to put it on but his hands trembled so much that he kept on missing the sleeve. Lenin, very pale, stood and looked at Martov.... Was he remembering the time, a little over two decades ago, when he and Martov — friends, fighting companions, comrades — were starting on their career as revolutionaries? ... Martov continued to struggle with his recalcitrant sleeve. At this moment he was a tragic figure. To one of the Left SRs he appeared

comic. Leaning back in his chair this Left SR roared with laughter, pointing at Martov. Martov turned on him furiously: 'You are wrong to rejoice, young man,' he croaked, 'in less than three months you will be following us.'* Exasperated he shook off his coat, flung it over his arm and walked unsteadily towards the exit. Lenin, still as pale, followed his slow progress with his gaze.[42]

The expulsion of the Mensheviks from the soviets was revoked on 1 December 1918, and that of the Right SRs on 26 February 1919, but their position was much weakened. They were not automatically reinstated in the VTsIK, merely allowed to stand for elections; and from many local soviets they were still barred. They were no longer elected to the congresses of the soviets, though they were sometimes invited to attend. There were still many inconsistencies in Bolshevik treatment of their socialist opponents. For instance, in early December 1919, Mensheviks and a few other socialists were invited to the Seventh Congress of Soviets and even allowed to address it. The Menshevik Central Committee sent Martov and Dan. Martov delivered a vigorous attack on Sovnarkom's internal policy: on its violation of the constitution and of electoral rights; on the degeneration of the government into bureaucracy; above all, on the development of the Cheka into an autonomous power practising mass terror and lawless repression.[43] Lenin devoted much of his closing speech to Martov's accusations, but he had no new arguments to offer. He merely protested that the Soviet Union was not a bureaucracy but a 'proletarian democracy', and affirmed that the constitution was observed to an extent unequalled anywhere in the world.[44] In short Lenin ended the year 1919 as he had begun it — supporting the Cheka and the terror, while paying lip service to 'proletarian democracy' and the constitution.

Throughout 1920 Mensheviks were still tolerated in the soviets: Martov was elected to the Moscow Soviet and there were many Mensheviks (and pro-Menshevik non-party delegates) in the provincial soviets. According to Fedor Dan,[45] there were 205 Menshevik deputies in Kharkov, 120 in Ekaterinoslavl, 78 in Kremenchug, 50 in Tula, and 30 each in Smolensk, Odessa, Poltava, Kiev and Irkutsk. They were never admitted to the praesidia, however, which were entirely reserved for Bolsheviks. They were again invited to the next Congress of Soviets, the Eighth, in December 1920, but it was the last they were allowed to attend.

*The fate of the Left SRs was less dramatic than Martov foretold. They were never officially expelled, but after their rising of 6 July 1918 and the imprisonment and the trial of their leaders in November of that year, they were systematically squeezed out of the soviets.

There were two sets of sessions at that congress. In the closed sessions, from which all but Bolsheviks were excluded, Dzerzhinskii argued that 'malicious criticism of the soviet authorities is [now] more inadmissible than ever,' and Trotsky insisted: 'Now that the Civil War is over, the Mensheviks and the SRs are especially dangerous and must be fought with particular ruthlessness.'[46] In the open sessions the two Menshevik delegates, Fedor Dan and David Dallin, criticised the government. Dan complained that the whole soviet system was being allowed to degenerate: local soviets were lapsing altogether while their praesidia acted on their behalf. As for the VTsIK, which was still supposed to be the highest legislative body in the country, it was totally ignored by the government: laws were passed without its authorisation and decrees which it did pass were not carried out. For instance, the general amnesty decreed by VTsIK on the occasion of the third anniversary of the October revolution was not applied to political prisoners, as the VTsIK had intended. The Cheka had applied the decree arbitrarily, and Dan read out a letter from the Cheka to support the point. In his closing speech Lenin defended the Cheka with the ambiguous statement that the head of the Cheka was a member of the VTsIK as well as of the Central Committee of the party — obviously implying that the Cheka had acted in full agreement with the government.[47]

The economic policy of the Bolsheviks was attacked by both Dan and Dallin. They pointed out that the Bolsheviks were forced to retreat from a fully nationalised economy and were offering concessions to private capital, which, said Dan, was the very idea for which the Mensheviks had been branded servants of capitalism. The trade unions had not been consulted, though it was of vital importance for the workers to know whether they would be allowed to defend their rights in private enterprises; they were denied these rights in state-owned industries. Dallin read out a resolution adopted by the Menshevik Central Committee in favour of free markets where the peasants could sell their surplus produce, which was another old Menshevik idea. Just three months later this idea was to become the basis of the government's New Economic Policy (NEP), which replaced War Communism. The congress, unaware of the coming change of government policy, was hostile to Dallin and passed a 'loyal' resolution in the spirit of War Communism.*[48]

Speaking at soviet congresses required 'maximum determination and moral courage'.[50] Usually only five or ten minutes' speaking time was granted to the opposition speakers, and during and after their

*After his speech at the congress, Dallin was dismissed from his post as teacher of history at a military school.

speeches they had to endure endless loud abuse. This was orchestrated by chekists masquerading as deputies, who usually surrounded the small group of Mensheviks, shook their fists in their faces and 'roared like wild beasts'.[51]

As the pressure on the electorate and the rigging of electoral results increased, the group of Mensheviks in the Moscow Soviet grew smaller year by year. Dvinov, who was himself a deputy, remembered the figure for April 1921 as eighteen,[52] but here his memory failed him — the figure of eighteen included six SRs.* Nevertheless, resolutions proposed by Menshevik deputies were sometimes carried, mainly owing to support by non-party deputies. During the election campaign the Bolsheviks had done their utmost to win over the non-party workers; in Petrograd, for example, the party boss Zinoviev convened a conference of 'honest non-party' workers. In the event, Zinoviev suffered a humiliating defeat, as the audience demanded that Fedor Dan, who was at the time in prison in Petrograd, be brought to the conference to confront Bolshevik speakers with 'learned marxist arguments', which they, the workers, could not produce as easily. The audience chanted 'We want Dan!' They did not get Dan. Zinoviev was furious. Non-party workers were henceforth renamed 'crypto-Mensheviks,'[53] and within a year repression of non-party workers began.

It was becoming less and less safe for Mensheviks to speak in the soviets: they were too obvious a target for the Cheka. The Menshevik deputy Boris Dvinov proposed in May 1921, that an immunity charter for deputies be adopted and the proposal was carried by the Plenum of the Moscow Soviet. This major triumph was mainly due to the support of non-party deputies. The charter stipulated that a deputy could be arrested only with the approval of the Soviet. The Bolsheviks, however, substituted 'approval by the Praesidium' for 'approval by the Soviet'; so that when the Menshevik deputies Deviatkin and Gonikberg were arrested, their arrest was approved by the Praesidium without being discussed by the Plenum.[54]

In August 1921, a Menshevik party conference in Moscow discussed their participation in the soviets, and related problems. Mensheviks were reluctant to give up participating in elections — it was their one remaining chance of being seen and heard on public platforms — and the conference decided in favour of continuing as before. But when in the next elections, in January 1922, only five Mensheviks managed to get elected, the Central Committee

*For this correction I am indebted to Richard Sakwa, whose forthcoming study on the Moscow Bolsheviks in the Civil War contains valuable statistics on the composition of the Moscow Soviet at the time.

reluctantly decided to boycott the elections thereafter. In a letter addressed to local Menshevik organisations, dated 7 September 1922, the Central Committee explained that 'everywhere the last legal opportunities have been destroyed. The deterioration of soviets has reached its limit....' A leaflet issued by the Central Committee explained to the workers that the elections to soviets had become 'a pitiful farce.... The spectres of prison, exile, loss of job stand at the gate of electoral meetings.'[55]

9 *Prisons, Camps, Exile*

Lenin's Russia had a constitution and a Code of Law, it had District Courts and City Courts and Revolutionary Tribunals and a Supreme Revolutionary Tribunal; it had Revolutionary Military Tribunals and even Revolutionary Military Railway Tribunals, but none of this is of any importance in the context of this book, because Mensheviks and other socialists were hardly ever brought to trial. When they were — as for instance, in the big show trials of the SRs in 1922 and of the Mensheviks in 1931, and in a few exceptional cases, such as that of the Rostov-on-Don Mensheviks[1] or of the Saratov workers[2] — the law was completely disregarded. And no wonder. Lenin made it perfectly plain that he had no use for the law and did not care whether it was broken. 'The revolutionary dictatorship of the proletariat,' he wrote in 1918, '. . . is power unrestricted by any law.'[3] In 1920 he said the same even more forcefully: 'The scientific concept of dictatorship means nothing else but this: power without limit, resting directly upon force, restrained by no law, absolutely unrestricted by rules.'[4] And in 1921 he said: 'Our courts are class courts'[5] — which was blatantly untrue, as not only bourgeois and black marketeers but also workers and peasants were tried and sentenced by Bolshevik courts as 'class enemies'.

Like everything else in the soviet state, justice was obscured by a dense cloud of euphemisms. The death penalty became 'the highest measure of punishment', prisons were called 'places of detention' and imprisonment 'isolation from society' or 'deprivation of liberty'.* Lenin introduced such vague concepts as 'revolutionary legality' and 'revolutionary justice', which served to disguise Bolshevik lawlessness. Under these guises indiscriminate killings were carried out. Whenever the Bolshevik government proclaimed an amnesty — usually timed to mark the First of May or the anniversary of the October revolution

*Only under Stalin were these obscurantist terms discarded, as can be seen from the journal *Soviet Justice* of 1937: 'A prison is a prison — why should we be so shy about calling it so? And punishment is punishment — why be afraid of the word? . . . We must overcome sugary liberalism, compassion towards the offender.'

—the Vecheka carried out a veritable holocaust of executions just before the appointed date.[6]

The routine punishments meted out by the Vecheka were either 'corrective' or punitive. The first was applied to criminals — pending such time as, according to Lenin at his most utopian, crime would altogether vanish in soviet society — and the second to 'class enemies', who were deemed to be incorrigible. In practice, many in both categories were shot out of hand. The rest were sent to camps to do 'socially useful labour'.

Socialists, however, presented a special problem. Could they be called 'class enemies'? Not really. And though Communists branded them as such, and as 'counter-revolutionaries' and 'social traitors', they could not make these labels stick. In fact the problem of what to do with socialists worried the Communist government considerably, and it is significant that the Politburo reserved for itself the right to decide their fate: it was too delicate a matter to be left entirely to the Cheka. Up to 1921 the Politburo repeatedly curbed the zeal of the Cheka where socialists were concerned. Executions of Mensheviks were rare. Periods of imprisonment, on the other hand, grew longer. According to SR data, the length of detention rose from three to four months in 1918 to eight to nine months in 1919, and to eighteen months to three years in 1920.[7] Menshevik sources give somewhat lower figures, but they too record the escalation. In 1919 and 1920 socialists were often imprisoned for 'the duration of the civil war' or until 'the outbreak of the world revolution'. Eventually deprivation of liberty became virtually lifelong as prison was followed by exile and concentration or labour camps,* from which very few returned alive. There are good grounds for thinking that in the end Stalin had most of the prominent socialists shot, some perhaps in 1937 but the majority in 1941. It is believed that amongst those shot at Krasnoiarsk in 1941 were Martov's two brothers, Sergei Ezhov and Vladimir Levitskii, with their families, Martov's nephew Andrei Kranikhfeld, Eva Broido and Cherevanin.[9]

Infringement of the law began when the chekists arrived, at dead of night, to search a house. Under the pretext of confiscating seditious material, the chekists helped themselves to anything they fancied,

*The terms 'camp', 'detention camp', 'concentration camp', 'labour camp' or 'forced labour camp' were used rather loosely in the first five years of Bolshevik rule. Lenin suggested that 'forced labour camps' be used as early as December 1917 and urged that 'unreliable elements' be 'locked up' in 'concentration camps' in August 1918. In both type of camp forced labour was in fact applied. By 1922 there were 56 concentration camps in Russia, with 2,750 inmates in them. In 1923 they were officially abolished, but in reality replaced by other camps, such as Northern Camps of Special Purpose (which included Solovki).[8]

from jewels or clothes to food and books. Priceless and rare collections of books and documents belonging to some of the socialists (the SRs Gots, Donskoi and Evgenia Ratner, and the Menshevik Boris Nicolaevsky) were lost in this way.[10]

Often, after taking the prisoner away, the Cheka would leave a few of its men behind as an ambush, to pick up any unsuspecting acquaintances or relatives who might drop in. But Menshevik (and, no doubt, SR) leaders were usually warned by anonymous well-wishers of the impending house search or arrest, in spite of the fact that the Cheka listened in on telephone conversations and swore to 'find and shoot those rotters'.[11] These well-wishers can only have been high-ranking Bolsheviks, who acted out of loyalty to old comrades, and perhaps also out of contempt for the Cheka. One of the most shameful practices of the Cheka was to encourage and even to force young people (the Komsomol) and school children (Red pioneers, the Russian equivalent of Cubs and Brownies) to spy upon and inform against their mates at work and at school, and against their own parents. Thus the Cheka had a huge unpaid army to reinforce its own spy net. Caretakers of town houses (*dvorniki*) were also recruited — as they had previously been by the Okhrana — to spy on tenants and their visitors.[12]

After arrest the prisoners were taken to Cheka headquarters. In Moscow these occupied a huge block of buildings on the Bolshaia and Malaia Lubianka Streets* — numbers 2, 9, 11, 13 and 14; while the Moscow Revolutionary Tribunal occupied number 19. Colloquially, this whole complex became known as the Lubianka. It contained the administrative offices of the Vecheka and the Moscow Cheka and their prisons, as well as interrogation rooms, cellars where executions took place, barracks for the Cheka troops etc. In addition several other prisons elsewhere in Moscow were administered by the Cheka: the Butyrki and the Taganka prisons, Lefortovo (formerly a military prison) and the Novinskaia prison for women. In Petrograd, the headquarters of the Cheka occupied the former police headquarters at 2 Gorokhovaia Street, where the tsarist secret police, the Okhrana, had been housed before the revolution. The old House of Pre-trial Detention, known familiarly as *Predvarilka* to countless revolutionaries, was still serving the same purpose. There were also several other old tsarist prisons reopened by the Cheka in Petrograd: the Kresty, a former prison for solitary confinement, at 5 Arsenal Embankment, the Deriabinskaia prison, former naval barracks, the Petrozhid, a former women's house of correction, the Poligon and the famous fortress prison of Peter and Paul.[13]

*Now called Dzerzhinskii Square.

In the provinces the Cheka headquarters often occupied the most commodious building available — the Town Hall, the Opera house, the House of the Nobility and the like.

Prison conditions were generally appalling. In spite of a huge increase in the number of prisoners, no new prisons were built by the soviet government, and some of the old prisons had been destroyed or burned down in the revolution, including the Litovskii Castle in Petrograd. There had been six to seven hundred prisons in pre-revolutionary Russia, but of these only 432 (apart from some small local ones) were still functioning in 1924. The result was monstrous overcrowding. It was estimated that on the average soviet prisons were made to hold one hundred to three hundred per cent more inmates than they were built for.*[14] In 1921, when the Menshevik Fedor Dan was imprisoned in the *Predvarilka* in Petrograd, this prison, meant for 700, held over 2,000 prisoners; Dan and twenty-one others were put into a cell with thirteen bunks and some prisoners slept on the floor in the corridor. Similarly, there were usually 2,500 to 3,500 in the Butyrki, built for 1,900.[15] The state of repairs in the prisons was lamentable: the official report for 1921 stated that only minor repairs had been carried out during the year under review, and only in fifty per cent of all prisons. These minor repairs included blocking broken windows up with plywood because of shortage of glass. The report commented on the shortage of wood for heating and the almost complete absence of prison clothing and soap.[17] The report made no mention of medical facilities.

Prisons were filthy and full of lice and bed-bugs which spread diseases, particularly typhus; washing and toilet facilities were often of the most insanitary kind or altogether non-existent. Food and fuel shortages, which affected the whole country, were made worse in prisons by careless and insanitary cooking; and administrators did not hesitate to appropriate most of the food rations and food parcels intended for the prisoners. The size and content of the food rations varied somewhat from year to year and from prison to prison, but not by much. The average consisted of half a pound to a pound of bread per day, often of very poor quality and mixed with chaff, and twice a day a thin gruel (*kasha*) or a thin soup (*balanda*) of potato peels or mouldy cabbage, rotten salted herring or a small amount of horse meat. In the prison at Ufa between seven and eleven prisoners died daily from starvation.[18] Prisoners commonly suffered from under-nourishment and scurvy as well as from consumption; but sick bays

*When labour camps proliferated all over northern Russia, the government hoped to solve the overcrowding problem by sending all those sentenced to over three years prison to the camps; but soon the prisons were as full as before.[15]

were so poorly equipped with medicines and comforts that the sick often preferred to stay in their cells.

This is how prison conditions were described by a group of British citizens who had been imprisoned in Soviet Russia and afterwards had communicated their impressions to the 'Committee to Collect Information on Russia':

> Of the Moscow prisons about which we had most evidence, the Extraordinary Commission* and the Butyrki were the worst.... More than one witness has likened the prison of the Cheka to the Black Hole of Calcutta. People were huddled together so closely that there was no room to lie or even to sit down.... The sanitary conditions in the prisons ... were painful and disgusting. In the prison of the Cheka the provision of latrines was totally insufficient. Those existing were so filthy and the excrement piled up to such an extent that the prisoners were unable to sit down when using them. In the Butyrki, access to the latrines was only allowed three times in the twenty four hours. At other times a tin in the cell had to be used.... With regards to parasites ... 'verminous' was not a strong enough word to describe the conditions of the prison of the Cheka. The lice were there by the million....The prisoners were impregnated with disease.... The healthy and the sick lay together: there was no general practice of removing the sick; they often died where they lay.

As for food: 'the rations ... were insufficient in quantity and of a quality so inferior as to undermine health.'[19]

This testimony agrees in all essential details with the numerous descriptions left by Russian socialists: whether in the large communal cells or in the 'solitaries', into which several persons were usually crammed — there was always the same picture of filth, overcrowding, nauseating stink from the tin latrine (*parasha*), lack of air and light, and miserable scraps of food on which nobody could subsist. Only the details varied — access to the toilets was sometimes allowed twice and sometimes three times in twenty-four hours; sometimes by night only; and sometimes for ten or even only five minutes at a time for a whole cell-full of prisoners. Though in a few prisons there were communal baths, in others there were no facilities even for washing. Nor did conditions improve with the years. In 1928, prisoners in the Lubianka and the Butyrki were still sleeping closely packed on verminous straw sacks, the food was mouldy and the bread contained all kinds of indigestible matter.

*Probably the so-called Inner Prison of the Vecheka.

Executions always took place by night, and as night approached the prisoners were gripped by fear. In the Butyrki the black car of the 'Commissar of Death', Ivanov, usually arrived at 2 a.m. Everyone listened horrified to the opening and closing of prison gates and to the revving of several motors in the courtyard (the usual prelude to executions, intended to drown the sound of shots), to the echoing steps of the guards in the corridors, the clinking of arms, the grating of keys in locks and the barked command. 'So-and-So, out — with luggage!' could mean either execution, or transfer to another prison, or release; 'Out — without luggage!' meant merely another session with the interrogators.

Armed guards took the prisoners down endless corridors towards their uncertain fate, while those left in the cell lay sleepless in their bunks thinking of the men, women and children taken away, stripped and shot in the back of the head; and of their relatives waiting for news for months or years or even forever.[20] Unable to bear the tension, some prisoners would cry out and bang on the door; but that only brought them a sojourn in the punishment cell, damp and dark and freezingly cold, where they might be left for days on end. In the daytime prisoners could relax and de-louse themselves and talk to each other, though always with caution as the Cheka had its spies in every cell — sometimes professional spies but more often ordinary prisoners who had been bullied and threatened into cooperation.

In the Inner Prison of the Vecheka in Moscow, prisoners were forbidden to read, to write, to play cards, chess or draughts, to sing, to talk loudly, or make any noise whatsoever; walks and visitors were not permitted, while visits to the toilet were allowed twice daily, under guard. These 'Rules' were nailed next to cell doors.[21] Communications between prisoners, such as knocking on walls according to the 'prison alphabet' (familiar to all revolutionaries who had been in tsarist prisons) or exchanging greetings during walks, were forbidden and were particularly severely punished.

Women prisoners suffered many more humiliations and indignities even than men. They were watched by armed guards when using the toilet or washing in the communal baths; they were subjected to insults and obscenities. In many prisons, and particularly in camps, they were often raped and had to choose between survival and sexual submission to the chekists.[22] In this respect women socialists were more fortunate than most, as their male comrades protected them whenever they could.

On arrival in prison, men and women were stripped and subjected to a search, during which all body cavities were thoroughly examined. This humiliating ritual was repeated at departure, at transfer and at other times as well. Next the prisoners were kept in quarantine for anything up to ten days. This so-called quarantine — which, of course, involved no health check — was usually a particularly dirty and dark room (or set of rooms) where criminals and other prisoners were crowded together, some sleeping on the floor, others on tables and window sills.[23] Finally, the prisoners were taken to their cells. Socialists were usually put into small cells which had originally been 'solitaries' but now housed two, three, or even four persons. In these cells the electric light was often switched on permanently.

The two most notorious prisons in Soviet Russia — the Inner Prison of the Vecheka in Moscow and the Cheka prison on the Gorokhovaia in Petrograd — had one particularly gruesome feature in common. In one very large room or hall, minute cage-like cells without ceilings were built along three walls and in a double row down the middle. Under the window in the fourth side of the room sentries stood on guard. People, including women and children, were kept in these airless and verminous cages for weeks and even months, never taken out for walks, given no books or paper or pen.[24] In Moscow this room of cages was used mainly for those sentenced to death and earned for itself the name 'The Ship of Death'.[25]

All political prisoners had to undergo lengthy interrogations. These were always conducted at night, when morale was at its lowest, and often they were spread over many weeks. Methods of interrogation varied, from open threats with the revolver to more subtle techniques of persuasion, though in Lenin's time socialists were not usually subjected to physical torture, as they were to be under Stalin.

Socialists were always interrogated by special chekists assigned to 'socialist affairs'. In Petrograd there was Chistakov, whom Dan described as an extremely ignorant and stupid man, politically illiterate, a liar and braggart, who tried to charm prisoners with 'intellectual' chit-chat.[26] There was the former worker Kozhevnikov, described as entirely devoid of moral sense, who perfected the system of cell spying. In Moscow there were Samsonov, and also the notorious woman chekist Broude, who came from Siberia, where, she bragged, she had the pleasure of executing 'the White scum'. She personally undressed and searched both men and women and openly regretted that she was not allowed to shoot socialists like 'the other scum'.[27]

Until 1921 Mensheviks regarded themselves as belonging to a 'legal' party and stood up for their rights within the Soviet constitution. For instance, on instructions from the party they refused to answer questions until they were told on what charge they had been arrested. Moreover, they demanded to be tried in open court or else released. All socialists and Anarchists, in fact, took this stand and this established them in prison as a very different category from the motley mass of other prisoners.* It was as a unified community that socialists and Anarchists in soviet prisons fought for political status, the same status that they had won, after a long and stubborn fight, from the tsarist police. Political status implied a great measure of autonomy. It included the right to elect elders (*starosta*), who conducted all negotiations with the prison authorities; the right to form a food commune, that is to share food from personal parcels as well as from official rations, and to cook their own food, to wash their own clothes, to disinfect their cells, exterminate vermin etc.; the right to have their own cells, separate from the criminals, and to have their cells open by day and to be allowed to visit socialists in other cells; the right to walk together in the prison yard; the right to receive visits and parcels from relatives and to possess books, journals, pens and paper.

It cannot be sufficiently stressed that under Communist rule the fight for political status was much more desperate than under tsarism. The only weapon of the political prisoner was the hunger strike, and while in tsarist times prison authorities and the government were reluctant to let prisoners starve themselves to death because of the adverse publicity it would arouse, the Bolsheviks were neither so soft-hearted nor so afraid of publicity, since there was no free press in Soviet Russia. They were afraid of public opinion abroad, however, and so — at least in the early days — they too yielded to demands backed by hunger strikes. This explains why the privileges enjoyed by socialist prisoners tended to be greatest at times when, for one reason or another, the Bolsheviks were most concerned to impress foreign opinion. At other times privileges were apt to be suddenly withdrawn, or else socialist prisoners would be moved to other, harsher prisons, where they endured the same treatment as all other prisoners. And, of course, even in prisons with political status, socialists shared with all other inmates the general privations and indignities of prison life under communism: overcrowding, lack of food and heating, and frequent body and cell searches. Occasionally there were completely unprovoked attacks on socialist prisoners. In 1920, and again in 1921, they were brutally beaten up in the Butyrki (see p. 124); in 1922, in Iaroslavl prison; and in 1929, in the Verkhne Uralsk prison, where the beating-up lasted three whole days.[29] The situation worsened year by year: hunger strikes were less and less effective, and finally became merely futile.[30]

*A former officer, Iurii Bezsonov, who was himself a prisoner in one of the northern camps, observed that socialists had earned for themselves many privileges owing to 'greater cohesion and inner organisation among themselves.' The only other privileged group were the criminals who, he said, also possessed an 'inner cohesion.' This enabled both groups to resist the authorities. The criminals also kept up their old traditions: one night in 1920/21, Bezsonov heard them singing the old convict song 'On the wild shores of the Baikal', in the prison of Ekaterinburg.[28]

Where the battle for the political status had been won, socialists took full advantage of it. In 1918, in the Butyrki, they were able to organise lectures and concerts. In 1921, also in the Butyrki, 'freedom' was almost complete: all day long, men and women socialists and Anarchists visited each other's cells and walked together in the yard. The Mensheviks had a 'party school' and even a 'prison university'; and concerts and theatrical performances were given in the evenings. Contacts with comrades outside were regular, and newspapers, both Russian and foreign, were received daily (the Russian papers even included some illegal publications). Socialist and Anarchist prisoners also established the tradition of accompanying those about to be released down to the prison gates, where they rendered, with great passion, one or other of the old revolutionary songs — 'Hostile storms' for a Menshevik, 'Boldly forward, friends' for a Right SR and so on.[31]

In the *Predvarilka* in Petrograd in 1921, conditions were also very good for socialists: they were all placed in the same wing of the prison, one or two to a cell, and cells were open from morning to eleven or twelve o'clock at night. Prisoners were allowed walks, visitors, parcels — even copies of the *Socialist Courier*.[32] Socialists often provoked the wrath of prison authorities by behaving in a manner to which the Communists could not easily object. One such incident was described in a letter received abroad in 1924:

> The only place in Russia where the First of May is freely celebrated is the prison. We, the political prisoners in the House of Pre-Trial Investigation, had red flags fluttering from the windows, loudly sang revolutionary songs, sent fraternal greetings to the socialists on the Solovki, and so on. The administration got alarmed and ordered the flags to be removed, but this met with vigorous protest from students. They demanded that an official report be made, to the effect that red flags had been removed on the First of May in socialist Russia.[33]

Provincial prisons were as a rule in a worse state of repair and even more insanitary than those of Moscow and Petrograd. In Vladimir, in 1920–21, neither laundry nor baths were working and there was typhus among the prisoners.[34] The prison of Iaroslavl was derelict (it had been out of use for several years) and the cells were damp and cold even in August; by November they became intensely cold, and the heating system was out of order. Here, as in Orel and several other prisons, prisoners were strictly forbidden to stand near, or even to approach the windows, and sentries posted in the yard were ordered to shoot without warning. Food was quite inadequate; food parcels from relatives and the Political Red Cross arrived half rotten and bearing the marks of rats' teeth.[35] The punishment cell at Iaroslavl measured two paces by one, and had no window. A woman SR, who was put into it for five days, says that she could not stretch out in it; it was icy cold and barely lit by a small electric bulb under the ceiling. She had been stripped naked, and given 'a huge coat of coarse soldiers' cloth, and bark sandals.'[36] The old convict jail at Orel had the worst reputation in tsarist times. It was here that both Dzerzhinskii and his deputy Unshlikht had been imprisoned before the revolution. Under Bolshevik rule, the Menshevik Grigorii Aronson found the cells there damp, floors slippery and walls mouldy to the touch; the *parasha*, a rusty tin, had no lid. Sewers and water supply were out of order.[37] Such conditions were typical for almost all provincial prisons. The two former monastery prisons, Solovki and Suzdal,* were a special case.

Solovki was the colloquial name for the monastery prison on the Solovetskii islands in the White Sea, some 250 miles from Archangel. The monastery was founded in 1437 and in 1584 it was surrounded by fortress-like walls with turrets. From that time on it was used as a prison for political and religious offenders. The prisoners were mainly heretics, recalcitrant clergy and insane monks and priests. In addition, 'state criminals' were incarcerated there on the direct orders of the tsars.[39] Thus two of the Decembrists were kept there.[40]

The prison attached to the Solovetskii monastery was abolished in 1905 and then revived under the Soviet government as one of the so-called Northern Camps of Special Purpose — SLON for short (*Severnye Lageria Osobogo Naznachenia*). The other components of SLON were situated on the mainland, at Kholmogory and Pertominsk (both former monasteries), at Archangel and at Kem. What happened to the Solovetskii monks is not known, but some were seen in prison in Moscow and some must have remained on the island; there is mention of two monks shot there in 1924. The first prisoners to be sent to the Solovki were officers of the defeated White armies; then came the sailors from Kronstadt after their revolt in February 1921. During 1921 and 1922 the Solovki camp was filled with criminals, with right-wing opponents of the regime and with the wives and relatives of convicted or executed political leaders. From 1923 onwards socialists and Anarchists were sent to Solovki, usually after some time at Pertominsk or one of the other northern camps.[41] By that time there were about 4,000 prisoners on Solovki; by 1925 there were about 7,000 and over the next two years the number grew to over 20,000. In 1929–30 the Northern Camps were extended to cover a territory stretching from the Arctic Ocean in the North to the

*In 1903 fifteen monasteries and five convents in Russia had prisons.[38]

river Svir and Lake Ladoga in the South and to the Finnish border in the West. By then the number of prisoners exceeded 100,000.[42] According to data supplied by the GPU official Kisselev-Gromov, who was more likely to understate than overstate the case, the figure rose to 662,000 by the middle of 1930.[43]

The administrative personnel of the SLON camps were recruited from among the prisoners of the camps, mainly from chekists convicted of fraud or some other misdemeanour or from common criminals. These men were hoping to earn their pardon or the chance of returning to lucrative jobs in the GPU by being particularly brutal to the prisoners under their command. Under their chief Nogtev and his deputy Eikhmans, they were the real masters of the SLON camps, even though officially all decisions had to be referred to the Board of the GPU in Moscow.

The Solovetskii islands were joined to the mainland by a causeway which terminated at the Kem transit camp on Popov island,* about forty miles from the Solovki proper. The other islands of the Archipelago were reached by boat only and for six to seven months they were completely cut off from the world by ice. All prisoners had to pass first through the transit camp on Popov Island and this, according to all descriptions, was a most traumatic experience. The camp was run on military lines; the prisoners were subdivided into patrols, companies, regiments and so on; the camp officials were called company commanders etc. Prisoners were drilled like soldiers, made to stand to attention and yell in unison; 'Good day, comrade commander,' while the commanders competed with each other in the abuse and maltreatment of the underfed, underslept and freezing prisoners. They carried heavy clubs and made liberal use of them —'Let them remember, sons of bitches, that they are now in the Solovki.' Every lapse was punished as a breach of military discipline; punishment cells were always full with men and women, stripped naked or to their underwear and left there to freeze for days and nights on end.[46]

There were three camps on the Solovetskii island: in the Kreml or Kremlin (that is the original walled monastery with its churches, towers and belfries)** and in the Muksomolskii and the Savvatievskii *skity* (hermitages). In addition there was a penal section on Sekirny mountain. On nearby Anzerskii island was another camp, called the

*Escape from Solovki itself was impossible; all attempts failed and all would-be fugitives were caught and shot. The few successful escapes were undertaken from Popov Island.[44] Popov Island (island of the priests) was renamed by the Bolsheviks Island of the Revolution, but the name did not stick.[45]

**Most of the churches and the cathedral of the Kreml were destroyed by fire in 1923. It is believed that the fire was started by the administration.[47]

Golgotha-Crucifixion *skit*. Over one of the camp gates was placed a huge placard proclaiming: 'We will build a better new world — Labour will rule the world!'* The Kreml housed the offices of the SLON and fifteen 'companies' of prisoners and administrative personnel. There was also a 'company' of women living in barracks outside the Kreml walls. The conditions in the Kreml were appalling. The prisoners were common criminals or 'counter-revolutionaries', commonly called C-Rs (pronounced Caiers), a category that included priests (several bishops among them), members of right-wing political parties, insurgent peasants from the Tambov province, Kronstadt sailors and students from Leningrad. All were compelled to do hard physical labour for unspecified hours on famine rations. They were beaten and abused and punished in the most fiendish manner, made to stand for four to six hours 'under the mosquitoes', that is exposed, with bared torso, to the vicious bites of swarms of the northern mosquitoes; or squeezed into the small, dark 'stone sacks' (punishment cells) in the outer walls, for one to two weeks.[49]

Socialists and Anarchists were housed in the Savvatievskii *skit*, in a compound surrounded by barbed wire and overlooked by several watchtowers. In the evenings the air was thick with mosquitoes. The two-storeyed former hostels for pilgrims in which these prisoners lived had room for about one hundred; but the number almost doubled in the course of a few months, and several smaller camps were set up at Muksolma and on Anzerskii island. A small group whom the authorities refused to recognise as political were put in the Kreml.[50]

At first socialists and Anarchists were allowed almost complete autonomy in their camps: their greatest affliction was the long interruption of all contact with the outside world during the six winter months. So it came as a complete surprise when, in December 1924, the camp commandant Nogtev ordered his soldiers to shoot at the socialists in the Savvatievskii *skit*, killing six and wounding two of them (see p. 146). When news of these events reached Moscow and the West, the Bolshevik government felt impelled to announce that the Solovetskii Camp for Political Prisoners was being closed. This was not true. Even as the steamers with the prisoners of 1923/24 were leaving Solovki, other steamers were already bringing new ones.[51] Nevertheless, there was a real change: from then on no political status was tolerated on the Solovki.

*Such placards adorned the gates of all labour camps: 'Long live the Third International!', 'The Soviet government does not punish, it reforms', 'Work without Beauty and Art is barbarism', and 'Work in the USSR is Honour, Glory, Valour and Heroism'.[48] One cannot but be reminded of the placard over the entrance to Ausschwitz: 'Arbeit macht frei' (Work liberates).

Of the other prisons and camps belonging to SLON, Pertominsk and Kholmogory, both on the mainland, had very harsh regimes. The commandant of Pertominsk was the notorious Bachulis: a sadist and possibly insane, he personally punished the prisoners or ordered them to be punished in the cruellest way.[52]

Another famous camp for political prisoners was established in November 1923 at the former Spasso-Iefimievskii monastery of Suzdal. Founded in the mid-fourteenth century and fortified in the seventeenth, it remains to the present day one of the glories of medieval Russia and one of the chief attractions offered by the Soviet State Tourist Office to foreign tourists. Like all prisons attached to monasteries, it originally held heretics, lapsed priests and monks, and 'state criminals' of both sexes sent there on special order of the tsars, usually for the duration of their lives.[53] It is beautifully situated on top of a high river bank, its outer walls impressively surmounted by twelve towers, while inside the walls there is a magnificent old park; and the central 'Kremlin' holds a multitude of churches and belfries, all with their many golden domes and crosses. The prisoners did not benefit from all this beauty. Their camp consisted of an old, damp, dark block and a somewhat newer two-storeyed building which had formerly served as a pilgrim hostel and which, though somewhat lighter, was equally damp.[54]

The first socialists to be sent to Suzdal included the Mensheviks Rubin, Liber and Levitskii, the Right SRs Rikhter and Vyssotskii, and the Left SR Braun. They were soon followed by hostages from Menshevik Georgia. By December 1924 there were some seventy political prisoners in Suzdal, including fifteen women.[55] Later on the Menshevik Eva Broido spent almost three years at Suzdal and in 1933 the SR Olitskaia was sentenced to five years there. According to her, all women prisoners were removed from Suzdal in 1937 and sent to other prisons and camps (she herself went to Kolyma).*[56]

There were many other prisons — too many to describe — in which socialists were kept. They were no better and possibly worse.

Exile

By 1924–1925, in accordance with the general hardening of the official policy towards socialists, the GPU extended the list of places of exile to include towns and villages situated on the polar shores of

*According to Professor Alec Nove, however, Suzdal was still used as prison in 1956, when he visited the USSR — 'there were NKVD guards at the gates' (verbal communication).

the White Sea, the taiga and the tundra of the Turukhansk and the Narym regions of northern Siberia, the sands of the river Pechora and the deserts of sub-tropical Turkestan. Most of these places were hundreds of miles from the railway and often no bigger than hamlets. Often the last stage of the journey had to be made on foot, by native canoe, on horseback or even by camel. In many of these places the climate was so bad that they were hardly suitable for human habitation.[57]

On arrival in the place of exile, a socialist had to report to the local GPU office. His or her life depended entirely on the goodwill of the local GPU: it could decide whether he or she was to report once a week, twice a week or even daily; whether he or she was to receive the official weekly money allowance* at once, much delayed or not at all; whether he or she would be permitted to rent a certain room or not and to accept a certain job or not. Exiles were barred from registering with labour exchanges, and from joining trade unions. Also they were altogether barred from employment in trade unions, cooperatives, all economic organisations (except those connected with foreign trade or with food), factories, mines and educational institutions.[59] As regards accommodation, they were further disadvantaged in that some flats went with jobs of a kind they could not aspire to. They were lucky if they could find a 'corner' or part of a room in a workman's or peasant's home, or in a native yurta. An undated letter (probably 1922–24) from an unidentified Menshevik describes the stupefaction one felt on finding oneself somewhere beyond the Urals, in a village, many miles from the railway, in which there were no houses, only earth hovels with small holes for windows. The new arrival was 'likely to wander around in a daze for a full week, wondering — could one live in such a place? — but one get used to it after a while.' The worst aspect was 'the complete impossibility of finding any work, though our people are extremely inventive — they are prepared to paint church roofs, tune pianos, clean the roots (a local item of export), to fish, to work in schools, to hunt moles and work for the natives. . . .'[60] In 1928, 1929 and 1930, three letters from Ienisseisk, in northern Siberia, still showed 'the usual picture': no work except physical work, such as cutting wood and helping in the fields in summer' — in other words it was seasonal work and by its very nature intermittent. And 'in summer the gnats are murderous; in winter, Siberian frosts nearly kill you'.[61] Cherevanin, a member of the Menshevik Central Committee, found that even in Moscow, in 1929, 'there was no place to live and no work and apparently no hope of any'.[62] From Saratov,

*This was in any case ludicrously small. Exiles to Oirot-Tura in Siberia received fifteen roubles per month in 1936 at a time when that equalled the price of 10 kilos of bread.[58]

where they found themselves in January 1928, the Ezhovs wrote that 'our affairs are worse than at any time during these years. We sold everything we could so as to exist from day to day.'[63] Eva Broido, in Tashkent since 1931, found only part of a room to rent for the first two years before she could move into a modest little room of her own. Later, in Oirot Tura, she could not find work — 'there is none and almost no chance of finding any' — until she bethought herself of earning some little money by making dresses for the wives of local commissars.[64]

In short, it was almost impossible to find either work or a place to live. Most exiles would have perished but for the help they received from their relatives and friends, their party, and the Political Red Cross (see p. 110 below). Even that help could not always reach the smaller localities, where climatic or geographical conditions interrupted all communication with the outside world and all postal services stopped either for the whole of the long northern winter (five or six months) or twice a year for about two months each time. In such places there were no books and often no company; isolation was complete.

Larger cities might offer greater cultural amenities; but even where schools and universities existed, children of exiles were not accepted because of their disfranchised parents. Medical facilities were non-existent in most places of exile, but even in comparatively populated centres provided with medical services, exiles were severely disadvantaged by a whole chain of circumstances: barred from employment and from the trade unions, through which all such facilities were channelled, they were not entitled to medical treatment. In fact, they could only get treated at great expense, privately.[65] As for correspondence, exiles were generally allowed to write and to receive letters, even from abroad,* and to subscribe to periodicals, including foreign ones; but all correspondence was of course severely censored.

For Mensheviks with established literary reputations there was a chance to earn some money by translating, or even by writing or editing works commissioned by Moscow publishers. Old friends in the State Publishing House would sometimes put some work in their way. Thus the exiled Sergei Ezhov edited and published Martov's *History of the RSDRP* in 1923; a book of his and his wife's reminiscences *From the Epoch of Iskra* in 1924; several translations and the booklet *Women in the Russian Revolutionary Movement* in 1927; a biographical sketch of the worker-leader Petr Moisseinko in 1929; and, in the same year, his and his wife's memories of their revolutionary work in Baku.[66] His brother Vladimir wrote his

*No letters from exiles or prisoners were received abroad after the summer of 1937.

Revolutionary Memoirs while in prison at Suzdal and they were published in 1925–27.[67] The memoirs of Eva Broido were published in Moscow in 1928 — without her permission and much abridged — at a time when she was in prison. Boris Nicolaevsky and Isaac Rubin were allowed to work for the Marx and Engels Institute. But such Bolshevik patronage was very limited and in the 1930s it dried up altogether. Censorship before and after publication was a reef on which several books written by Menseviks in exile foundered. Such probably was the fate of the book written by Andrei Kranikhfeld, under most trying conditions, on the parliamentary representation of workers in different countries,[68] and of a book by Boris Ber on the ideological crisis of the war and post-war period, and no doubt of many others.

The pattern of prison and exile for socialists was as follows: After prison or camp — usually for three or more years (after 1937 it could be fifteen to twenty years; and after 1947, twenty-five years) — came exile, usually for two to three years. But in fact these people were never allowed to stay for long in any place, no matter what their sentence stipulated. Thus a socialist or Anarchist sentenced to a specific prison or camp for, say, three years, was often shifted to another prison or camp long before the first year expired; or if exiled for three years to a specific locality might find himself or herself re-arrested and exiled to a more distant and worse place. Sometimes, too, the term of exile might be prolonged by an order from Moscow. Only a minute number of political offenders were released altogether or allowed to emigrate, and none after 1923. Some were occasionally given the chance to settle in any place in European Russia (under GPU supervision), except for certain major cities. This was called 'exile minus five' or 'exile minus ten', according to the number of cities banned. In 1924 several Mensheviks were offered a 'minus ten' exile — that is in any place except Moscow, Leningrad, Kharkov, Kiev, Odessa, Rostov-on-Don and any place in the provinces of Nizhnii Novgorod, Ekaterinburg, Ivanovo-Voznessensk, and Tula.[69] Even then the possibility of sudden arrest and further exile was not excluded. In fact the vicious cycle never stopped: socialists had to face the fact that they had been sentenced for life.

A few personal histories will serve to illustrate GPU policy. Rosa Elman, a member of the Menshevik Youth League, born in 1901, was first arrested at the age of twenty in 1921 and became one of the victims of the beating in the Butyrki in April 1921; she was taken from there to the Orel prison, then returned to the Butyrki and unexpectedly released. Re-arrested in 1922, she was sent to the Iaroslavl politisolator and then sentenced to two years' exile in the province of Perm. Arrested again in September 1923, she was sent to the Solovki camp and from there to Tobolsk prison. In 1925 she was once again exiled and in 1926 was back in prison. In 1927 she was in the prison of Verkhne-Uralsk, where she was to remain for another two years — and that is the last information available.[70]

Andrei Kranikhfeld, born in 1902, was first arrested by the Cheka in February 1921 and was a victim of the beating in the Butyrki; transferred to Vladimir prison, he was released late in the autumn. A year later he was arrested again, kept with ten other young Mensheviks in the notorious Inner Prison of the Vecheka in Moscow and then sent into exile. Distributed between two small localities in European Russia, all ten managed to escape and return to work in the underground. Andrei Kranikhfeld went to Kharkov, where he was arrested at one of the periodic raids on the local Menshevik organisation; escaped from the Cheka building, was caught and put back in prison. In January 1923 he and another of his closest comrades — Lev Lande — were sent under heavy guard to Moscow, but escaped on the way, at Orel, where they were hidden by comrades. There followed a very active period of work in the Menshevik underground, in preparation for the eagerly awaited First Congress of the Youth League at Irpen. But all the participants of that congress were arrested in September 1923 and sentenced to three years in the Solovki camp. From there Andrei Kranikhfeld was transferred to Tobolsk and then sent into exile in Turt-Kul in a remote part of Turkestan, on the borders of Khiva. Turt-Kul was followed by exile in Saratov, followed by a long stretch in prison; he was last heard of under GPU supervision in Stalingrad in 1934.[71]

With calculated cruelty the GPU sent very young socialists to the most remote and lonely places. The eighteen-year-old Anarchist Olga Romanova was exiled to a hamlet in the Narym region, where she had to share a native hut with eight orthodox priests, the only other exiles there. There were no books, no newspapers, no paper; and often no food except bread and hot water.[72] A young girl Menshevik from Moscow, Riskina, was exiled to a hamlet in the Turukhansk swamps where there were only a dozen dwellings and where there was no chance whatsoever to earn anything or to buy anything.[73]

Sergei Ezhov (Tsederbaum), a member of the Menshevik Central Committee and a brother of Martov, had been one of the founders of the Social Democratic Party in Russia. He spent all of his active political life inside Russia, in the trade union and the cooperative movements. Under tsarism he had spent many years in prison and exile and acquired quite a reputation for successful escapes. Under Bolshevik rule Sergei Ezhov was hardly ever out of prison or exile. In 1921 he spent a year in prison and was then exiled to Viatka, where he was once again arrested and in 1923 exiled to Kashin; arrested there in 1925 he was exiled to Minussinsk, then in 1928 to Saratov and in 1932 to Kazan.[74] Ezhov's wife, Konkordia Zakharova, herself a prominent Menshevik, had also been arrested in 1921 and again in 1922 and sent from one place of exile to another until she was allowed to join her husband in Minussinsk, where their son and daughter also joined them.[75]

Another member of the Menshevik Central Committee, Boris Ber (Guzervich), a leader of the party organisation in the Ukraine, was arrested in Kharkov in 1920 and exiled, with ten or twelve other Mensheviks, to Georgia; then arrested in Moscow in late 1921 and exiled for two years to Perm. In 1924 he was exiled to Kashin and in 1925 arrested there and exiled to Tashkent. Arrested in Tashkent in 1928, he was exiled to Vizinga, the most northern point in European Russia, and then to Voronezh. During the preparations for the Menshevik trial in 1930–1931, Ber was arrested and spent some six months in prison but could not be 'persuaded' to confess to crimes he had not committed. He was next heard of in January 1931 in Tobolsk (where he and his wife had been in exile fifteen years earlier). In July 1931 he was transferred to Obdorsk, at the delta of the river Ob, beyond the polar circle, where he spent a full year; then back to Cherdyn, near Vizinga, where he had been in 1928. In 1935 he surfaced in exile in Vladimir, where he was again arrested in 1937. He died in 1938 in Moscow during interrogation by the NKVD. His wife, the highly popular Secretary to the Menshevik organisation in Kharkov Lidia Abramovich, had also been exiled to Georgia in 1919–1920. She joined him in 1921 in Moscow, where she became Secretary to the Menshevik Central Committee. In August 1922 she was arrested and went on a hunger strike demanding to be allowed to join her husband, who had meanwhile been exiled to Perm. After twelve days her demand was granted. From then on she stayed with him and their two children until his arrest in Voronezh. In 1937, when Ber was arrested for the last time, his wife was also arrested; she spent the next fifteen or sixteen years in the labour camps of Siberia and was released only after Stalin's death.[76]

Eva Broido, a member of the Menshevik Central Committee and of the Delegation Abroad, had left Russia in 1920 but returned to it in 1927 on a secret mission from the Delegation. Like most 'old' Mensheviks, she had spent many years in tsarist prisons and in Siberian exile — she had been arrested in 1901 and then again in 1911, 1913 and 1915. On her return to Russia in 1927 she was arrested after six months of extensive journeying in the country and sentenced to three years solitary confinement at Suzdal. But before her term expired she was taken to Moscow in March or April 1931, that is during the preparations of the Menshevik show trial. Like Ezhov, Ber and most other 'old' Mensheviks she could not be broken; later that year she reappeared in exile in Tashkent. In 1936 she was arrested, and spent three months on a journey, during which she seemed to have stayed at most transit prisons in Siberia, to arrive, utterly exhausted, at the place of her new exile, the village of Oirot Tura in the Altai mountains. She was not heard of after August 1937.[77]

Transport, Étapes, and Transit Prisons

The interminable journeys between prison and prison and between prison and exile were generally held to be infinitely worse than either prison or exile. Such a journey could take three to five months,[78] some of the time being spent on trains and the rest in the *étapes* or in transit prisons. Both had already existed under tsarism and socialists had understandably hoped to have seen the last of them, but here they were once again, only worse.[79] The *étapes* dated from the times when convicts were made to walk all the way to the gold mines of eastern Siberia; they were primitive compounds meant to serve as overnight stops on the way. Under the rule of the Cheka and the GPU, prisoners were often kept in these half ruined, dirty compounds for days and weeks on end. Many fell ill and many died in the *étapes* or soon after, for instance the Menshevik Anna Krasnianskaia[80] and the SR Avtonomova,[81] both from typhus.

Transit prisons were more solidly built but hardly less dirty. Still, the worst part by far was undoubtedly the travelling — usually in the so-called 'Stolypin trains', named after the tsarist minister who had originally introduced them. This is how the Young Menshevik Boris Sapir described a Stolypin train: 'one of the walls was blind and the other had iron-barred windows. A wire partition running the whole length of the car left an aisle along the wall that had windows. In this aisle guards were posted who watched the prisoners through the partition, while the prisoners were put into the compartments arranged between the partition and the blind wall.' Sapir, who travelled in such a train from Moscow to Archangel on the way to the Solovki camp, says that the trip took them three days and three nights and that during that time 'the prisoners received nothing but bread and water'.[82]

Sometimes prisoners were transported in cattle or freight cars, either heated (the so-called *teplushki*) or unheated. One of the earliest and fullest accounts of such a journey dates from October 1920. Written by a prisoner of the Ivanovskii concentration camp, it tells how he and ninety-five other prisoners were sent from that camp to the labour camp at Ekaterinburg. They were assembled at about 7 p.m. in the courtyard and told of their transfer, for which no reasons were given. Among the prisoners selected for this transfer there 'were criminals (*bandity*) and politicals and communists and speculators.' There were 'people over sixty and seventy years of age who were very ill, whose entreaties to be left behind were in vain ... many (probably the majority) had no warm outdoor clothes' though 'the first big snow had fallen, followed by a snow-storm; many had no shoes, only bast sandals; many had no food.' Marched under heavy armed guard to the railway station, they were made 'to stand for over three and a half hours in the open, exposed to wind, snow and snow-storm' until the train was ready for them. It consisted of sixty unheated freight trucks (not even *teplushki*) and one heated one, for the chekists and the soldiers. The prisoners were herded into them, thirty-five to each truck, which had 'holes in the floors and walls through which the cold wind was blowing'. It was clear that they were likely to die of cold, but fortunately they managed to equip most trucks with stoves 'simply by stealing some iron or tin stoves from empty freight trains' while they were waiting — for another five to six hours — for departure. The filth inside the train was unbelievable: 'because of overcrowding ... it was not surprising that after four or five days masses of parasites were discovered ... lice which under the existing conditions could not be got rid of.' There were, of course, no toilets on the train and prisoners were taken to relieve themselves under trains or anywhere on the rails, whenever the train stopped, 'with a frost of ten or fifteen degrees below zero'. It took twelve days to reach their destination and during that time 'sometimes no bread was issued for over twenty-four hours' (at a rate of approximately three-quarters of a pound per person). Other food (small portions of raw meat or salted herring, a few potatoes, a little butter and sugar) was given out only very occasionally. Hot water was another rare commodity and snow had to serve both for cooking and washing. To supplement their totally inadequate diet prisoners bartered away any articles of clothing they had on and such valuables as sewing cotton, soap, pencils — 'You could get almost nothing for money'. Such bartering was carried out at the infrequent stops on the way and, because of the eagerness of prisoners to get food, the exchange rate 'rose monstrously and really valuable objects were exchanged for one or two pounds of bread'. And still their hunger was such that at the end of the journey many fainted.[83]

Seventeen Mensheviks transferred from exile in sub-tropical Turkestan to the extreme north of Siberia — the Narym and Turukhansk regions — began their journey some time in October 1923, but after three months they had got no further than the prison in Novo-Nikolaevsk, still far from their destination. They had begun their journey in summer clothes and were still wearing them in temperatures of 30 degrees below zero: the GPU had not kept its promise to supply them with warm clothes. Yet they could expect even worse frosts in Narym and Turukhansk. When the exiles reached Narym they were so exhausted and weak that only five or less out of a party of twenty-five could still carry their belongings.[84]

Relatives of Prisoners and the Political Red Cross

No account of Soviet terror should omit the suffering inflicted on the families of the victims. The great Russian poet, Anna Akhmatova, whose husband, the poet Nicolai Gumilev, had been shot in 1921, and whose son, Lev Gumilev, was imprisoned in 1935, had dedicated her cycle of poems, the *Requiem*, to the nameless and countless women in prison queues. This is her short introduction to the *Requiem*:

> During the terrible years of Ezhovstchina,* I spent seventeen months in prison queues in Leningrad. One day somebody recognised me. Whereupon the woman with pale blue lips who stood behind me ... woke up from the stupor that held us all and whispered into my ear (there everybody spoke in whispers): 'And this — could you describe this?' and I said 'I can'. And something like a smile flitted over what once had been her face'.[86]

Akhmatova kept her promise — her verse spoke for all the women whose hearts had 'turned to stone'.

If the estimated number of the victims of Bolshevik terror runs into thousands for the Lenin period and into millions for the Stalin period, the number of their closest relatives (father and mother, brothers and sisters, spouse and children) must at all times had been at least five to six times that. Some of these relatives were shot or imprisoned along with the offenders, but most were punished in other ways. They became under-privileged in respect to jobs, education, rations and other rights of Soviet citizens; they were often evicted from houses and ostracised at work and school and university. The Vecheka and all its successors elaborated an ever more cruel policy of making relatives suffer maximum anguish and anxiety. To refuse information or to give misleading information was routine procedure; 'So-and-so has been shot' was not necessarily true, just as 'So-and-So has been sentenced

*The name of Ezhov, head of the NKVD (the successor of the GPU) from September 1936 to December 1938, is associated with the worst period of Stalin's terror.[85]

to . . .' might mean that So-and-So had already been shot. Crypto-information was used even more widely under Stalin. The writer Lidia Chukovskaia, whose husband, Matvei Bronshtein, a professor of physics at Leningrad University, was arrested in 1937, thus described her experiences: 'A little wooden window on the Shpalernaia Street into which I pushed a sum of money saying "Bronshtein, Matvei Petrovich", answered me in a deep voice: "Exiled!" and a man whose face was out of sight of the visitor, pushed away, with elbow and belly, my hand with the money in it.' To get further information, she stood two to three days and nights on the stairs of the procurator of Leningrad, but was told to go to Moscow. 'In the military Procurator's Office in Moscow . . . I was told the sentence, quite a standard one in those days — "Ten years without right of correspondence; and confiscation of property". . . . We knew already by that time that such a sentence meant arrest and camp for the wife [and indeed they had come for her when she was already on the train to Moscow] but not yet that "ten years without correspondence" was a synonym of death.'[87]

Even if he or she was spared the ultimate horrors, every step on the way of a questing relative was like a step on the way to Calvary. To obtain permits to visit and to send parcels to So-and-So, the afflicted spouse or parent had to brave innumerable and endless queues, all terminating at similar 'little wooden windows' with the bored, disembodied voice which had the power to shatter all hope. However far away one might live, one had to go to Moscow to obtain all these permits, including a certificate that one was indeed related to So-and-So. Moreover, since all Soviet citizens must work and visiting an 'enemy of the people' was no valid reason for special leave, such a visit meant in most cases giving up a job and with it wages and food rations. The journey itself was often very long and tiring. Thus an exile to the Archangel Province wrote in 1928 that he had just had a visit from his brother and wife, who stayed for three and a half weeks. 'To the stay here one has to add the time of travel here and back, that is a week and a half . . . and owing to the tides and to the fact that the steamer does not get near the town but docks some seven versts outside it, one has to leave twelve hours before the departure and wait all that time for the steamer.' The exile felt that it was too great an effort for anybody to make.[88]

The Menshevik Vera Aleksandrova has left a detailed account of her efforts to locate and to visit her husband, Solomon Schwarz, who had been arrested in February 1921. After the beatings up in the Butyrki, Schwarz was, she found, taken to Vladimir prison. She decided to go to Vladimir to see him, but this proved very difficult. Moscow was then in a state of emergency and nobody was allowed to travel for a distance of over one hundred versts from Moscow without a special permit. To obtain such a permit, one had to have some very powerful connections. She was lucky enough to get an official *komandirovka*, that is a commission to go to Vladimir on a special task connected with metal supplies. There were only army trains going to Vladimir at the time, starting at 1 a.m., and the night journey was most tiring. Arriving in the morning, she went straight to the Cheka office, but was categorically refused permission to see her husband. Disconsolately she walked round and round the prison hoping for a glimpse of she did not know what. She was lucky again: a Serbian PoW, who was seemingly employed in the prison, saw her loitering and told her that prisoners were sometimes sent to fetch water from a well outside the prison. And indeed that was where she met Schwarz. They decided that she should move to Vladimir after collecting the rations and money that were due to her in Moscow. There were many wives and mothers of prisoners in Vladimir at the time and she found a room not far from the prison, which she shared with the wife of another Menshevik. Mensheviks in Vladimir prison included Andrei Kranikhfeld, whose mother also came to visit him, and many printers, including Deviatkin, who was visited by Ludmila Radchenko, daughter of the old socialist couple Stepan and Lubov Radchenko. Vera Aleksandrova managed to see her husband almost every day and to hand over parcels to him in the prison office. She even found a job. But then, suddenly, Schwarz and the others were taken back to Moscow. Once again she had to uproot herself. The Information Department of the Moscow Cheka refused to give any information about her husband's whereabouts, so that, carrying a parcel of food and clothes, she had to make the round of all Moscow prisons — the Inner prison of the Vecheka, the Taganka etc. — everywhere waiting in the queue, everywhere being told he was not there. Finally, she located him at the Butyrki, the very prison from which he had been moved to Vladimir. Again she had to look for a job and a room; and again there began the interminable routine of finding food and perhaps medical supplies for a parcel and, after a heavy day's work, standing in the queue before the prison.[89]

Relatives intending to visit somebody in the Solovki camp had a particularly disheartening time. The usual endless waiting at the Moscow Cheka office might terminate with the information: 'no navigation for the next six months'. Even if this was not the case, the journey was long and very tiring and at the end of it the total of visiting hours permitted was usually four or five, at the rate of an hour or even half an hour per week. This meant staying for several weeks. Visitors to Solovki in 1923–24 were lodged in filthy barracks on Popov Island, where they were badly treated and almost starved, and for each visit to the camp itself they had to travel a further twelve versts. The visits could hardly have been worth the nerve strain and fatigue endured; and the prisoners were equally strained and worried.[90]

Visits to Suzdal, a much less remote place, were complicated by the fact that the permits to visit obtained in Moscow had to be confirmed in Vladimir. And since Suzdal was thirty-six kilometres from the railway line, the last part of the journey had to be made by horse cart.[91] In 1929, when the Menshevik Eva Broido was in prison at Suzdal, her eldest daughter Alexandra, who lived in Leningrad, went to visit her. Taking her two small children with her, she went to Moscow, where she was given permission to visit her mother, but was told that she was allowed three hours visiting hours per month — to be used up as she chooses, either all at once or one hour or half an hour at a time. Only after much desperate pleading was the rate increased to five hours for one month. She found the journey with small children, by train and by horse cart, quite exhausting. And when she went to the prison for the first time ('a marvellous piece of architecture to look at', she wrote), she was made to wait for three hours outside before she was allowed to enter. There was no shelter of any kind, the sun beat down mercilessly, and she sat on the grass wondering whether she would get sunstroke. The visit itself took place in a low vaulted room with damp patches on the wall — as in all rooms in that prison — in the presence of a guard who sat at the same table as themselves. They rationed themselves to two visits per week, to make the stay not too ruinous. Already the fares and the rents had cost so much money that there was little left for food parcels. This was the last time mother and daughter saw each other; Eva Broido's subsequent places of exile were too remote and visits would have been too costly.[92]

However, political prisoners and their relatives had the enormous advantage of having the Political Red Cross to assist them. The Political Red Cross collected money, food, clothing and medical supplies for distribution among the prisoners, it interceded with the Cheka and the GPU on their behalf, and it gave sound advice when there were problems to solve. The mere existence of an organisation that was friendly, that was 'on their side', was an enormous morale boost. There was hardly a letter from prison or exile, or from relatives, that did not refer to Peshkova, the indefatigable President of the Political Red Cross.

The Political Red Cross had existed since the 1870s, when it was founded and run by the *Chaikovtsi*, a group of early Russian revolutionaries. The tsarist police had rounded up many members of this and other revolutionary groups, and prisons were bulging with many hundreds of young offenders, most of whom had never been in prison before and were bewildered and helpless. The Political Red Cross gave them material and spiritual support, and later, after the trials, this support was also extended to those who had been sent to hard labour (*katorga*) prisons and to exile in Siberia.[93] Under tsarism the Political Red Cross was not officially recognised and its staff was mainly composed of 'illegal' revolutionaries (including Martov, who worked for it in 1892).[94] Under Bolshevik rule it was recognised but its activities often annoyed the authorities and it was repeatedly closed down. Its central office was in Moscow, under its President, Ekaterina Pavlovna Peshkova (first wife of Maxim Gorky) and the Vice-President, Dr Michael Vinaver; the Leningrad branch was run by the old Narodnik Shevtsev; and the Kharkov branch by Mrs Sandomirskii. While Lenin and Dzherzhinskii were alive, they showed a certain respect for the organisation and allowed it to exist. Under Stalin it was totally demolished. The Kharkov branch was probably the first to go. The Leningrad branch was closed down in 1926 and its leaders sent into exile. The Moscow branch survived until 1937, when Dr Vinaver was arrested and shot and Ekaterina Peshkova retired (she is said to have survived to 1965).[95] This was the end of the last voluntary humanitarian organisation in Soviet Russia. Its name and the name of its courageous leaders and workers should not be forgotten.

10 A Chronicle of Persecution and Resistance

This chapter tries to give a month by month account both of the persecution of Mensheviks and of the resistance they put up. It is based mainly on memoirs, reports, articles and books written by Mensheviks themselves.

1917–1918

The first victims of Bolshevik persecution were newspapers. The central organ of the Menshevik Central Committee, *Rabochaia Gazeta* (Workers' Paper), was closed as early as December 1917. The Mensheviks immediately replaced it with *Novyi Luch* (The New Ray), and, after its suppression in February 1918, by *Vpered* (Forward) and later still by *Vsegda Vpered* (Always Forward). Menshevik papers were never allowed to appear for long periods. For instance, during the negotiations for the treaty of Brest-Litovsk, *Novyi Luch* was closed down for criticising the proposed terms, but was allowed to appear again once the treaty was signed. Eventually the entire Menshevik press was banned on 6/7 July 1918 (after the uprising of the Left SRs in Moscow). For some time after that, resolutions, declarations and appeals by the Menshevik Central Committee were occasionally allowed to appear in the paper of the printers' union *Rabochii Internatsional* (Workers' International) or their weekly periodicals *Utro Moskvy* (Moscow Morning) and *Vecher Moskvy* (Moscow Evening) until these papers were closed down in their turn.[1]

In March 1918 the trial of Martov took place before the Supreme Court in Moscow. He and fourteen other Mensheviks were accused of criminal libel by Stalin. Martov had published an article describing Stalin's involvement in Bolshevik bank robberies of 1907 and Stalin's subsequent expulsion from what at that time was a united party. Stalin denied having ever been tried or expelled from the party and demanded documentary proof. Martov asked for a postponement to get the relevant documents from several Bolsheviks in Georgia who had taken part in the examination of Stalin in 1907; he also asked for a trial by jury and for witnesses to be heard. The Court granted a postponement and Boris Nikolaevsky went to Georgia and obtained the desired affidavits. But when the court reconvened, it transpired that all records of the first session had disappeared; the affidavits were not examined, witnesses were not called and the 'trial' was wound up in a hurry. Martov was dismissed with a reprimand for 'insulting and damaging the reputation of a member of the government'.[2]

The following months saw the beginnings of a systematic repression of Mensheviks. Throughout 1918 Menshevik deputies to provincial soviets were arrested. In April they were expelled from soviets in Rzhev, Kaluga, Vitebsk, and Kineshma. In May they were expelled from the soviet in Saratov and in June put on trial there for allegedly displaying a declaration of the Petrograd Assembly of Factory Representatives (see p. 76) in the window of their party committee room. The trial was represented as a 'large scale struggle against the counter-revolutionary actions of the Menshevik party and of that of the SRs'; however the accusations proved to be unfounded, the public clearly sympathised with the accused and the judges merely declared them 'enemies of the people' and ruled that they should be expelled from 'the ranks of the working class'.[3]

In June, Mensheviks were expelled from the VTsIK of the soviets (see p. 82); and in June and July the Assemblies of Factory Representatives were suppressed; during these two months the number of arrests mounted, both of rank and file and of the leaders.

In August 1918, after the attempt on Lenin's life, the decree 'On Red Terror' started a wave of mass arrests and executions all over the country; and several Mensheviks — Krakovskii in Sestroretsk, Ridnik in Sormovo, Levin and Romanov in Rybinsk, Sokolov in Tambov, Smyshkin in Vitebsk — were shot 'without trial ... and for no apparent reason'.[4]

In November–December 1918, with the outbreak of the revolution in Germany, an unexpected thaw set in in the political life of Russia, most of the imprisoned Mensheviks were released and Mensheviks were once again allowed to stand for elections to the soviets. In the provinces, however, this official liberalisation was often ignored.

1919

The thaw continued into early 1919. Menshevik clubs were allowed to reopen, meetings were held and lectures given without interference. The newspaper of the Menshevik Central Committee, *Vsegda Vpered*, resumed publication on 22 January 1919 under Martov's editorship and was 'spectacularly successful'. Though its ration of newsprint was cut, 100,000 copies were printed and after the fourth issue it came out daily. Mensheviks attributed this comparative leniency to the fact that at that time Lenin and Zinoviev were making enormous efforts to attract western socialists into the Third International (Comintern) but were being rebuffed precisely because of the persecution of socialists in Russia. When socialist papers were allowed to appear, Moscow radio was ordered to broadcast the fact to the world. But the success and the aggressively critical contents of *Vsegda Vpered* angered Lenin and the paper was closed down again, on 26 February 1919. A similar fate befell the SR newspaper *Delo Naroda* (People's Cause), which had been appearing under the editorship of Victor Chernov: in late March that too was closed down.[5]

By that time the Bolsheviks had stopped courting western socialists. The German revolution had collapsed and Germany had become a parliamentary democracy. The uprising of the Spartakus Bund (the nucleus of the future German Communist party) had been smashed in January 1919, and the Comintern had opened in Moscow on 4 March 1919. From then on the Bolsheviks went over to an open attack on western democratic socialists and their Russian counterparts, the Mensheviks and the SRs.[6] Lenin gave the Vecheka its head. There were many arrests of individuals and of entire meetings in Moscow and in the provinces. On 20 March the Cheka invaded a joint conference of the Menshevik Central Committee and the Moscow Regional Committee. All those present, including Martov and Dan, were kept at the Cheka headquarters for a day or so; the party premises on Miasnitskaia Street were sealed.[7] Next the Cheka forbade the government presses to print anything 'of a Menshevik character'. This ban also covered the printers' union paper *Gazeta Pechatnikov* (Printers' Journal),[8] and soon not a single Menshevik paper was allowed to appear anywhere in the country. The last was closed in Moscow in 1919.

In April 1919 the Menshevik Central Committee issued a leaflet about the new wave of terror. It argued that the ruling party had been so corrupted by the use of terror that it could no longer tolerate any independent force. As for the provinces, where the Bolshevik party organisations consisted mainly of politically 'new people', the very concept of legal opposition as represented by the Mensheviks was not understood.[9]

1920

In January 1920 Martov was writing to Pavel Axelrod abroad: 'After the closure of our last paper in March 1919 and the subsequent break-up of the Petrograd committee and the Moscow committee, we have no means for broad open work among the masses.... Illegal agitation is infinitely more difficult under a regime like the Bolshevik ... than under tsarism.'[10]

In March 1920 a trial of Mensheviks took place in Kiev, in the Ukraine. When the Whites had taken the city for a short time in 1919 they had decreed that all paper money issued by the Bolsheviks should be exchanged for other money at the State Bank. No sooner did the Red Army occupy Kiev than the Bolsheviks accused the Mensheviks of 'taking money' from the Whites. They arrested the entire trade union council, on which Mensheviks were strongly represented, and then the local Menshevik committee. About twenty people were tried; the best known among them — Kuchin (Oranskii), Romanov and two others — were sentenced to concentration camp 'for the duration of the Civil War', which was explained to them as meaning 'until the victory of the world revolution'. The rest were deprived of electoral rights. As the accused were leaving the court, crowds of workers gave them an ovation.[11]

Also in March there were strikes of printers in Samara against the arrest of their delegates to the All-Russian Congress of Trade Unions. The strike spread to factory workers, who demanded, in addition to the freeing of the delegates, freedom of the press and an improvement in food rations. The local Menshevik committee supported the political demands of the workers; whereupon all well-known Mensheviks were arrested, together with several hundred strikers. Several Mensheviks, SRs and non-party men were tried and sentenced to terms of compulsory labour, and many were sent to the Russo-Polish front.[12]

In the course of March and April, it is estimated that some 1,400 Mensheviks were arrested in the Ukraine.[13]

In May a few young people formed a group in Moscow which became in due course the Menshevik Youth League. Most of its members were between sixteen and nineteen years of age and full of energy and optimism — the League's motto was 'The future belongs to us!' The League was an autonomous organisation, but in the main it followed the programme of the Menshevik party. The much depleted cadres of the Mensheviks were glad of this infusion of new blood. It was also a great morale boost to have attracted young followers at a time when the party was at such a low ebb. These young people were often impulsive and reckless and had to be restrained by their elders; but they showed exceptional courage under terror and indeed quite enjoyed fencing with the Cheka. The League established links with workers in factories and held spirited debates with the

Komsomol. Sometimes the young Mensheviks were beaten up and thrown out of factory meetings, but usually they were listened to with lively interest by the workers, who were tired of official speeches.

The membership of the League (estimated at between eight and nine hundred) came mainly from among men and women students and also workers. The central core of the League — Kranikhfeld, Sapir, Lande, Rappiport, Zingarevich, Gurvich, Falk, Iakubson and Rosa Elman — gave proof of abundant intellectual power and literary talent.[14] Andrei Kranikhfeld, a nephew of Martov, was the 'soul' and leading spirit of the League. He was frail and of poor health from adolescence but was quite fearless and possessed great reserves of mental energy. The best speaker of the League was one of its youngest members, Lev Gurvich: he was a first rate debater and was not afraid to cross swords in debates with the most senior Bolsheviks (see p. 123).[15] But, in fact, they were all remarkable young people.

The League embarked at once on a wide range of activities: proselytising among students and workers (particularly among women workers); producing and distibuting — secretly, of course — typed or hectographed leaflets and even periodicals. In Moscow it produced its central organ *Young Proletarian*; in Kiev *Young Action*; and in Odessa a regular bulletin and later a journal. It formed groups and opened clubs in Moscow, Petrograd, Kiev, Kharkov, Odessa, Kremenchug, Poltava, Ekaterinoslavl, Rostov, Smolensk and Vitebsk. In addition the League distributed leaflets produced by the party itself and helped it in its many activities. This help included the providing of sentries to watch out for the Cheka and the GPU during meetings and of 'hosts and hostesses' for the party's secret presses and stores of literature. Even in prison, members of the League continued to proselytise among young fellow prisoners, with some success. Exiled to 'distant parts' they managed to keep in touch and to compose a report to the Socialist Youth International about the activities of the League and a booklet (secretly published in 1923) on the aims, tasks and tactics of the League.[16]*

In May there were arrests of members of the Petrograd Menshevik committee: its secretary Shevelov was sentenced without a trial to two years compulsory labour, the metal worker Shpakovskii, a member of the committee, to six months and another metal worker, Zimnitskii, to three months. After the elections to the Petrograd soviet the leader of the Menshevik faction in the soviet, Kamenskii, was arrested and was still in prison a year later.[18]

Also in May, a major disaster struck the Menshevik committee in Rostov-on-Don. At the first session of the newly elected soviet,

*Only about twenty of that heroic band of young Mensheviks survived the camps.

Vassiliev, the chairman of the Menshevik committee, was expelled from the soviet after his first speech, and he and fourteen other Menshevik delegates were arrested. Vassiliev had been editor of the Samara paper *Nash Golos* (Our Voice) during the War and chairman of the Rostov-on-Don soviet during 1917–1918. Others arrested were: A. Lokerman, a trade-unionist of long standing, S. Gurvich, chairman of the Rostov-on-Don soviet in 1905 and twice sentenced to hard labour under the tsars, Pleskov, who had also done hard labour under the tsar, and the worker Bibik, a poet. Local workers protested so vigorously that the authorities promised that the accused would have a public trial. They were charged with collaborating with the Whites. This was a stock accusation levelled at the Mensheviks during and after the Civil War (in Ekaterinburg in 1919; in Kiev and Kremenchug in 1920), though in reality, the Mensheviks had opposed both the Whites and the Reds in defence of the rights of trade unions and other workers' organisations. In the event no trial was held at Rostov-on-Don and the prisoners were spirited away to Moscow, where they were kept in prison until February 1921 (see p. 124).[19]

In May, too, a strike by the workers of an armanent factory in Tula against the commissar assigned to their factory was joined by all other workers in Tula, including Bolshevik workers. When the Cheka arrested some strikers, all the others, and their wives, showed their solidarity by insisting on being arrested too. The Cheka found itself with several thousands of detainees on its hands: they disposed of them by sending many of them to the front and sentencing twelve workers to compulsory labour for life. When the Menshevik delegates to the local soviet appealed for a peaceful solution to the conflict, their entire faction was arrested and kept for a month in prison; most of them were then expelled from the region.[20]

The leaders of the 'old' printers' union, who dared to arrange a meeting of welcome for the British Labour Delegation in May, (see p. 69) were arrested and kept for three months in prison and then sentenced without trial or any explanation: Buksin, Deviatkin, Tsipulin and Romanov to two years in concentration camp; seven others to one year; yet others to six months; while some were freed.[21]

In June, the entire Menshevik committee of Samara was arrested and the most influential of its members expelled from the region.[22] Throughout the summer of 1920 arrests of Mensheviks continued all over the country. At Ekaterinburg the local Menshevik committee was arrested, along with a member of the Central Committee, David Dallin. In Tomsk, Irkutsk and Cheliabinsk there were arrests of individual Mensheviks, while in eleven other towns whole groups were arrested.[23]

In August the Cheka delivered two major blows, in Moscow and in

Kharkov. In Moscow, just before a party conference, fifty-six people were arrested, including two members of the Central Committee and delegates from parts of Russia; all were freed within a month, but the conference could not be held. The Moscow branch of the Menshevik Youth League was also broken up by the Cheka, though within six months it was active again. In Kharkov, just before a South-Russian party conference, all delegates and many other people were arrested — altogether 120 people, including seven members of the Ukrainian party committee. As part of the same campaign, two Menshevik leaders were arrested in Odessa. Of all those arrested forty-six were kept in prison to the end of the year; then fifteen of them were charged with 'belonging to the right wing of the party' and administratively sentenced to concentration camps 'for the duration of the Civil War'. Seventeen others were exiled to Georgia* because 'they had tolerated a right wing in their ranks'. Somewhat later, eight Mensheviks from Poltava and three from Kremenchug were also exiled to Georgia. Seventeen Mensheviks were arrested in Samara, and twenty in Rostov-on-Don; in Vitebsk many Mensheviks were arrested, including the well known and popular Baturskii.[24]

In August, the German Independent Socialist party held a congress at Halle. The Bolsheviks, anxious to persuade that party to join the Communist International, sent Zinoviev to Halle (he was a colourful though somewhat theatrical speaker, with a good command of German). When the Mensheviks announced that they too would like to be represented at Halle, the Bolsheviks thought it a good occasion to impress the foreigners with soviet 'liberalism'. So Martov and Abramovich were granted exit visas on orders of the Central Committee of the Communist party. It proved a miscalculation. Martov delivered a speech (later printed as a booklet — *Bolshevism in Russia* — in Berlin in 1925) in which he described the persecution of socialists in Russia. The speech made a deep impression; the Independents split and only one part joined the Communist Third International.[25]

In November, the entire local committees of the Mensheviks and of the Jewish Bund were arrested in Mogilev: sixteen were sentenced to compulsory labour in various concentration camps 'for the duration of the Civil War'. There were arrests in Stavropol, Briansk, Nizhnii Novgorod, Gomel, Perm, Kazan, Saratov; and house searches in Vologda and Smolensk, including the home where Fedor Dan was living in exile. Many of these repressive measures were connected with re-elections to soviets or to trade unions.[26]

*The Georgian government protested against their country being used as a place of exile, but in the end agreed to take the exiled Mensheviks for their own good.

In early December a workers' conference on the food situation came under attack in Kiev. The conference had attracted over a thousand participants, of whom 170 were Mensheviks, about 100 were Bolsheviks and the rest non-party. Anti-Bolshevik feelings ran high: Bolshevik candidates for the Praesidium were voted down while the Menshevik Pavlovskii, a member of the Board of the dissolved Union of Metal Workers and only just out of prison, was elected chairman and given an ovation. Discussions were lively and could not be cut short — each time an attempt was made to do so there was a chorus from the floor: 'We have kept silent long enough.' This produced the usual result: the Bolsheviks closed the conference and the Cheka arrested sixty-seven Mensheviks.[27]

Also in December, the prominent Menshevik Baturskii, earlier arrested in Vitebsk, died of typhus which he had contracted in prison. A crow of no less than three thousand factory and office workers attended his funeral.[28] In Kaluga, still in December, a house search was conducted at the home of Alexander Smirnov, the well known Menshevik worker, who had been exiled there for his part in the Assembly movement. Among the books confiscated were two of the three volumes of Marx's *Das Kapital*.[29]

1921

At first the new year seemed to bring little change to Menshevik affairs. In January Fedor Dan, only just returned from exile in Smolensk, was exiled to Petrograd, which again reduced the size of the Central Committee in Moscow. In February there were two big raids on the Menshevik club *Vpered*. On 20 February the Cheka arrested five members of the Menshevik Youth League, who were producing, on a rotator (a kind of duplicator), the second number of their journal *Iunyi Proletarii* (the Young Proletarian). They also arrested the entire Central Committee of the Jewish *Bund*, which was, however, released two days later. On 25 February the Cheka netted a really large number of Menshevik leaders, including five members of the Central Committee, and many more members of the Youth League. These arrests — altogether some 160 Mensheviks in Moscow, followed by large scale arrests in Petrograd, Samara, Saratov, Briansk, Odessa and other cities — put the Central Committee members Dan, Ezhov, Nicolaevsky, Pleskov and Cherevanin behind bars, as well as such prominent members of the party as Bienstock, Aronson, Volin, Deviatkin, Dubois and Schwarz. Though after a few days 38 of them, including 35 women, were released, members of the Central Committee and of the Moscow regional committee announced that they themselves would not leave the prison until all were set free. They were told that 'those in power' had in any case no intention of releasing them.[30]

Also in February, the Mensheviks from Rostov-on-Don, who had been in prison since May 1920 (see p. 118), were unexpectedly set free — 'We shall wait,' said Dzerzhinskii; 'circumstances may arise when it would suit us to have a case against SDs [Mensheviks] in the courts — we shall then make use of them.' In the meantime they were informed that the Vecheka had closed their case.[31]

February proved a black month for Menshevik Georgia: overrun by the Red Army and undermined from within by a well-timed Bolshevik revolt, it was forced to surrender to Bolshevik Russia (see p. 50).

However, February also brought an unexpected bonus to Russian Mensheviks: the first number of the *Sotsialisticheskii Vestnik* (Socialist Courier) came out on 1 February in Berlin and reached Russia in March. It is impossible to exaggerate the impact and lasting importance of that journal both abroad and inside Russia. Edited by Martov and written by people with intimate knowledge of Russian trade unions, soviets and government, it mirrored Russian life in all its complexities. It was infinitely more informative than the official soviet press and thus commanded respect even among Bolsheviks. In fact it was regularly read by high ranking Bolsheviks, including Lenin. To the Russian reader it offered information on events inside the country which the official press did not mention, as well as reports on the socialist movement abroad. In each number there was an up-to-date account of the reverses as well as the successes of the Menshevik party in Russia.

Martov had not intended to remain abroad after the congress at Halle, but he never saw Russia again. A very sick man, he died in Germany in 1923 from his throat affliction. But in those few last years of his life he proved a greater thorn in the side of the Bolsheviks, and a greater help to his own party, than ever before. In Russia the Menshevik party had no means to make its voice heard, but now it found its voice in the *Socialist Courier* which was smuggled into Russia in great numbers.[32]

Martov had arrived in Berlin in September 1920; Abramovitch joined him there in November. Together they formed the Menshevik Delegation Abroad (its correct name was the Delegation of the RSDRP Abroad — *Zagranichnaia delegatsia RSDRP*). At first it consisted of Martov, Abramovitch and Eva Broido (who was already in Berlin, having left Russia in the spring of 1920). In early 1921 they began to publish the *Socialist Courier*, doing all the work between them — writing, editing and taking the paper to a cheap provincial press to be printed. Later they were joined by David Dallin and in 1922 by Fedor Dan, Boris Nicolaevsky, Iudin and Iugov, all members of the Menshevik Central Committee. Other prominent Mensheviks were co-opted: Grigorii Aronson in 1922, Mark Kefali in 1924, Solomon Schwarz in 1926. The appearance of the first number of the journal in Russia was a complete surprise and made an overwhelming impression. Dvinov, who was in Moscow when it arrived, said: 'Everybody was pining for a free word, there was such a general mental stagnation, such general lassitude . . . that the appearance of the *Socialist Courier* was greeted enthusiastically by everybody: inside prisons and outside them.' What did it matter that 'ninety per cent of the party was in prison . . . we had the *Socialist Courier*'.[33]

The appearance of the journal was equally surprising to the Bolsheviks, and they were particularly enraged by the publication of information from Russia. They were also curious and could not resist begging for copies from Moscow Mensheviks. To the latter, copies of the *Socialist Courier* were infinitely precious; they were passed from hand to hand and read and reread until they were in rags. People drank in the contents like an elixir. The journal infused new confidence and new energy into the party, at the centre as well as in the provinces — 'in short,' said Dvinov, 'it united the party in that terrible time, so its value was incalculable.'[34]

At first funds and people were in desperately short supply at both ends, and only single copies could be got into Russia. Eventually the smuggling, or the 'transport' as it was called, was properly organised and consignments of 50 copies each of numbers 1, 2, and 3 were received and thereafter 100 to 150 copies of each number. Later still, 200 to 300 and even up to 2,000 copies could arrive. The journal was distributed throughout the country; in the winter of 1921–22 it was sent from Moscow to seventeen other towns and to the Far Eastern republic. The demand always exceeded the supply. Since the Bolsheviks, in tsarist days, had an equal expertise in smuggling illegal literature, it was indeed a matter of special pride to the Mensheviks that not a single consignment fell into the hands of the Cheka.[35]

The first three months of 1921 were black months for the Bolsheviks: there were mass strikes of workers, particularly in Petrograd, peasant risings, a mutiny at Kronstadt* and threat of

*In March 1921, the population of Kronstadt, a naval base on a small island in the Baltic Sea — sailors, soldiers of the garrison, dockers, shipyard workers and civilian employees of the naval establishments — formulated a protest against War Communism and political repression. This was a genuine and spontaneous expression of popular anger and it had not been influenced by any political party, except, to a limited extent, by the Anarchists. It was even supported by many of the local Bolsheviks. When the government learned of the protest, it chose to regard it as a mutiny and Trotsky sent an army of 50,000 against the 15,000 Kronstadters. In spite of desperate resistance the islanders were overwhelmed: many were killed in the fighting, but many more were shot afterwards and thousands imprisoned and later shot.[36]

famine everywhere. This, said the Mensheviks, surely signalled the bankruptcy of Bolshevik policies. Lenin, with characteristic suddenness, reversed those policies. In March he announced the introduction of the New Economic Policy (NEP), which he quite blatantly cribbed from the Menshevik party program of 1919. NEP marked a partial return to capitalism. The Mensheviks welcomed it, since they had been consistently demanding a return to a mixed economy and now felt vindicated. They were in a state of euphoria. They were also hoping for a general democratisation of the regime —a 'political NEP' — for they were convinced that a semi-capitalist society could not function without it; but in this they were disappointed. Lenin had no intention of relaxing his dictatorial regime. Repressive measures against socialists were tightened: administrative exile, so hated in tsarist times, was introduced again and a network of politisolators (security prisons for political prisoners) was created. Lenin himself used stronger language than ever before: 'For public profession of menshevism our courts must order execution.'[37]

The Russian people were perplexed, and even many Bolsheviks were dismayed, by the unexpected change of government policies. Lenin tried to explain that NEP would in no way deflect soviet Russia's progress towards socialism: there was nothing wrong in borrowing some forms and methods from capitalism. When Trotsky spoke in the same vein to a Youth conference, he found an unexpected opponent in the eighteen-year-old Young Menshevik Lev Gurvich, who argued that the NEP was simply a return to capitalism. Trotsky was sufficiently worried to write at once to Lenin urging him to publish an article on the meaning of 'state capitalism' as applied to a proletarian country on the road to socialism. Lenin immediately dictated a reply over the phone: 'Comrade Trotsky, I am in no doubt that the Mensheviks are intensifying now and will further intensify their most vicious agitation. Therefore I think that we must intensify our supervision and repression against them. I have spoken to Unshlikht* about it.... But as he was very busy himself it would be most useful if you were to start an open battle in the press, name this Menshevik, explain the vicious and counter-revolutionary nature of his speech and address a significant warning to that party to behave itself.'[38]

NEP did not bring any improvement in the treatment of socialists or of workers. In March, railwaymen in Saratov came out on strike against a further reduction of their barely sufficient bread rations.

*Unshlikht was deputy to Dzerzkinskii. Lev Gurvich was indeed arrested, not once but repeatedly.

The strikers also demanded freedom of speech, freedom from arbitrary arrest, and independent trade unions. Meetings in support of the strikers were held at all the major factories in town. A suggestion made by the Bolshevik Zhuk that a commission should be elected to investigate and control food supplies in Saratov was promptly acted upon and some three hundred were elected, though there were only four Bolsheviks among them. The elected Control Commission began to investigate not only food warehouses but also the District Food Committee, the local Cheka, the prisons and many other Soviet bodies. One can imagine the consternation of the local authorities. For about two weeks the Control Commission carried on with its work; then mass arrests of its members and other workers began. In the overcrowded local prisons, under the most inhuman conditions, they were kept for the best part of six months and then, to their surprise, almost all were released. (That was not the end, however: there was more to come a year later.)[39]

In April, elections were held to the Moscow Soviet, and the Mensheviks protested that 're-elections are scheduled at a time when over a hundred members of the RSDRP ... are kept at the Butyrki, the Taganka, the Novinskaia prison [for women] and the Lubianka.... Thousands [of workers] will be unable to express their will freely by casting their votes for those whom they trust.'[40] The Vecheka judged this to be a suitable moment to reopen 'the case against the Menshevik committee of Rostov-on-Don' (see p. 117). Since many of the members of the Rostov committee had never been arrested, or had been arrested and released, only seven persons could be produced in court, some being found and arrested and one coming of his own accord. The indictment against them was based on unsigned documents, no witnesses were called, and the accused were denied the help of counsel. The prosecutor Krylenko demanded death sentences, but in the end five of the accused were sentenced to five years' solitary confinement in prison with compulsory labour.[41]

The elections to the Moscow Soviet over, Mensheviks expected that their comrades would be released from prison, as was the usual practice of the Cheka. Instead, they heard that on April 26 a brutal beating of political prisoners had taken place in the Butyrki prison.*

*This was not the first brutal beating of political prisoners in that prison. On 11 August 1920, some thirty SRs, including five members of their Central Committee, Victor Chernov's first wife and the worker Berg (former chairman of the Petrograd Assembly of Factory Representatives), were beaten half unconscious by armed soldiers. These had been chosen from among Hungarian, German and Czech prisoners of war who had been told that there had been a riot of White guards, dangerous bandits who had massacred the warders: they were ordered to overpower the prisoners suddenly and brutally.[42]

The story has been told independently by Menshevik[43] and by SR[44] prisoners, and they agree in practically every detail. At dead of night, between 3 and 4 a.m. a lot of noise was suddenly heard from the political wing of the prison — screams from the women's cells, and the sound of breaking glass. Next the doors of the men's cells were flung open and, on the orders of a chekist, Red Army soldiers with rifles took up position by the windows. The prisoners were ordered to dress, take their belongings and leave the cells. The prisoners were mostly seasoned revolutionaries and accustomed, both under tsarism and under bolshevism, to fight for their rights. On this occasion too they demanded to see their *starosta*, the Menshevik Pleskov, before they would obey orders. The chekist in command repeated the order, adding that they would be removed by force. Thereupon some forty soldiers and chekists invaded each cell, three for each inmate. The prisoners were given no time to dress or to put on shoes but were kicked, pushed and beaten with rifle butts and then dragged down stone stairs to the guard room, while soldiers hit them on head and stomach and stamped on their bare feet. Women were treated even worse — after being beaten and kicked, they were dragged down the stone stairs by their hair or their feet. No exception was made for men or women with weak hearts or for pregnant women. Only those taken from the prison hospital were not maltreated. In the guard room, surrounded by crowds of armed soldiers and chekists, among whom two women chekists with revolvers were conspicuous, the prisoners saw their comrades in torn underwear, bruised and wounded, some fainting from shock or pain. When the chekists tried to take some of the women away, the men linked arms and formed a ring around the women. Some women were taken away nevertheless, to return shortly afterwards in a far worse condition. In the end some three hundred Mensheviks, Right and Left SRs and Anarchists were taken to railway stations and dispersed to the provincial prisons of Vladimir, Orel, Iaroslavl and Riazan. Some managed to throw notes from the truck in which they were being transported. One such note duly arrived with a scribbled P.S.: 'found accidentally near the railway station of Pavlovo on the Moscow–Nizhnii Novgorod line. We figure the prisoners are being taken to Vladimir ... sympathise with all our hearts ... are outraged!!!' Two other notes were found and forwarded without comment.[45]

In Moscow, attempts to ascertain the whereabouts of individual prisoners remained unsuccessful for a considerable time. Up to a thousand relatives of the deported prisoners besieged the Political Red Cross and the Vecheka headquarters, but the Vecheka refused to give information; as became clear later, they had in fact kept no records.[46] The worst uncertainty concerned the fate of thirty-one women, among whom were many sick and injured. Eventually it transpired that prominent members of all the parties had never left Moscow: the Mensheviks Nicolaevsky, Ezhov, Pleskov and Vassiliev were being kept in the Inner Prison of the Vecheka; Dubois, Melsitov, Petrenko, Lokerman and several prominent SRs were in the military prison of Lefortovo, one of the worst in Moscow.[47] Within a few months all the prisoners were returned to the very prison from which they had been so violently removed, the Butyrki. Protests about the beatings in the Butyrki flew in all directions. The Menshevik Central Committee brought out a leaflet on 7 May addressed to factory and office workers urging them to send protests 'to all organs of soviet power'. The Central Committee also sent protests to the police, to the militia, to the Procurator General, to the VTsIK, to the Praesidium of the Moscow Soviet and so on.[48] The deported prisoners themselves also protested: those deported to the Vladimir prison sent a declaration to the Praesidium of the VTsIK in which they described the events in the Butyrki and pointed out that these took place under the eyes of high ranking Cheka officials. They also noted that the beatings were equally brutal whether the prisoners defended themselves (like the Anarchists in the clock tower, who believed that they were being taken to execution) or offered no resistance. The declaration named the eleven men grievously injured; and denounced as particularly vicious the maltreatment of women prisoners. The prisoners at Vladimir also sent a written protest, signed by fifty-five Mensheviks, seven SRs and three Anarchists, to the Praesidium of the executive committee of the Vladimir district soviet (with copies to all and sundry) in which they complained about the highly unhygienic conditions and the inhuman regime of the prison and accused the Cheka of trying to destroy socialists by means of epidemics and hunger.

The Menshevik Delegation Abroad issued an appeal to all socialist parties and trade unions. It explained that terror was once again raging in Soviet Russia, the Bolshevik government having begun a new exterminatory campaign against Mensheviks, Social Revolutionaries and Anarchists, that is against all organised political groups that could help the working and peasant masses to formulate and express their legitimate discontent with the regime. In the last three months no less than two thousand Mensheviks had been arrested in Russia and the other revolutionary parties had been similarly decimated. Prisons were overcrowded; in the House of Preliminary Detention in Petrograd, seven people were packed into one 'solitary'; 'conditions of detention, in their cruelty and unhealthiness, surpassed anything known under tsarism.'[49] Prisoners were worn out, particularly if they had suffered repeated arrests, and their health was already undermined. Many prisons were hotbeds of infection: Boris Baturskii, for example, had died in prison from typhus, Karavkin from tuberculosis. The SR Tarabukin had died after a sixteen-day hunger strike.[50]

The case of Anna Drozdova, head of the Vologda Menshevik committee, was typical of the way the Cheka worked. She was arrested in April 1921, when she was ill with influenza, and interrogated the same night. Having refused to name members of the committee, she was kept for four months in prison hospital for 'agitation against soviet rule'. When, in the end, she was released 'for lack of evidence', it was to find that her apartment had been emptied of all her belongings, including warm clothing.[51]

At the first session of the new Moscow Soviet, on 14 May, a member of the Menshevik faction, Terekhov (a worker in the chemical industry) protested against the beating of political prisoners in the Butyrki and demanded that a commission be elected to investigate the incident. The Soviet elected a commission but no Menshevik or non-party deputy was allowed to serve on it.[52] Lenin again announced merciless repressions of socialists. Arrests of Mensheviks, SRs and non-party men and women took place in Riazan, Orel, and Kharkov. In Poltava the Menshevik K. Liakhovich, the son-in-law of the writer Vladimir Korolenko, was arrested and afterwards died in prison.[53] Fourteen Mensheviks imprisoned in Kremenchug were ill with typhus. Death from typhus in prison was reported from Kremenchug and Kiev; Alexandrov died in Moscow, Tuchanskii in Odessa and S. Dizhur in Kiev.[54] Kuchin was arrested in Kiev after he had made a speech at Dizhur's funeral; and some twenty Mensheviks were exiled from Kiev to Kharkov. Altogether about 1,400 Mensheviks were arrested in the South of Russia. All were pressed by the Cheka to leave the party, but only five agreed to do so.[55]

In Moscow, twenty wives and mothers who came together to make food parcels for their imprisoned relatives were arrested, and some were exiled. On 20 May the Cheka made a raid on the Political Red Cross and arrested its entire council, together with some 140 persons only casually connected with it. They were set free later after all letters and notes had been taken from them. There were some 600 socialists (including 350 Mensheviks) in the prisons of the Moscow region in dire need of help; but the general shortage of food and clothing made effective help almost impossible.[56]

In June, seventy to eighty Mensheviks and Anarchists in the Orlov prison began a hunger strike in protest against prison conditions. They were joined on the fourth day by Left SRs, who decided not to take even water. Two women Left SRs — Surkova and Iagelskaia

—tried to set fire to themselves. Conditions in Orel were particularly harsh: prisoners were forbidden to approach the windows of their cells and the sentries fired without warning at any they saw. Of the well-known Mensheviks, Cherevanin (a member of the Central Committee) and Aronson took part in the hunger strike. It was terminated on the ninth day and during that period no medical help was available and no Cheka official appeared; while to enquiries made in Moscow, the Cheka boss Unshlikht responded with a laconic: 'Let them die.' The hunger strike left many in a very weak physical condition.[57] In the Lefortovo prison in Moscow, the Central Committee members Ezhov, Nicolaevsky and Pleskov fasted for five days in an effort to secure either release or a trial. It ended in a compromise; they were allowed books and newspapers and visits from relatives, which they had been hitherto denied.[58]

Protests against the beatings in the Butyrki prison found an echo among students in Moscow; they held protest meetings and passed resolutions of condemnation. The Cheka responded with arrests, which led to further protest meetings. Finally, on 8 June, the People's Commissar for Education, Lunacharskii, temporarily closed the universities and high schools. Students not resident in Moscow were ordered to leave town within a few days. A little later ten women and nine men students who had taken part in the protests were seen in the Butyrki.[59]

Elections to provincial soviets brought the usual crop of arrests or else expulsions from the soviets. Thus in Odessa, where twenty-four Mensheviks were elected in May 1921, two were arrested before the elections and twelve were disqualified.[60]

In June a member of the Menshevik Central Committee, Sergei Ezhov, protested against prison conditions. Twenty years of revolutionary work under tsarism had failed to break his health, he said, but one and a half months in a Vecheka prison did; he had acquired a heart complaint, and he, Boris Nicolaevsky and others were also suffering from acute scurvy. After their hunger strike in Lefortovo prison they had been transferred to solitaries in the Inner Prison of the Vecheka, allowed walks of only one hour, always at night, denied hot water and permitted to wash themselves only once a week.[61]

Altogether the Cheka continued to behave inconsistently. It transpired that it had in fact little say in the matter and that the fate of the Mensheviks was in the hands of the Politburo. This made little difference and the persecution continued.

On 30 June, the Moscow Soviet was to hear the report on the beating of political prisoners in the Butyrki. The investigating commission had not interrogated prisoners or witnesses; the prison doctor, Kuznetsov, who had twice examined the injured and had entered such injuries as broken skulls into the medical records, had been exiled to the Archangel district; and the medical records themselves had been removed.[62] Before the report was read out, the Deputy Head of the Vecheka, Unshlikht, announced the discovery of yet another secret plot to overthrow the Bolshevik government, involving everybody from the Mensheviks to the monarchists. Then the commission read out its report. It was as short as it was preposterous: the socialists imprisoned in the Butyrki had *attacked and beaten the soldiers and the chekists*, having first incited the criminal prisoners to start a riot!

Boris Dvinov, who was a Menshevik deputy to the Soviet at the time, has left a vivid description of that unbelievable scene. The small group of Menshevik deputies, about ten strong, was surrounded by a dense crowd of chekists who always attended the sessions of the Soviet. The first speaker after the report was Bukharin, one of the best-known Bolshevik leaders. He played up 'to the lowest and crudest instincts in his listeners'. The chairman Kamenev threatened more repressions against the Mensheviks. The Menshevik deputy Iudin was prevented from speaking. Mensheviks were used to 'roars as of wild beasts', says Dvinov, but what was happening this time surpassed everything known before. The hall resounded with a deafening noise; the chekists shook their fists into the faces of the Mensheviks and yelled: 'Shoot them!' They were lucky to escape unharmed.[63]

A Menshevik conference held in Moscow in August coincided with two major waves of arrests. On 27 August the entire Committee for Famine Relief was arrested, with the sole exception of the veteran revolutionary Vera Figner. The Petrograd branch of the Committee, headed by Maxim Gorky, closed down of its own accord.[64] The Cheka also discovered yet another, probably fictitious, conspiracy among Red sailors, and hundreds of them were arrested; it was rumoured that the entire staff of the Baltic Fleet was arrested at the same time.[65]

The arrests continued in the following months. Thus on 27 October, over a hundred socialists (fifty-four Mensheviks among them) were suddenly arrested in Kharkov, probably because of impending local elections. It was the same in Petrograd, and on 5 November several prominent Mensheviks were arrested in Moscow, among them Rubin and Iudin, members of the Menshevik Central Committee and deputies to the Moscow Soviet.[66] Moreover the amnesty announced for the fourth anniversary of the Bolshevik revolution, which was applied to criminals and to former soldiers of Wrangel's White Army, was not applied to socialists. Some of the

Mensheviks then in prison had in fact fought against Wrangel in the Red Army. For instance, A. Stoilov had been divisional chief of staff in the Red Army throughout the Civil War and fought against Denikin and Wrangel, as well as against Poland. He was arrested soon after his return home and was kept in the Taganka prison in Moscow before being exiled to Tashkent.[67]

In mid-November about thirty Mensheviks were released, while others were exiled for two or three years. And then the Cheka was encouraged to tighten its grip. Lenin declared the Mensheviks to be 'the most dangerous enemy'. Sentences of exile, mainly to remoter parts of inhospitable Turkestan, were thereupon meted out to whole groups of Mensheviks. They were arrested in Odessa, Zhitomir, Tagonrok, Rostov and elsewhere. Members of their Central Committee, including Iudin, remained in prison.[68]

In Moscow another batch of eleven Mensheviks was released and thirty others were exiled to Tashkent, some of them to be kept in prison there. On the other hand, fourteen Mensheviks were returned from Tashkent to be kept 'under surveillance' in Moscow.[69] All of this seemed part of a deliberate policy to wear the victims out, physically and morally. The extent to which nerves had become worn out was shown by the number of (sometimes ill-considered) hunger strikes in prison. From October 1921 onwards hunger strikes threatened now here now there. From Orel prison came urgent protests against the harsh regime and demands for a transfer to Moscow, as 'further delay would result in tragedy'. From Vladimir prison came one ultimatum after another. Anarchists and SRs were constantly starting hunger strikes in Petrograd. In Moscow the leader of the Left SRs, Maria Spiridonova, starved herself for fifteen days. It was apparent to their comrades outside that these hunger strikes brought no appreciable gains and might well cause avoidable deaths; and the Menshevik Central Committee forbade them. Fortunately, most Mensheviks from Vladimir were soon in any case released.[70]

The September issue of the *Socialist Courier*[71] had a leader on the terror in Russia. It pointed out that a year had passed since the Civil War ended, yet the Cheka was continuing to fabricate conspiracies to frighten people with executions. 'Why were sixty people shot in Petrograd?' it asked. The conspiracy uncovered there was blamed on an organisation of 'Anarchists, Bolsheviks,* Mensheviks, SRs, Kadets and monarchists.... Why were they not tried?' Among those shot were the sculptor Ukhtonskii, the poet Gumilev (husband of Anna Akhmatova), Professor Lazarovskii, as well as a woman accused of

*The first oppositional Bolsheviks, members of the 'Workers' party', were seen in the Butyrki around this time. The reference might be to them.

'being her husband's accomplice' and another woman, completely unpolitical, who let an 'illegal' sleep at her place. It seemed that many people picked up at random were made to suffer for a very small core of real conspirators, if there were any. The chairman of the Petrograd Cheka, Ozolin, who was responsible for these executions, was a notorious drunkard, lecher, and taker of bribes.

During the winter of 1921–22, practically all Menshevik papers being closed down, the party produced only occasional illegal leaflets and bulletins. But the distribution of the *Socialist Courier* was maintained, at great personal risk to the distributors. By the end of 1921 the number of copies smuggled into Russia increased from 50 to 400, and by the end of 1922, to 800.[72]

A grim comment on the year February 1920 to February 1921 was contained in a secret report by the Odessa Cheka, which fell into the hands of the Mensheviks. According to that report, 3,675 persons were tried during that year and 1,418 executed.[73]

1922

The year started with a hunger strike in the Butyrki — led by four members of their Central Committee (Dan, Cherevanin, Iudin and Nicolaevsky). The Mensheviks started to fast on 4 January and, made desperate by privations and harassment, they determined to hold out 'to the death' if need be. They protested against the threat of exile to remote villages far from railways; they demanded immediate release or trial. Though the Central Committee had advised against the strike, it now gave it all possible support. Two thousand copies of a proclamation were speedily printed, of which three hundred were pasted on walls and the rest distributed by hand.[74]

The Delegation Abroad was immediately informed by a telegram sent by Lev Lande to his father in Berlin. It read 'Pass on to Uncle that Gurvich, Lipkin with family literally starve. Long journeys ahead. Very necessary to respond.' It was easily decoded: Gurvich equals Dan; Lipkin equals Cherevanin; his family — all the other Mensheviks in the Butyrki; long journeys — threat of exile. The news was read out by Abramovitch at the Congress of the German Independents which was then in session at Leipzig. The congress responded at once: the official organ of the Independents, *Freiheit*, published the facts and the whole press followed suit. At the same time, the Menshevik Stchupak informed the Congress of the Latvian Social Democratic party in Riga. Foreign public opinion was roused, much to the discomfort of the Russian Bolsheviks who only recently had been declaiming about the plight of German Communists on hunger strike in Germany.

The first reaction was anger. Kamenev said to Iugov: 'We shall be forced to arrest every one of you.' But the Politburo considered the moment unsuitable and it restrained the Vecheka. Instead, new proposals were made to the hunger strikers: small towns and not villages were to be their places of exile, and those who so desired could go abroad. The hunger strike ended on 10 January, when all were released, though some were too exhausted to go home at once. All were given seven days to settle their private affairs; those who opted for going abroad were allowed to take their families with them and their fares were paid by the Soviet government. Clearly the Bolsheviks had decided that their old opponents were better out of the country. In this they were mistaken: it was not in the power of the Bolsheviks to control the activities of the Mensheviks abroad, and they were often most prejudicial to Bolshevik prestige.[75]

The departure of so many prominent leaders threatened the very survival of the party in Russia, and an enlarged plenum of the Menshevik Central Committee was urgently called to discuss the situation. The discussions were very heated. Many considered that going abroad was 'running away from the field of battle'; others thought that they would be more useful abroad. In the end, the Central Committee approved the departure of all who wanted to go; only Cherevanin and Ezhor did not avail themselves of the permission. After further obstacles from the Vecheka, including the re-arrest of some of the released, twelve Menshevik leaders with their families were handed $13 each for travel expenses and were escorted, by train, to the Latvian border. This was on 26 January 1922.[76]

This date proved a watershed in the fortunes of Russian menshevism. Its ranks were now so depleted that the party found it almost impossible to maintain its legal status, that is, to participate in the elections to the soviets. Nevertheless, against even greater odds than usual, five Mensheviks got elected to the new Moscow Soviet (Deviatkin and Gonigberg among them). The main activities of the party were now centred on smuggling the *Socialist Courier* into Russia and distributing it to all parts of the country; on collecting material for the journal; and on maintaining correspondence with the Delegation Abroad. Superhuman efforts were also made to print, whenever possible, protests, appeals, proclamations, bulletins, even newspapers. One of the main concerns was to find money, people and time to help comrades in remote places of exile, in prisons and politisolators, to supply them with books and journals, clothing and food; often also, to support their dependants. These were enormous tasks in themselves, and made no easier by frequent interruption through arrests. 'Life gave us no rest and no time,' said Dvinov, one of the few leaders still left in Russia.[77] A sinister new affliction was the appearance of Cheka agents-provocateurs, particularly in the Menshevik Youth League. Clearly, the Cheka was determined to 'gather in' the remains of the party.

On 15 February, some twenty members of the Youth League were arrested and of these all the 'inner core' (Kranikhfeld, Sapir, Rappiport, Iakubson and others) were taken to the dreaded Inner Prison of the Vecheka. They at once began a hunger strike demanding transfer to the Butyrki. After four days they got permission to have books and 'normal' prison conditions were introduced.[78]

The old Menshevik M. Alexandrov died of typhus in the Taganka prison in Moscow. His funeral, which took place in Orel, turned into a demonstration in which four hundred people took part, carrying wreaths and banners. The crowd listened to speeches at the graveside and sang revolutionary songs.[79]

On paper the Menshevik Central Committee counted no less than nine members in February–March 1922, but most of them were suffering from the after-effects of prison and were in very poor health. In a letter to Martov of 19 February Ezhov wrote: 'Iugov is very poorly, hardly able to work, Pleskov is recovering very slowly; Ber is consistently ill (and very exhausted); the less said of Rubin the better. . . .' There were many others in similar plight. In addition, the Central Committee lost the distinguished economist Groman, who decided at that point to 'rethink the tenets of marxism'. His close friend Cherevanin, to whom he confided his doubts, urged him to leave the party, as he had 'ceased to be a marxist'.[80] Some ten years later Groman, who had risen to great eminence in the Gosplan (State planning office) was to figure as a defendant in the Menshevik show trial (see Appendix II).

A government decree of 6 February 1922, abolished the Vecheka. It was replaced by the GPU (*Gossudarstvennoe politicheskoe upravlenie* — State Political Administration), but it proved a change in name only. Not only did the GPU keep most of the Vecheka personnel, it also kept most of its methods. The decree announced that under the GPU every arrested person would be formally charged within two weeks; all cases would be completed within two months; all detainees would be tried by a revolutionary tribunal; the GPU would bring in an era of 'revolutionary legality', of 'revolutionary justice'.[81] All this was welcome news, and arrested Mensheviks demanded even more persistently than before to be tried in an open court. The Menshevik Central Committee instructed all party members to give only the most essential information (name, age, and party affiliation) at the time of arrest, and to refuse to answer any further questions except in court. In practice, however, very few Mensheviks were brought to trial. The era of 'revolutionary legality' was nothing but a cloak to cover old lawlessness; a pretence at a change when there was none; in Martov's words, 'an attempt to legalise terror'.[82]

No sooner did the GPU hang its new shop sign over the Lubianka than it decided to demonstrate to the world how this new legality was carried out: it staged a monster political show trial against the SRs. It was the first trial of that kind, no more than a rehearsal for the bigger and better trials that were to follow, but precisely because it was the first, it has great historical importance. A full report on the trial will be found in Appendix I.

The anniversary of the Kronstadt rising of February 1921 was marked by mass arrests in Petrograd: between 400 and 460 were already in prison by 26 February (all sailors and workers except for 60 intellectuals). There were 800 prisoners in the House of Preliminary Detention in February; in May there were 2,300. There were also at least 2,000 Kronstadt sailors held at detention centres at military barracks: about 1,800 of them were sent to penal servitude in the Murmansk district, where there was outright famine and widespread scurvy. But that was not all. In June some 3,000 Kronstadt sailors and soldiers who had fled to Finland but had been later promised a pardon, returned to Russia; they were immediately arrested and kept under dreadful conditions in prisons and barracks. Those who survived were released at the end of the year, except for ten Menshevik sailors who were exiled to Siberia.[83] Mensheviks had in fact played hardly any role in the Kronstadt rising. In particular Fedor Dan, who was in prison at the time, knew nothing of it. Yet he was accused of having prepared the rising and Lenin publicly denounced him (and Professor Rozhkov, another Menshevik in prison with Dan) as 'organisers of Kronstadt'. This absurd accusation was based on the fact that when he was being interrogated by the Cheka in early February 1921 — *before the Kronstadt mutiny* — he said without meaning anything specific: 'Now you call workers "scum" and praise the sailors, but let's see what you will call the sailors, should they mutiny.'[84]

In February 1922 the case of the Saratov workers was resumed (see p. 124). Forty of them were rearrested and taken to the Taganka prison in Moscow, where about half of them fell ill with typhus, four died (including the old Menshevik printer Peter Kolesnikov), and others contracted pneumonia. On 10 April, thirty-one of them were tried before the Supreme Revolutionary Tribunal, accused of having caused disturbances in Saratov a year earlier. Among the accused were twenty-nine highly skilled metal workers, railwaymen and printers, one professor of engineering and one office employee; some were Mensheviks, SRs, Anarchist-Communists and former Communists who had left the party, but the majority were non-party. All the accused were still weak from illness and other privations in the Taganka and had to testify sitting or lying down. Even though no witnesses for the defence were called, the testimony of the accused presented such a picture of unbridled power of officialdom and the Cheka over the lives of Saratov citizens, that the judges found themselves in a dilemma. Sentences of five, three and two years in labour camps were passed and then annulled under the amnesty of the previous October. Practically all the accused were set free. But by then four had died, nineteen had become invalids and all had lost their livelihood. There is no knowing what their families had suffered.[85]

At the end of March mass arrests of Mensheviks again took place in Kharkov, Poltara and Ekaterinoslavl. In Kharkov, where twenty Mensheviks were arrested, including such prominent leaders as Astrov, Kuchin and Malkin, and several Young Mensheviks, the immediate reason for the arrests was the emergence of the so-called '*smenovekhovtsi*' (signal-switchers), so-called because they wanted to change their previously anti-Bolshevik attitudes for pro-Bolshevik ones. This partly sincere and partly opportunist movement of Russian expatriates was hailed by Bolsheviks as a truly Russian social phenomenon and given wide publicity. In Kharkov a two-days' public discussion on the subject was arranged in a large theatre and in the presence of a very large audience of students, *Komsomoltsi*, Red Army men and others. The local Menshevik committee decided to take advantage of this opportunity to address a large public. And indeed, speeches made by Astrov, Kuchin and Grigoriev found a great response from the students and others; Menshevik ideas aroused interest. Needless to say that put an end to all public disputations and the Kharkov Mensheviks landed in prison. Sentenced to exile in Turkestan, they were first taken to Moscow where they were kept in their prison train for four days outside the station; eight wives who were voluntarily going into exile with their husbands were not allowed to go into town.[86] On the journey to Turkestan two of their number fell ill with typhus: one, Iarin, was taken off the train at Riazan and survived, Astrov was not taken off and died on the train. His wife, who was following him into exile, also died of typhus a month later. The death of Astrov, a member of the Central Committee of 1917, with fifteen years of revolutionary work behind him, shocked the party deeply. His funeral was held in Moscow on 8 May. The GPU had announced that the body would arrive at the Kazan station but instead shifted it to a small halt (Kutuzovo) near the Briansk Station, at the opposite end of Moscow. Nonetheless, almost four hundred people made the journey on foot to Kutuzovo, where friends and relatives had to pay high freight charges before being handed the body. The mourners carried the coffin of their old comrade to an ancient cemetery, to the sound of an old revolutionary song and of the funeral march; speeches were made by members of the Menshevik Central Committee, the Youth League and the *Bund*. Meanwhile, GPU photographers took numerous shots of the funeral.[87]

In Ekaterinoslavl twenty-one Mensheviks had been arrested on 17 March, mainly from the local party organisation and the dissolved printers' union, including one very seriously ill man. Their progress on foot and under armed convoy from prison to railway station was truly triumphal: accompanied by work mates, comrades, relatives and friends, showered with flowers and good wishes, they boarded the train to a thunderous singing of revolutionary songs and the Internationale. In Kharkov they were kept for a few days in an unspeakably dirty cell and then packed like sardines into a prison train. One of them, who had seen the inside of many tsarist prisons and twice measured the length of the *Vladimirka*, the notorious road along which convicts walked to Siberia in tsarist days, said that this prison train was unlike anything he ever saw before — dirty, airless and so tightly packed that one could neither move nor breathe. The prisoners were told that they were going to Moscow and only learned from their guards that they were being taken to Tashkent.[88]

In April there was a lockout at the First State Printing Works, formerly Sytin's, following a one-day strike. The printers, who among other things printed the official newspaper *Izvestiia*, were protesting against the systematic non-payment of their wages, something which, incidentally, was a common occurrence in the whole of industry. The Moscow Menshevik committee published and widely distributed a leaflet condemning the lockout and explaining the reasons for the strike. That very day several prominent Mensheviks were arrested, among them Ber, a member of the Central Committee, Deviatkin and Gonigberg, both members of the Moscow committee and of the Moscow Soviet. Deviatkin and Gonigberg appealed against their arrest, invoking the 'immunity of deputies charter' (see p. 85); but the chairman of the Soviet, Kamenev, insisted that the arrest had been sanctioned by the Praesidium of the Soviet and did not permit any discussion of the matter.[89] This was the last time the 'charter' was invoked. On 16 June, Deviatkin and two other Mensheviks arrested in connection with the lockout, started a hunger strike in the Butyrki prison and demanded to be released. On the 28th they were told to go home, but they were too weak to leave the prison.[90] When, after two days, Deviatkin was moved to a sanatorium to recover, a chekist arrived to rearrest him. Luckily Deviatkin managed to escape.[91]

At the Eleventh Congress of the Russian Communist Party, which was then in session, Lenin once again said that since Mensheviks would not refrain from criticism, they had to be destroyed. It is interesting to note that many Mensheviks thought that Lenin was 'already suffering from a mental illness' at that time.[92]

The leader in the *Socialist Courier* of 2 May, entitled 'Terror Against the Proletariat', pointed out that after the end of the Civil War, the categories of 'speculators' and 'White guards' were less thickly represented in soviet prisons, while there were many more socialists and non-party workers as well as peasants, all of whom were fighting for their class interests. Official statistics issued by the People's Commissariat of Justice for the first four months of 1922 showed that sixty per cent of all political prisoners were socialists: fifteen per cent were non-party workers: and twenty-five per cent were 'counter-revolutionaries' (a category that included monarchists as well as participants in peasants' revolts).[93]

The Central Committee member Ezhov was again arrested in Moscow and started a hunger strike on 23 April. Later he was seen and recognised in a Moscow street, under armed guard, in an open droshky; he managed to call out: 'I am being taken to Viatka!'[94] Boris Ber and others arrested in Moscow in April were exiled to Turkestan. A group of 160 Mensheviks from the southern towns of Kherson, Nikolaev and others were also on their way there.[95] In Turkestan the exiles were distributed among some five or six remote small towns, most of them ridden with malaria and fever, where they could not find employment as they were forbidden to work in State offices and there were no others. They were legally entitled to a small State support, but in many places the GPU did not pay up.[96] In the Caucasus, socialists were accused of arson in the Baku oilfields.[97]

In June, the trial of the SRs took place in Moscow (see Appendix I). Though that trial naturally dominated the public scene, the persecution of Mensheviks continued. On 3 July a meeting at which the entire Menshevik Central Committee, two members of the Central Committee of the *Bund*, two members of the Menshevik Moscow committee and one member of the Youth League were present, was surprised by a GPU officer and two soldiers. The Mensheviks escaped instant arrest only because of the extreme stupidity of the GPU man, who took down their names but failed to recognise them and let them go. But that very same night some eighty-five Mensheviks were rounded up, though three members of the Central Committee luckily escaped arrest and the contacts with the Delegation Abroad and the *Socialist Courier* were not disrupted.[98] Of those arrested six were released, but on 4 August many others were conveyed to Iaroslavl jail and thence into exile, without money or clothing, to places situated six to eight-hundred versts from the railway. Some were very ill, notably Petr Garvi, who was exiled to Cherdyn, in Perm province. Boris Ber, Boris Sapir, Rosa Elman and others were also exiled to the same province; Anatole Dubois, Berlin and others were exiled to Turkestan, all the sentences being for two years. Ezhov's wife, Konkordia Zakharova, was exiled to Viatka for a year and a half.[99]

In spite of the intense terror, the Menshevik Youth League in Odessa, where a branch had been founded in 1921, had managed during the first year of its existence to issue eight numbers of its *Bulletin* and Number 1 of *Proletarian Youth*. In Kharkov, the League continued to publish the newspaper *Young Social Democrat*.[100] Zinoviev's threat, delivered at the Conference of the Russian Communist Party, to 'liquidate politically' both the Mensheviks and the SRs was answered by the Menshevik Bureau of the Central Committee in its Circular Letter No. 2 of 8 August. It urged all party members to keep to their 'battle positions' and to be careful not to take needless risks. 'Keep up your spirits! The future is ours!'[101]

A wave of arrests in Moscow engulfed scores of university professors, writers, scientists and others. Trotsky attacked them in the press as *potential* 'agents of the Entente'; should there be a war they would have to be shot: the present arrests and exile were 'preventive' measures. 'What logic is there in this madness?' asked the *Socialist Courier*.[102] Obviously, though the NEP had brought in its wake a revival of arts and sciences, the Bolsheviks wanted their NEP 'without dangerous frills'. Soon after the arrests many of the liberal professors with their families, altogether two hundred persons, were exiled abroad. There were also many arrests of students protesting against the persecution of their professors.

In August the first escapes from places of exile took place: five Mensheviks unexpectedly arrived in Moscow from Turkestan, including Kuchin and Bernstein, a member of the Youth League. Lodgings, false documents and money had to be found for them. It meant that ever greater numbers had to lead an entirely clandestine, 'illegal' existence,[103] though it also meant a welcome addition to the depleted ranks of the party. In mid-September the Political Red Cross was closed by the authorities in Petrograd, at a time when there were some fifty-six socialists (including twenty-three Mensheviks) in the *Predvarilka* dependent on its support.[104]

Most of the Menshevik publications were by then being produced and distributed secretly. There was an impressive number of new publications, very few printed, most of them produced in other, more amateurish ways: in Odessa, a collection of articles (on a rotator) and a *Bulletin* of the Odessa committee (typewritten); in Moscow, the *Bulletin* of the Moscow committee (typewritten); in Ekaterinoslavl,

Iskorka (Little spark, on a hectograph); in the Ukraine, the *Bulletin* of the Chief Committee of the Ukraine (on a rotator) in Kharkov, the organ of the committee *Social Democrat* (on a rotator) and an organ of the Menshevik Youth League *Young Social Democrat* (on a rotator); in Moscow, an organ of the Youth League *Young Proletarian* (on a hectograph) and the *Bulletin* of the Central Committee; in Petrograd, the monthly organ of the committee *Workers' Page* (typewritten).[105] Thus in 1922 the Mensheviks already tasted all the difficulties and dangers of the Samizdat.

In October, socialists in the Iaroslavl prison were several times severely beaten, some were injured. A few attempted suicide by setting fire to themselves or by throwing themselves out of the windows. No doctor came to see the prisoners, fearing, no doubt, to be arrested like the doctor who recorded the beating of prisoners in the Butyrki in April 1921 (see p. 129). There were hunger strikes in Iaroslavl and also in the Novinskaia prison for women in Moscow.[106]

Also in October the Mensheviks in Moscow held a conference in the utmost secrecy. Delegates from the provinces reported that local organisations continued their work in spite of the constant threat of detection; some new groups had even been formed. It was generally agreed that extra caution and more elaborate conspiratorial techniques had become essential. Nevertheless, the party was not giving up 'legal' work: under the impact of the terror it was closing its ranks. The conference took some major decisions. The old Central Committee, elected in 1917, was dissolved. Instead a Bureau of the Central Committee was to supervise and direct all party work in Russia, while the Delegation Abroad was to represent the party centre outside Russia and to publish the *Socialist Courier* as the central organ of the party.[107]

Under tsarism, 'illegal' revolutionaries could always count on moral and material support from friends and acquaintances in the liberal intelligentsia. They were helped with money and clothes, were fed, were invited to stay the night. Now it was no longer so. The GPU had thrown a cordon of fear around them. Nobody wanted to be found associating with them or helping them. They were shunned. It was almost impossible to find a room, a night's lodgings or a place to leave a parcel or a message. Also it was impossible to find a room to hold party meetings, even of only a few persons; or a room to store the *Socialist Courier* and illegal leaflets. On one occasion, warned that the GPU was looking for him, Dvinov just managed to slip into his flat and carry away two large and heavy attaché cases with party records and archives. But where could he take them? There was literally no place safe enough in the whole of Moscow, so he roamed the streets under torrential rain for hours until he decided to risk asking a neighbour — a simple working-class woman — for shelter. And she let him in. From her window he could watch the GPU men lying in wait for him in his own flat.[108]

In November several Mensheviks were notified that they were to be exiled abroad: Boris Bogdanov, Boris Dvinov, Mikhail Braunstein, Petr and Sofia Garvi, Iakov Novokovskii and a few others. They were given time to settle their affairs before departure, but when Bogdanov asked for additional time he was instead arrested and sent into exile. They were to leave Russia in January 1923. That made it possible to celebrate, in greatest secrecy, the New Year. To prevent all of them being caught, they separated into two groups. But all went well, neither group was discovered by the GPU. And, says Dvinov: 'Our spirits were high. Morally and ideologically we felt we were winning, in spite of all our troubles.'[109]

1923

On 25 January Boris Dvinov and other Mensheviks exiled abroad left Russia. This was the last group of prominent Mensheviks to leave Russia and the remaining few went into deepest 'underground'. There was a new leader — Georgii Kuchin (Oranskii), a great organiser and a man of great moral courage. The period that followed has rightly been called the 'Kuchin era' by Boris Sapir, who worked with him.[110] The underground was run on strict conspiratorial lines: there were false passports and letter coding and decoding and secret printing presses; every activist was known by a nickname and towns were known by personal names. When Kuchin took over he had to memorise all 'safe' addresses, all nicknames and codes, and then destroy all written notes. When the 'illegals' met, they disguised themselves: some grew beards and others shaved theirs off, some put on dark glasses, and all wore inconspicuous clothes. They met in the parks, a few at a time; sometimes they went out of town into surrounding forests. Thus the leafy suburb of Petrograd, Lesnoie, a favourite retreat in tsarist times, became once again a welcome hideout. At times party leadership was reduced to four, three, or even two people. The only cheerful note came from the Youth League, which in spite of constant arrests never stopped being optimistic.[111]

A new camp was opened at the old monastery of Pertominsk, on the shore of the White Sea, near Archangel. The first party, of SRs, arrived there in December 1922, but early in 1923 some Mensheviks were also sent there. The conditions in the camp were terrible: cold in the barracks, hunger, no drinking water. The SR Krykov went mad; the Anarchists tried to commit mass suicide by fire, were saved and then declared a hunger strike. After eleven days the regime was somewhat improved.[112]

In January 1923, in Semipalatinsk, a member of the Menshevik Youth, N. Treiger was terribly punished for making an oppositional speech. Treiger had been exiled to Semipalatinsk from Odessa and he and other exiled Mensheviks took exception to the behaviour of the former Menshevik Isaev on the occasion of a meeting organised by the Living Church, an anti-religious, Communist organisation which was usually most active around Christmas and Easter. As its chairman, Isaev behaved in a most arrogant and provocative manner — in true 'Bolshevik style'. Treiger, though seriously ill at the time, rose to protest against the behaviour of Isaev; he also explained the Menshevik position with regard to religion: the Menshevik had always exposed religious prejudices but were careful not to offend true religious beliefs. Treiger was arrested on the spot; local workers were indignant and left the meeting in protest against his arrest. Ill as he was, Treiger was kept for two days and two nights in a 'box' together with an insane Chinese, a convicted murderer. This 'box' was a cell, three paces long and two paces wide, dark and airless and unspeakably dirty. When Treiger reached complete exhaustion, he threatened to start a hunger strike if not transferred to a proper cell. He was interrogated, accused of having supported the White Admiral Kolchak, of having favoured the international bourgeoisie and so forth, and was threatened with execution. He countered these absurdities with a firm affirmation of his loyalty to the international socialist movement and the RSDRP, and asked to be tried by a truly working-class court. After that he was taken to a cell which was hardly better than the 'box', overcrowded with criminals, full of vermin and stink, and with a broken window at a temperature of fifteen and twenty degrees of frost. Here his condition deteriorated to such a degree that he had to be transferred to the prison hospital. He was then released and brought to trial. The trial was held on a Sunday and the courtroom was crowded — there were many Communists and Komsomol members as well as non-party people, both intellectuals and workers. The judge, in language better suited to a soap box, denounced the policies of the Mensheviks since 1905. Treiger answered with a big political speech which was listened to with great attention. After the trial almost the entire audience accompanied him back to prison. He was refused visits and was at first put into a cell with syphilitic Kirghiz tribesmen; later he was transferred to a 'solitary'. He found prison conditions appalling: filth, typhus epidemic, threats and insults. Treiger had a serious heart and lung condition, but a doctor was not allowed to see him until after a short hunger strike (two days on water and three days on nothing at all).

Soon afterwards he was sent to Pertominsk. His mother was later arrested in Odessa.[113]

In February the Bureau of the Menshevik Central Committee finally decided not to participate in the elections to the soviets. This marked the official break with 'legality'.[114] At that time there were still fifteen to eighteen more or less solid Menshevik organisations in the country, including the Moscow organisation with some two to three hundred members; and the *Socialist Courier* was distributed in thirty-three to thirty-five places.[115]

In March, a heavy blow fell. The house where the party archives and literature were kept was discovered by the GPU, the stores seized and the 'hostess', Rosa Lurie, arrested.[116] This seriously disrupted the work of the Bureau. On 13 March the Mensheviks commemorated the anniversary of the foundation of the RSDRP in 1898. In a festive mood the party literally plastered the walls of working class districts with leaflets, in Moscow, Petrograd, Briansk and other towns. The GPU retaliated with many arrests: in Moscow it arrested Liubov Radchenko, who with her husband Stepan was one of the original founders, Anna Krassnianskaia and Konkordia Zakharova.[117] But fortunately it failed to discover the clandestine printing press. The setting up of that press, and the printing of the party paper *Social Democrat*, had been the greatest concern of Kuchin. It proved somewhat easier in Petrograd than in Moscow, but even there the difficulties and frustrations were daunting. Kuchin's description of the enterprise recalled similar endeavours of the *Norodnaia Volia* of the 1870s. However, after several moves, always just before a GPU raid, from one house to another, with every man and woman connected with it carrying away up to two tons of type and printing equipment concealed under their coats, a 'safe' address was secured. Indeed it managed to function so secretly that the GPU failed to discover it until 1925.[118] In the meantime the successful appearance and distribution of the party paper and various leaflets and proclamations exasperated the GPU.

On 14 March, after many arrests, Bolshevik authorities staged a congress of 'former' SRs (the Russian word for former, *byvshie*, has the connotation of 'people of the past'). On an even larger scale, a hunt for former Mensheviks took place all over Russia. The official press, provincial and metropolitan, was deluged with letters, in which these people disowned their old party and defamed it, while declaring their admiration of the Bolsheviks. The Bolshevik papers described the surprising emergence of hundreds of such breast-beating penitents as a grass-roots movement, that had started in small cities and eventually grown to nation-wide proportions. From confessing to past crimes committed by the SR and Menshevik parties, the 'movement of the formers', as it became known, turned to demanding their liquidation. The 'self-liquidation' congress of the SRs was the first of its kind; it was followed by scores of 'liquidation' congresses of former Mensheviks. Throughout 1924 congresses of that kind took place in Moscow, Rostov, Ekaterinoslavl, Tiflis, Kutaiss (there were 326 participants in that town) and other cities. There was even an All-Russian 'liquidation' conference in Kharkov.[119]

In reality the whole movement was fabricated by the GPU.* It started with mass arrests, not only of active Mensheviks, but of people who had left the party years before, and even of people who never had been party members. All alike were subjected to great pressure by the GPU, and were threatened with reprisals to themselves and their families if they did not 'repent' and sign a promise to recant in public if called upon to do so. They were promised instant release if they submitted; the alternative was prison or exile. Naturally, most of them chose to save themselves and their families; the temptation was especially strong for workers, who faced not only exile and labour camp but also blacklisting and the knowledge that, deprived of their earnings, their families would simply starve. There were some who honestly hoped to be left alone after they repented, some who hoped for better opportunities for socially useful jobs, but there were also some who simply saw a chance to foster their careers. Finally there was a very small number of people who had really changed their political views and were ready to work for the Bolsheviks.

It is not surprising that so many submitted to GPU pressure; rather that so many resisted it. In Tiflis, where the prison was bulging with Mensheviks, only thirty-eight yielded. They were immediately marched off, under red banners, to the 'liquidation' congress then in session.[121] In Ekaterinoslavl, thirty-two 'repented'.[122] There is some evidence that workers treated 'former' Mensheviks with contempt as 'traitors to the cause'.

On 4 April, Iulii Martov died in a sanatorium in Germany, in the Black Forest, and was cremated in Berlin on 10 April. The crematorium was packed with Menshevik and other socialist expatriates and with foreign socialists. Meanwhile, in Russia, Lenin was also nearing his death. His wife recorded that he reflected sadly: 'They say Martov is dying too....'[123]

Also in April the Menshevik leaders arrested in Moscow in February were sentenced: Rubin to three years in camp, Bialovskii to two years in camp, and Drabkin to two years' exile in Turkestan. In

*Official Soviet historiography pretends to the present day that these congresses were genuine and that the SRs had liquidated themselves in earnest in 1923 and the Mensheviks in 1923–24, instead of being driven underground by the GPU.[120]

Viatka all exiled Mensheviks were arrested as a reprisal for having sent information to the *Socialist Courier* about the life of exiles in that town.[124] The Viatka exiles were told that they would be sent to Pertominsk. Thereupon Sergei Ezhov threatened to commit suicide, so in the end he was exiled to Kashin and the rest to equally distant places.[125]

In May an international socialist congress was held in Hamburg with the view of fusing the Vienna and the London Internationals. There were 620 delegates at the congress and the Russian Mensheviks were represented by Pavel Axelrod, Fedor Dan, Raphail Abramovitch, David Dallin, Eva Broido, Peter Garvi, Mark Kefali, Aaron Iugov, Solomon Schwarz, Boris Nicolaevsky, Grigorii Bienstock, Boris Gurevich-Dvinov, and Gonigberg; and the Bund by Aronson and Iudin. The Russian SRs were also represented. During the preparations for the congress there were protests against the persecution of socialists in Soviet Russia and there were more at the congress itself. The 'underground' Bureau of the Menshevik Central Committee sent warm greetings to the congress.[126]

In Russia the terror was again intensified. In Moscow seven Mensheviks and thirty-five Anarchists were sentenced to the camps. In the Butyrki prison two Anarchist women were brutally beaten 'for insubordination', whatever that might mean. One of them was pregnant and miscarried in consequence; whereupon all political prisoners went on hunger strike. The twenty-two SR *smertniki* (those sentenced to death in the big SR trial) starved themselves for seven days before they were allowed slightly longer walks and a greater number of parcels and visits. In Moscow up to a thousand Mensheviks, Young Mensheviks and 'former Mensheviks' were arrested — obviously in preparation for the congress of 'former Mensheviks', as all were pressed to give written promises to recant. The arrests were conducted according to old lists of party members and included relatives of Mensheviks ('almost to the seventh degree!'). Owing to these arrests and ambushes, contact with the Menshevik Delegation Abroad was temporarily disrupted.[127] In Kharkov, seven Mensheviks recently released because of illness were rearrested and each sentenced to three years' camp in the frozen Archangel area. The GPU had begun to use tracker dogs to trace Mensheviks who were pasting leaflets on walls. In Rostov-on-Don fifty Mensheviks were arrested, mainly among workers. In Turkestan exiles had their terms of exile prolonged or were sent to the Amu-Dariansk district or the town of Turt-Kul situated four hundred versts from the railway station, so that the journey had to be completed on camels. In Vitebsk the arrested Mensheviks were at first, for a week or two, put into the same cell with some twenty or more criminals who insulted and beat up the newcomers. The cell, six paces wide and six paces long, had only twelve bunks; and it was so full of lice and bed bugs that one could scoop them up with one's hands; there were also huge rats. In one case, the GPU arrived to arrest a Young Menshevik, found him away from home and arrested his mother and sister instead; they were kept in a cellar for over a week. In Orenburg the local exiles had assembled to celebrate the twenty-fifth anniversary of the RSDRP, when the GPU arrived to arrest them. Twelve Mensheviks and eleven SRs were kept in a cellar for a week. When the prisoners asked for the reason for their arrest, the GPU man Uglov ordered sixty Red Army men and some fifteen of his own men to attack and beat them.[128]

In the summer of 1923 an astonishing number of illegal publications were brought out by the party: in Kharkov, the paper *Social Democrat*; in Odessa, a party bulletin and a bulletin of the Menshevik Youth; in Petrograd, the *Workers' Page*; while in Moscow preparations were made for the publication of the Bureau's central organ. Some local organisations, particularly in the South, showed remarkable resilience. Particularly active and disciplined were the groups in Kremenchug (composed solely of young workers), Rostov and the neighbouring towns of Taganrog, Ekaterinodar, Berdichev, Belaia Tserkov, Ekaterinoslavl, Vinnitsa, Poltava, Iusufka and several other places in the Don valley; and in central Russia, in Briansk, Tver, Kostroma, Sormovo, Tula, and Orel. On the other hand, in some industrial centres there were only a few individuals active; and in the country as a whole contact with the masses had been lost: many of the small local groups were simply groups of readers of the *Socialist Courier*.[129]

By June it was no longer possible for the members of the party centre to meet anywhere in Moscow, not even if two or three of them arranged to meet, as by chance, in the street, in a park, or at a *dacha*. To meet at a private flat was quite impossible, for the GPU had spies and ambushes everywhere. There were further arrests of leaders. Kuchin escaped arrest only because he happened to have gone to Petrograd. There too, the local comrades had to be exceedingly circumspect. Kuchin and a few others settled at Lesnoie and met in the forest.

In July and August contacts were re-established, including contacts with abroad; a new 'centre' was elected; there were even plans for a small conference. The financial situation was desperate, the available cadres were minimal, work in Moscow and the whole of central Russia seemed to be finally destroyed. But the members of the Menshevik Youth League were as fearless and daring as ever and it was mainly due to their energy that the South was not lost too. Young

Mensheviks were constantly arrested and exiled, but equally constantly escaped from exile. At one time no less than nine of them were on the run: Kranikhfeld, Sapir, Iakubson, Zimin, Gurvich, Zingarevich, Lande, Rappiport, Falk.[130] In tsarist times it was a revolutionary tradition to escape from prison and exile whenever possible; it had become infinitely more difficult to do so, but Young Mensheviks did their utmost to keep the tradition alive.

In July the old monastery on the Solovetskii islands in the White Sea was converted into yet another concentration camp (the notorious Solovki). The administration of the camp consisted of convicts, including Communists and Red Army soldiers with criminal records.

The first prisoners to be taken there was the amorphous mass of the so-called 'counter-revolutionaries' — former officers and clergy —as well as criminals of all kinds. Socialists and Anarchists followed, some being transferred from the concentration camp at Pertominsk. During the early months, some 175 Socialists were lodged in the Savvatievskii *Skit* (hermitage of St Savvatii), though there was room for only eighty; later more and more prisoners arrived, to be lodged in two other hermitages. All arrivals and departures went through the transit camp on Popov Island, where there was also a prison hospital; but the conditions there and the treatment of patients was so barbaric that the sick preferred to remain in their barracks. Mensheviks in Russia and abroad protested against Solovetskii islands being used as a prison and against the conditions there.[131]

On 25 July, Martov's sister and Andrei Kranikhfeld's mother, Nadezhda Ossipovna Kranikhfeld died after a long and painful illness, at the age of forty-eight. She had been subjected to house searches practically once a week, and on the day the news of Martov's death was received in Moscow, the GPU set up an ambush in her flat in the hope of catching any who might come to offer condolences.[132]

The August number of the illegal *Social Democrat* gave the following news: there were 54 Mensheviks on Solovki, including Bogdanov, Sapir, Zorokhovich, Treiger, Malkin; there were 43 in other remote places. Some 20 were transported to the north from Kharkov.[133] A young member of the Menshevik Youth League, Lusia Kogan, was first sent to Pertominsk and then exiled to the Pechora district, to a place deep in the forests. She had only just recovered from an illness of the lungs, but the GPU doctor certified her as fit.[134]

Moscow Mensheviks were gratified to hear that the Bolshevik Stukov reported to a special session of the Moscow committee of the Communist party that 'the obnoxious activities of the Social Democrats [Mensheviks] considerably increased their influence among the workers'; and that the illegally printed leaflets were enjoying a great success: 'they are pasted nightly on walls in the working-class districts and in the mornings whole crowds of workers stop and read them. So that members of the Communist cells have to leave for work half an hour earlier to tear those leaflets down.'[135] An interesting light on the feelings of workers was shed by the open letter to the official press from the worker A. Novikov from Archangel, in which he announced his resignation from the membership of the Communist Party — a brave man — because of its dictatorship over the workers.[136]

On 6 September the entire conference of the Menshevik Youth League was arrested at Irpen, near Kiev. This was a tremendous and irreplaceable loss. Older comrades had advised them to keep some of their members in reserve, not to risk all of them being taken at the same time, but, says Kuchin 'for all of them "their" conference was truly a question of personal happiness and nobody wanted to be left out.'[137] So they were all captured and taken, without warm clothes (there is a considerable difference in temperature between Kiev and Moscow) to the Inner Prison of the GPU on the Lubianka, where they were kept in 'solitaries', without visits or parcels. On the 25th they started a hunger strike, which lasted eight days. After that they were sentenced to three years each in the Solovetskii camp.[138] The loss of all these energetic and dedicated young people very seriously impaired the work of the party. Kuchin's letter to the Menshevik Delegation Abroad, dated 14 September 1923, reflected the seriousness of the situation: 'you must realise in what truly monstrous conditions of terror, of general demoralisation . . . we have to work . . . Old cadres of local groups are broken up. Broken up, terrorised is the entire surrounding population. . . . We are reduced to a very few and they battle on in conditions of unparalleled difficulty.' Further: 'Never in the history of the working-class movement in Russia had there been such terror . . . [clearly] the aim is to destroy us. . . . Masses of people are exiled.' All the same, he warned against pessimism: 'Raging repressions failed to kill us altogether and *potentially* we are strong. . . . Without doubt . . . we are going just now through a most critical moment, under the onslaught of utmost universal reaction.' Even the fact that the party had gone underground had many advantages: members were no longer so conspicuous and visible to the GPU, and there was greater cohesion within the party. And though the working class was on the whole passive, mainly as a result of six years of terror, there were some signs of growing political awareness among some workers and among students. The situation of the party could be compared to that of the revolutionaries of the 1880s: now, as then, a small but compact political group could have an influence far in excess of its numerical strength. In spite of immense losses, the party had weathered the GPU attack of the first half of 1923. 'There has never been a more difficult, a darker, a more repelling time.... How shall we emerge from the second half? Nobody can say.'[139]

The October number of the *Socialist Courier* printed the news that eighty-six Mensheviks from Georgia had been arrested 'as hostages' for the good behaviour of the Georgian people and taken to the Iaroslavl prison. They had protested first to Chicherin and then to Stalin, then People's Commissar for nationalities, but had received no replies.[140]

The December number of the *Socialist Courier* carried an obituary of nineteen-year-old Iakov Aronovich, who had committed suicide at Kem, the transit camp for the Solovki. He had joined the Menshevik Youth League at the age of sixteen, was at one time secretary of its Moscow branch and had been arrested for the first time in July 1922. He had been sent to the Iaroslavl central prison, then into exile at Soligalich, a little town of the Kostroma district, eighty versts from the railway station. He was all alone there and ill; letters reached him only after much delay. He requested transfer to some more central place, but instead he was sent to Kem. Worn out and discouraged he hanged himself.[141]

The same number of the *Socialist Courier* announced the opening of yet another prison camp, at the former monastery of Suzdal. The Mensheviks Mark Liber, Vladimir Levitskii and I. Rubin along with the Georgian Mensheviks, the SR Vyssotskii and others were transferred to the new prison. All the administrative staff had previously worked in the Inner Prison of the Vecheka in Moscow and the notorious woman interrogator Andreeva was appointed to supervise both Suzdal and the Solovki.[142]

Those who had completed their terms of exile in Turkestan were sent to the Solovki or to the Narym and the Turukhansk regions of Siberia. Conditions were particularly bad in the Pechora region, where there was no food and one had to pay for everything with fish or game: 'The exiles lack the most elementary things, including clothes. The poverty is enormous. If the conditions do not improve they will be in danger of ... dying.'[143]

A letter from the Solovki reads: 'Soon the long winter — eight to nine months long — will begin. And the long northern night. The day is only two to three hours long.' The prisoners on the Solovki had little warm clothing or boots, and only kerosene lamps. But 'our mood is buoyant. Some few lucky ones have been visited by relatives. They brought letters, books, parcels. These are the last meetings [with outsiders], the last news for many long months.'[144] It is surprising under the circumstances that the mood could be 'buoyant', yet one finds this and similar assurances in many letters of the time. The paradox is perhaps best explained in a letter from a non-party exiled student arrested along with many others after a students' seminar on 'the death penalty' and on 'Soviet financial policy'. The arrested students were put into separate cells in the Inner Prison of the GPU in Moscow. In his letter he wrote: 'I would never have thought that *nowadays* such a regime was possible in Russia. We were allowed neither walks nor visits nor books nor papers.' After prison they were exiled to 'distant places'. 'So far no chance of getting any work. . . . It's difficult, but in the course of the last months I have become convinced that it is much more honest to be here at such a time. Much more decent towards oneself. That is why my spirits are high.'[145] Many socialists, particularly the young, felt that to be in prison or exile 'at such a time' was indeed a badge of honour, something to be proud of, and their spirits were buoyed up by the thought.

In the night of 2/3 November there were again mass arrests of Mensheviks in the whole country, comparable in scale to those of February and May of that year. In Moscow several hundred were arrested, including printers and students who had recently returned from exile; there were house searches in the flats of wives of exiles. In Petrograd, where the 'illegal' press had fortunately been moved out a few days earlier, there were also many arrests, including among students. There were fifty arrests in Rostov-on-Don; forty in Tula; and in Riazan, Cherevanin, a member of the Menshevik Central Committee, was arrested, along with his daughter. House searches at the flats of the Ezhovs and other exiles took place in Kashin.[146]

The December number of the *Socialist Courier* gave a few interesting quotes from Soviet publications. Thus *Itogi partiinoi raboty za 1922–23 gg.* (The results of party work during 1922–23) stated that of the total of 372,900 members of the Communist party only ten per cent were workers.[147] According to commentaries of the soviet press itself, on the occasion of a Congress of Worker-Correspondents and Worker-Journalists, only ten per cent of the rank and file of the Communist party read the party's central organ, *Pravda*; the reasons given were that 'words and style were difficult, monotonous; lies, abuse — one can no longer believe them. . . .'[148]

On 19 December there was a completely unprovoked armed attack on the socialists in the Solovki (see p. 146). Armed soldiers were ordered to occupy the political compound just before the evening roll call, when some sixty prisoners were strolling in the yard. After the briefest of warnings, the soldiers opened fire, killing five and wounding three prisoners (one of the wounded died soon afterwards). Communications with the islands having been, as usual, interrupted in December for the winter, news of the event reached Moscow only on 10 February 1924, in the form of a very brief paragraph in *Izvestiia*. The paper gave a list of those killed and wounded and eventually also supplied a reason for the incident: there had been a riot on the island, it alleged, which had been planned 'abroad', and the prisoners had attacked the soldiers.[149] In March 1924, once the news of the killing and wounding of socialists on the Solovki was confirmed, the Delegations Abroad of the Mensheviks, of the *Bund*, of the Right SRs and of the Left SRs addressed appeals to socialist parties and workers' organisations abroad.[150]

The well-known Menshevik Mark Liber had no sooner arrived at Suzdal that he was exiled to Semipalatinsk.[151] The twenty-three dockers arrested after a strike at Odessa in June 1923, were taken to Kharkov and hence to Moscow, on the way to the Archangel province. They had no other clothes than the light summer ones, suitable for the South, in which they had been arrested. In Moscow they saw the first newspapers since their arrest and from them they learned that there was a strike of dockers in England — and the newspapers were appealing to soviet workers to support the English strikers![152]

Some sixty exiles in Viatka assembled to see in the New Year — an old tradition respected even by the tsarist police but not, it appeared, by the GPU. At midnight five completely drunk GPU men burst into the house where the exiles were celebrating and ordered everybody to get ready to come to the GPU office. The exiles refused; whereupon a detachment of soldiers on horseback and on foot arrived and took them all to the local prison where they were kept for three days.[153]

1924

In January 1924 Lenin died. He had been ill for over a year and had spent most of 1923 away from state and party affairs. But he continued to write or plan articles until the last moment. Two of his last published articles[154] concerned Rabkrin, that is Workers' and Peasants' Inspection, a body created to control the efficiency of the state apparatus, while there was also a Central Control Commission of the party. That Lenin's last thoughts were centred on such matters is not surprising. It reflected a deep-seated and lifelong distrust of his colleagues and, in fact, his fellow men at large. He trusted nobody but himself. While he was well and stood at the helm, he was a one-man control commission; there was no matter, great or small, that he did not deem worthy of his personal attention. But, of course, one man cannot oversee everything and work and authority had to be delegated to others. Lenin, one feels, was never very happy about this — hence the multiplication of control commissions controlling each other. The Vecheka, as Lenin originally conceived it, was perhaps the first inspection and control body. In his last articles Lenin proposed not only yet another reform to improve the work of existing organs of Rabkrin but also the creation of a new super control commission to control all the other control commissions. He seemed to pin exaggerated, even frantic hopes on this reform: his preoccupation with it seemed insane. And indeed the autopsy revealed later that he had been for a long time suffering from cerebral arteriosclerosis.[155]

In its obituary of Lenin, the *Socialist Courier* deliberately refrained from attack; it spoke not of the political enemy but rather of the 'outstanding figure in the working-class movement', of Martov's comrade-in-arms.[156]

The death of Lenin made no difference to the persecution of Mensheviks: the routine was too well established by then and Stalin proved a worthy successor to Lenin. Several prominent Mensheviks were arrested in Moscow, among them Anna Krassnianskaia, Vassilev and Ikov.[157] In exile in the Narym region, the Menshevik Vladislav Kamenskii died at the age of thirty-seven. He had been in tsarist exile; after the revolution he was elected chairman of the Novo-Nikolaevsk soviet and later member of the VTsIK of the Petrograd Soviet. In 1922 the workers at a big metal works (formerly Lessner's) elected him to the Petrograd Soviet; but he was promptly arrested and kept for a whole year under a particularly harsh regime in prison, where he fell ill. After his release he returned to party work; during the strikes in Petrograd preceding the Kronstadt rising, he addressed workers' meetings, and soon found himself sharing prison with Fedor Dan and Professor Rozhkov. When the rising began, this whole group of Mensheviks was transferred to the Peter and Paul Fortress on Zinoviev's orders. Zinoviev, the political boss of Petrograd, urged their execution, but got no permission 'from above'. This was very lucky for the Mensheviks, as Zinoviev quite often had people executed out of hand; having on this occasion asked for and failed to obtain permission, he was checkmated. The group was returned to the *Predvarilka*. Kamenskii, who underwent a serious operation in the prison hospital, was, after a year in prison, exiled first to Vologda for one year, and upon his return to Moscow, rearrested at the railway station and exiled to swampy Narym. As he was suffering from acute tuberculosis, this was the worst possible climate for him.[158]

In accordance with an established tradition the Petrograd Menshevik committee printed a leaflet to mark the anniversary of the February revolution, and on the night of 11/12 March it was pasted on walls and widely distributed among workers and students, in spite of a special effort by the GPU, the militia, the communist cells and the Komsomol. The leaflet was much read and discussed. As a reprisal many printers in various printing works were arrested.[159]

The officially organised congress of 'former Mensheviks' in Petrograd was held with great pomp and ceremony: a great demonstration marched through the streets with banners. It was given great publicity; it was even filmed. The Bolshevik cry was: 'We have buried the Mensheviks!' However, Menshevik leaflets and proclamations soon appeared again. The Bolshevik Zalutskii, speaking at the local party conference explained that though the Mensheviks had been well and truly liquidated . . . they have sprouted new organisations, 'composed of sons of NEP-men'.*[160]

Many printers and metal workers were arrested in Petrograd and imprisoned in the *Predvarilka* for refusing to participate in the congress of 'former Mensheviks'.[161]

During March, the GPU arrested 150 Mensheviks in Moscow and some 75 in Nizhnii Novgorod, Rostov-on-Don, Kharkov and elsewhere. Early in April some 300 were arrested in Moscow and some 500 in Petrograd. At the same time some 300 students were reported as arrested in Petrograd, accused of 'treacherous Menshevik ideology'. Further information from Petrograd gave the number of arrested as 600, of which seventy-five per cent were students (and a few professors) and fifteen per cent workers.[162] The arrests of students were connected with a sweeping purge of universities. According to Lunacharskii, the People's Commissar for Education, some 30,000 were expelled. Some of the expelled were at the very end of their studies. There was an epidemic of suicides among the students. In Moscow the purge led to complete demoralisation among them, everybody being afraid — for themselves and of each other.[163] Nor did the students who were thus persecuted belong to the groups which the regime had labelled as 'class enemies': admission to a university had long been conditional on descent from sound proletarian stock.

When a group of sixteen students from Moscow arrived in Petrograd on their way to the Solovki, they exhibited all the signs of having come in contact with socialists in prison. First they refused to stand up when counted by the warders (this was an old tradition of political prisoners); when told that they were to be separated and distributed among the criminals they resisted, and won the first round. Next morning, when they were being taken out for a walk with criminals, they began to do physical exercises (another old tradition); this was stopped and they were taken to the prison office under armed guard. Here they were again told that they would be put into criminal cells; in protest they laid down on the floor and would not budge though they were kicked, beaten, strangled and had their hair pulled;

*NEP-men: profiteers from the NEP.

finally they were dragged away to the punishment cells. They immediately started a hunger strike, as a result of which they were returned to their original cells. When they were leaving the prison to continue their journey to the Solovki, and again at the railway station, the students sang traditional revolutionary songs, to the great delight of a large crowd.[164]

In May a new party programme was adopted in Berlin and was published by the *Socialist Courier* as *The Platform of the RSDRP*. Its fifty-four pages were the result of prolonged discussion among the various trends abroad and in the Russian underground. In Russia, Menshevik party workers wanted above all a clear formulation of Menshevik views which would guide them in their work and assist them in the composition of their leaflets. It cannot be said that the new programme satisfied the right wing of the party or the Russian underground. It repeated the old criticism of the Bolshevik regime: it condemned terror and the dictatorship of the Bolshevik party, it warned that the NEP must not be allowed to restore capitalism, it advocated greater scope for the intelligentsia and the peasants, and nobody could quarrel with that. But it also demanded 'the establishment of a democratic republic based on universal, equal, direct, and secret suffrage, the broadest political freedom, an elected and accountable administration' and so forth; and furthermore suggested that 'the proletariat [was] the basic force to steer the liquidation of the Bolshevik dictatorship into the channel of democracy.'[165] These assumptions and demands showed that the Mensheviks had not outgrown their old illusions and still believed the Bolsheviks willing to change their regime. Unfortunately Kuchin, who had secretly come to Berlin to help to compose the new programme, was arrested on his return to Russia and sentenced to ten years in prison — to disappear for ever.[166] His was the strong hand on the rudder of the Menshevik 'underground'; with him gone, things went from bad to worse. Thus the year 1924, the year of Lenin's death, proved a year of crisis for the Menshevik party in Russia, not as a result of 'self-liquidation' by 'former Mensheviks', but as a result of relentless persecution by the GPU.

There is little to report of the years that followed. The GPU had started arresting people whose names appeared in the *Socialist Courier* on the grounds that 'if the *Courier* is interested in you, you must be an active Menshevik.' The editors of the *Socialist Courier* therefore found it necessary to announce that it would refrain from printing information about arrests, except where the cases had been concluded.[167]

Arrests of Socialist-Zionists were becoming more frequent. Some were sent into exile but others were offered the alternative of going to

Palestine.[168] Those who went abroad usually contacted the *Socialist Courier* or individual Mensheviks and gave them the latest news of Russian prisons and prisoners.

A detailed account of the events of December 1923 on Solovki reached the Menshevik Delegation Abroad only in September of the following year. It confirmed all that had transpired from other sources and gave a dismal picture of the conditions during the months that followed. Food rations were reduced by approximately forty per cent and no natural fats, fresh vegetables or tinned meat were distributed at all. Instead dried fish was issued, but this was so rotten that it was uneatable. As supplies of money and parcels had been completely exhausted, prisoners were unable to supplement food rations from any source. It was assumed that tuberculosis and scurvy would therefore claim even more victims than in the preceding winter when twenty-five per cent and forty-five per cent respectively of prisoners had suffered from these diseases. Overcrowding was getting worse: both the original socialist *skits*, Savvatievskii and Muksolomskii, as well as the newer one, on the Anzerskii island, were filled beyond reasonable capacity. Newly arrived students, male and female, were put into the Kreml, among the criminals; they were denied political status and were threatened with punishment cells for the least protest.[169] On 25 September 1924, the four hundred socialists and Anarchists on the Solovki began a hunger strike demanding to be transferred to the mainland.[170]

In Moscow groups of prisoners surrounded by armed guards with drawn sabres were more and more frequently seen being marched to railway stations on the way to northern camps. The GPU had opened a new camp beyond the polar circle, on the island of Hey in the Ob province. Solovki was becoming the destination of bandits and so-called economic criminals — officials of government and industry and Red Army men convicted of fraud. None of the politicals were any longer granted visits before going to the Solovki, and heart-rending scenes were daily taking place in front of the Butyrki, as women learned that their husbands, sons, daughters had already left.[171]

On 25 July up to sixty people were arrested in the Ukraine 'on suspicion' of being Mensheviks: old workers and intellectuals as well as many entirely unpolitical people. In Kiev the 'purge of universities' had begun.[172]

In Georgia, conquered by the Bolsheviks in February 1921, a popular rising against the occupation broke out on 28 August 1924 and was drowned in blood. Under the slogan 'Physical extermination of the Mensheviks', the Bolsheviks began by shooting twenty-four Mensheviks, including eight of their leaders, in spite of the fact that the local Mensheviks had tried to dissuade the Georgian masses from starting an uprising. A telegram from Iraklii Tsereteli and the former Prime Minister of Menshevik Georgia, Noah Zhordania, to the Menshevik Delegation Abroad named forty-three socialists shot as 'leaders of the rising', though all these men had in fact been held in prison, as hostages, since 1922. Somewhat later the official soviet press admitted to four thousand shot. The *Socialist Courier* addressed an appeal to 'The workers of all countries' to protest against Bolshevik treatment of Georgia.[173]

At the end of December, thirty political prisoners in Suzdal began a hunger strike, demanding the transfer of the sick to a hospital and a general improvement of sanitary conditions; the strike was maintained for two weeks.[174] In Petrograd, now renamed Leningrad, there was a bacchanalia of arrests following one of the periodical floods. A state of emergency was declared and up to 150–200 people were being arrested daily, sometimes picked up in the street. Among those arrested were many students and workers. The queue of relatives outside the *Predvarilka* stretched to the very end of the street. More arrests were to follow — at the very end of the year some 400–500 were picked up.[175]

1925 and After

From then on there were more frequent notices of death in prison and exile.

Boris Bogdanov, the *starosta* (Elder) of the Mensheviks on the Solovki, was exiled to a place in the Petchora region, 750 versts from the railway station.[176] Georgii Kuchin, after three months in the Inner Prison of the GPU, was sent to the Cheliabinsk politisolator for ten years of solitary confinement.[177] The exiles in Tashkent were dispersed to much smaller towns, where they could find no work and no lodgings and no doctors, though all these places had tropical malaria. The old Menshevik and poet Marfusha (Anna Dobrokhotova), who had been in perpetual exile in eastern Siberia from 1903 and in prison and exile again since October 1917, died in exile in Kaluga.[178]

The Menshevik Delegation Abroad supplied the Twenty-second Congress of the French Socialist party at Grenoble in February with a collection of illegal publications in Soviet Russia, which were put on display.[179]

In Russian prisons hunger strikes were no longer effective and achieved nothing: in Suzdal, where some new arrivals were put into the damp old disused wing, two SR men went on a hunger strike of twenty-two days and several women on one of fifteen days, without results. Eventually they were all sent to the concentration camp at Cheliabinsk. The Menshevik Lokerman, sentenced to three years of strict solitary confinement, was lodged in the old wing at Suzdal.[180] In Moscow the GPU was arresting relatives and even mere acquaintances of Mensheviks, who were then, even if released, thrown out of their apartments and jobs, dogged by spies and harassed by house searches.

Sentences lost all their meaning: people were constantly moved from one place and prison to another. In Kachin, twice-exiled Sergei Ezhov, his wife and his son were arrested and so were Boris Ber, a sister of Boris Bogdanov's wife and several others. The terms of Ber's and Ezhov's exile to Kachin were due to expire in May, but the Ezhovs were sent to Minussinsk in Siberia before that, and Ber to Turkestan.[181]

Boris Bogdanov was once again arrested in exile and taken to the Inner Prison of the GPU in Moscow.[182] In the summer of 1925 the camps on the Solovki were officially closed and socialist prisoners transferred to the camp at Kem, to the Siberian prisons of Tobolsk (the Mensheviks Rozhkovskii, Bernstein and dozens more) and of Cheliabinsk. Some were also sent to the former penal prison at Iaroslavl (Georgii Kuchin was there, transferred from Cheliabinsk). The Menshevik Pechorskii died of scarlet fever in the Iaroslavl prison.[183]

Alexander Deviatkin, the former leader of the printers' union, caught while working in the Menshevik underground, began a hunger strike for the release of his daughter, gravely ill with tuberculosis, whom the GPU had arrested when they could not find her father. His demand was met on the twenty-fourth day of his hunger strike.[184]

In the course of 1925–26 all Kuchin's comrades were picked up by the GPU.[185] Nonetheless, occasional leaflets and bulletins appeared, even as late as 1928.[186] And miraculously the connection with the party abroad was not broken, though one consignment of the *Socialist Courier* disappeared, probably seized by the GPU.[187]

From time to time secret emissaries made the journey to and from Russia. In 1926, Boris Sapir, one of the core of the Menshevik Youth League, who had gone through Solovki and escaped from his place of exile, was sent to Berlin, where he was later co-opted into the Delegation Abroad; he represented the Menshevik Youth League on the Executive Committee of the Socialist Youth International. In the same year, two people (one man and one woman) seem to have been sent to Russia, but they remain unidentified. In 1927, Eva Broido and in 1928, Michael Braunstein (Valerianov)[188] went secretly to Russia: both were eventually arrested and died 'somewhere and at an uncertain date', after many years in prison and exile.

Letters from the Russian underground of the late 1920s showed a catastrophic dwindling of resources and personnel. All the letters were carefully coded and signed by first names only. The letter of 8 March 1926 described the *Socialist Courier* as the only life-line left: 'If you only knew with what enormous impatience comrades here are waiting for the latest number.... For it we are prepared to bear material sacrifices and all the blows and troubles, however heavy.'[189] The letter of 6 July 1927 explained: 'It is not easy to find anyone prepared to carry out dangerous work. All those capable of heroism for the sake of the party have long since been used and are now paying for their heroism, while the remaining people are too careful of themselves.... That is why all current work rests on the shoulders of three or four people; there are a few sympathisers who are ready to pass on [letters or literature], to enquire, but not by any means to offer us their room or a night's lodgings.'[190] The letter of 21 August, 1927 further explained that three 'illegals' and one other person for purely technical tasks were considered to be the absolute minimum needed to maintain the work of the Bureau, yet there was no money to keep the 'illegals' or to pay for travel and postal expenses. 'We have wonderful heroic youngsters. But they lack experience and cannot be entrusted with just any task. We have also wonderful comrades among the workers' groups but they are almost all married (and there is no way to support their families if they are arrested.)' The whole of the experienced old group in Moscow had been arrested. Plans to help exiles to escape and join the 'illegals' would demand lots of money; material help for the imprisoned and exiled comrades was insufficient; and the illegal press was in constant peril of being closed down for lack of funds.[191] The letter of 28 December 1927 described the mood of the workers as deeply depressed; unemployment was rising steadily while wages were falling; and in the provinces drunkenness was universal. Political activity, either inside the trade unions or outside them, was nil, since the workers did not trust official trade unions or the government, and were mainly preoccupied with their own most elementary economic needs.[192] Yet they avidly read the *Socialist Courier*, if they could get hold of it, seeking the answers to their many bewildering problems.

A letter from Kharkov, dated 29 December 1928 described how since 1925 their conspiratorial rules had been tightened so much that each member of the group knew only one other person: 'This has greatly reduced the number of arrests (there have not been any in Kharkov recently), but has also reduced to zero all companionship and the chance to exchange opinions; it has also considerably lessened the psychological readiness to perform dangerous tasks.'[193] Nevertheless 'illegal' leaflets were strewn in Kharkov by local Mensheviks at the gates of two factories at night and the workers were most intrigued by the very fact that the leaflets had appeared at all![194]

A letter of 23 September 1928, signed by Zoë (the other correspondent, Victor, was apparently arrested in September of that year) showed the Bureau to be at its last gasp: 'I am not suited to be in charge, I have insufficient theoretical grounding.... Also the baby has taken and is taking great toll of my time and health. Possibly I had no right to have it, but it is too late now to talk of that.' She would continue the work until she was caught: 'I shall carry on but do understand that it is dreadfully difficult.... I am tired out, spiritually and physically.'[195] This *cri de coeur* of a despairing young mother, shouldering almost alone the leadership of a hunted political party, heralded the demise of menshevism in Russia. The Russian Bureau indeed continued to exist and to correspond with the Delegation Abroad for a few more years.[196]

Abroad, the Menshevik Delegation battled on well into the 1960s, first in Berlin, then in Paris, and finally in New York. And the *Socialist Courier*, more than once threatened with closure through lack of funds, continued to speak out against Bolshevik tyranny.

Long before then, underground activities in Russia had finally ended. From 1932 onwards Mensheviks survived, or died, only as prisoners. Yet we are told by the Young Menshevik Till, who himself survived many years in camp and prison, that not one of the Mensheviks he met there regretted the political position they had taken. When Till met Lev Gurvich in 1933/34, both agreed that in the long perspective of history, the Mensheviks had been proved right; by using evil means the Bolsheviks had betrayed the aims which had originally been shared by all Russian socialists. And forty years later, in 1975, Till found that all of his old comrades who survived* were still proud to have belonged to a party which, though physically annihilated in the end, had always upheld the principle of moral and political freedom.

*Till estimates that only twenty members of the Youth League survived to be released in 1954–1958, which would mean that ninety-seven to ninety-eight per cent of the League had perished; and only two to three per cent of the entire party (including the League) seem to have survived.[197]

Appendix I: The Trial of the Right SRs

The two show trials of socialists — Social Revolutionaries and Mensheviks — appear in retrospect to have been rehearsals for the more spectacular trials, of Bolsheviks and others, in the late 1930s.

The first of the two, the trial of the Right SRs,[1] took place when Lenin was still alive, and therefore with his full knowledge. It opened in Moscow on 9 June 1922. The SRs were accused of having, during 1917–1918, accepted money from the Entente; of having planned and carried out the assassinations of the Bolsheviks Volodarskii and Uritskii; and of having attempted to assassinate Lenin and Trotsky. The indictment was based on a brochure written and published just before the trial by the GPU agent Semionov-Vassiliev. This man had been previously expelled from the SR party 'for disreputable behaviour incompatible with revolutionary honour'. The accused denied having taken money from the Entente at any time, or having authorised assassinations: these, they stated, had been perpetrated by individuals for whom the SR party took no responsibility. The accused admitted that they had planned to establish a rival government in 1918 — a democratic and not a counter-revolutionary one — a plan which they later recognised to have been a mistake. The party had decided that it would never again attempt to overthrow the Bolshevik government by force of arms and had been pardoned under the amnesty of 1919, a fact that the indictment specifically denied.

In preparation for the trial, many SRs were arrested months in advance. Those arrested in Petrograd were brought to Moscow in chains,[2] something which had not happened since tsarist days. Meanwhile the leaders of the party had already been in prison for one to three years. They were now taken to the Inner Prison in the Lubianka and kept there in complete isolation from each other, without books or papers, without letters or visits from their relatives.

Long before the case came up to trial the official Bolshevik press began a campaign of hate, denouncing the SRs as guilty and demanding the death penalty for them.* The press campaign was a signal for an outburst of what was described as 'popular wrath' — factory workers, soldiers, sailors, students all began to demand the death penalty for the accused. This 'popular wrath' was carefully orchestrated: mass demonstrations were assembled in front of the courthouse, carrying banners with slogans such as 'Death to the murderers!' and sometimes 'Death to the bourgeoisie!' and even 'Death to the Social Democrats!' Coaches full of school children also displayed the same slogans. Such a demonstration took place on 1 May as part of Labour Day celebrations, and another bigger one on 20 June. Everybody in Moscow knew that the workers were driven into the streets by hunger and fear of losing their jobs; the students by fear of losing their places in the university. The same fear made them sign innumerable petitions and resolutions demanding 'Death to the SRs'.

The arrival of foreigners as counsel for the defence — three western socialists, Vandervelde, Liebknecht and Rosenberg, had volunteered to act for the accused — was accompanied by particularly spectacular demonstrations of 'popular wrath'. At the frontier and again at the railway station in Moscow, these men were met by dense crowds demanding death not only for the SRs but also for their defenders. Howls of rage and cries of 'string them up' continued until the foreigners were 'rescued' by the militia, which had stood by inactive for quite some time before coming forward.** For as long as Vandervelde and his colleagues remained in Russia, the GPU continued to pretend that they must be protected and, in consequence, kept them practically under house arrest.[5]

When the trial opened, the number of the accused was reduced from forty-seven to thirty-two, there being apparently absolutely no evidence against the other fifteen.*** The others were divided into two groups: the first group consisted of twenty-two genuine SRs and included their entire Central Committee; the second group consisted of ten former members of the party who had defected to the

*Mensheviks were considerably startled to read that 'cases against ... Dan, Martov, Abramovitch' would be set aside for the time being as not 'directly relevant to the present case'. They had no idea that any such cases were pending.[3]

**A letter from Moscow, signed S. Dvinov and dated 21 June 1922, described the background to these events: 'for two weeks prior to the arrival of the foreigners, students of the Sverdlov University were excused lectures and study and were told to "get ready!..." On the day of arrival, these students ... marched to the railway station early in the morning and camped there.' Suddenly Bukharin arrived: 'driven slowly in a car, he reviewed his "troops" ... a rehearsal was enacted and the effect was found satisfactory.'[4]

***These fifteen were nevertheless sentenced to exile. Five of them refused to go, demanding release or trial.

Bolsheviks, including the GPU agents Semionov-Vassiliev and his wife Konopliova. The first group was defended by Vandervelde, Liebknecht and Rosenberg and by a few Russian lawyers including Muraviev and Tager. The second group was defended by Bukharin, Sadoul, Felix Kohn, Lunacharskii, Pokrovskii and Klara Zetkin. The public was admitted by ticket only and only twenty-two tickets were allotted to the relatives of the accused. The first group of accused, its counsel and its witnesses were constantly interrupted by cat calls and roars of abuse, with the president of the Tribunal saying that he could not forbid expressions of 'the people's wrath'. Meanwhile the second group of accused and its counsel vied with each other, and with the Prosecutor Krylenko, in incriminating the first group and themselves.

The high point of the trial was the demonstration of 20 June. The turnout was impressive. Column after column, including many school children, marched for five solid hours past the House of the Soviets in which the Tribunal was sitting. Each time a column reached the building, on the command 'One, two three!', it roared in unison 'Death to the SRs!' The columns were mainly composed of soldiers, sailors, Komsomoltsi, and chekists — people who had to obey orders. Workers were much less in evidence. It had proved very difficult to whip up 'the people's wrath' among the workers, in spite of a ferocious press campaign led by Trotsky and in spite of the usual threats of loss of jobs and reductions of wages and the rest. Thus of the fifteen hundred workers at a Moscow power station, only some two or three hundred came out to demonstrate; of the four thousand workers in a railway repair shop, only sixty or seventy; and at two tramway depots the workers altogether refused to participate. And these are only a few examples. In several factories the workers protested against being told to carry the banners with 'Death to the SRs'.* Nevertheless, sufficient numbers were mustered to make an impressive show. According to Menshevik eye-witnesses it was 'frightening to see ten thousand workers, old and young, marching under a veritable forest of red banners with the words on them: 'Death! ... Death! ... Death!' But this was not all: at about 10 p.m. on the same day, a huge crowd led by Bukharin was allowed to invade the court room, and, according to a witness, 'for two and a half hours ... raged and raved, shook fists and shouted insults' at the accused. And for two and a half hours the SRs sat silent but composed: even the Communists admitted later that they had shown true heroism on that occasion.

Counsel for the defence lodged a last protest and then left the court

*Only three banners were seen with a different inscription — they read 'Down with the death penalty!' The people carrying them were arrested the same night.[6]

room. Vandervelde and his friends left Russia and later published the full truth about the trial; their Russian colleagues behaved with great courage in making their protest and were later made to suffer for it.* The accused also protested and declared that they would not attend the trial any longer, as they had no respect for the judges. The sentences were therefore pronounced *in absentia* on 8 August: twelve members of the first group of accused were condemned to death and the rest to from two to ten years of strict prison and compulsory labour. Semionov and Konopliova were also sentenced to death but the sentence was quashed.

The official press was not allowed to publish the verdict, and in fact it was said that 'a battle was raging in the bosom' of the Communist party. After two days the government announced that it had pardoned the twelve *smertniki* (those sentenced to death): they were to be kept in life-long confinement in prison as hostages for the good behaviour of their party.[8] One of them, Morozov, killed himself in the Inner Prison of the GPU in December 1923;[9] the remaining eleven are thought to have died in prison or exile.

The most striking difference between the trial of the SRs and later political show trials is that the accused in this trial had not been tortured and were not made to confess publicly to crimes they had not committed. In all other respects, this trial offended in every way 'against the elementary principles of natural justice'.[10]

*Muraviev, in particular, made a most valiant speech, ending with: 'Woe to that country, and woe to that nation which treats the law with disrespect, and mocks at those who stand up in defence of it.'[7]

Appendix II: The 'Menshevik' Trial of March 1931

The trial of alleged Mensheviks that took place in Moscow between 1 and 9 March 1931[1] was an early example of the new technique devised by the GPU — extortion of confessions by means of torture. This technique had been successfully applied in the so-called economic trials, against the Shakhty engineers in 1928 and the fictitious 'Industrial Party' in 1930; in both cases the accused were forced to confess to sabotage and wrecking of the soviet economy. This time it was a political party that was put on trial for sabotage and wrecking; and it was the first time that torture was applied to socialists.

The fourteen defendants were accused of founding, in 1928, a 'Union Bureau of the Central Committee of the RSDRP' for the purpose of overthrowing the Communist government and re-establishing capitalism in Russia. It was further claimed that, with financial help from the western bourgeoisie and the Socialist (Second) International, channelled through the Menshevik Delegation Abroad, this 'Union Bureau' had organised sabotage and wrecking inside the country; while the Delegation was supposed to have been organising intervention (invasion) by foreign powers.

In fact the real Bureau had been founded not in 1928 but in 1922, and the only one among the defendants who was a member of it at the time of his arrest was Vladimir Ikov.* Isaak Rubin had worked in the Menshevik underground until 1923–1924, while the others either had never belonged to the Menshevik party (e.g. Professor Fin-Ienotaevskii and one other) or had left it between 1920 and 1921. Nikolai Sukhanov, the well known memoirist, had called himself a Menshevik for a short time during 1918. Most of the defendants had worked loyally and devotedly for the Communist state and had risen to key positions in their work: Vladimir Groman, the 'father' of soviet planning, in the State Planning Commission (Gosplan), Vassilii Sher

*I remember Ikov from Minussinsk, in 1915: he was in exile there at the same time as my mother. I remember him as a highly strung, nervous person, which might explain why the GPU was able to break him.

in the State Bank, Abram Ginzburg in the All-Russian Council of National Economy, Mikhail Iakubovich in the Commissariat of Domestic Commerce. It was inconceivable that any of these men would plot to wreck the soviet economy which they had done so much to build up. Yet here they were confessing to doing exactly that.

According to Michael Iakubovich, the only one to survive into the 1970s and to publish his recollections of the trial (in the Samizdat),[2] they were tortured for a very long time before they agreed to act as the GPU wanted them to act. They were beaten about the head and face and on the genitals, kicked to the ground and stamped upon with heavy boots; they were throttled. Or else they were kept standing, without sleep, for many days and nights, while they were interrogated by shifts of chekists (the so-called 'conveyor belt'); they were put, half naked and barefoot, into icy punishment cells; they were threatened with execution.* Vladimir Groman, a very sick man (*angina pectoris*) and an alcoholic, was deprived of spirits but promised a pardon if he would cooperate.[3] Iakubovich and Ginzburg tried to commit suicide but were revived. When, finally, the fourteen were broken, the GPU made them compose and work out the plan of their fictional activities and then coached them in their roles until they were word-perfect.

At the trial, all the accused pleaded guilty and gave full accounts of their subversive work. Groman testified that he and the other accused had organised the 'Union Bureau' with the aim of carrying out sabotage in preparation for an overthrow of the government. It was to be replaced by a provisional government composed of representatives of the Menshevik party, the Industrial Party, the peasant party *Trudovaia partia* and some Bolsheviks who had left the Communist party. Sher testified that the 'Union Bureau' received altogether 480,000 rubles from the Menshevik Delegation Abroad which, in turn, had received considerable sums from the German Social Democrats and the Socialist International. Groman declared that in 1925 and 1927 he had seen Dan and Abramovitch in Berlin and had made arrangements for the transfer of funds. Much prominence was given to the alleged journey of Abramovitch to Russia during June and July 1928. All the accused described meeting him, told the court what he had said, where he had gone. Even the name of the man who drove him from the station was mentioned. Other accused, particularly Sukhanov, delivered lengthy lectures on the fallacies of Menshevik ideology, even on the psychology of menshevism.

The self-accusations of the defendants were nothing but a pack of

*This was clear also from the testimony of Sher, who said that when, in 1905, after taking part in the Moscow uprising, he had been in prison awaiting execution, he had not feared death, 'but now I no longer have the same courage.'

lies. In Berlin, Abramovitch easily established the fact that he never went to Russia in the summer of 1928; the German Social Democrats and the Socialist International denied having supplied the Delegation with any money for the purposes of sabotage. The procedure in court was farcical: counsel for the defence made no effort to disprove the accusations and no credible witnesses were called. Nor were any documents produced except three letters from the Delegation Abroad found in Ikov's home and one letter from Ikov to the Delegation intercepted by the GPU — and not one of these referred to sabotage. Sabotage was in any case not the main point of the trial: it was there to link the Mensheviks to the 'Industrial Party' and other bodies already convicted and pilloried for counter-revolutionary activities. The main purposes of the trial seem to have been, firstly, to defame the Socialist International, and secondly to intimidate the so-called right deviationists within the Russian Communist party. To make the first point the accused were forced to name such respected western socialists as Kautsky, Bernstein, Léon Blum, Hilferding and Breitscheid as being involved in the financial transactions. It was for that reason that Abramovitch was given a star part in the trial: he was prominent both in the Menshevik party and in the Socialist International. As for the oppositionists in the Communist party, Ginzburg testified that 'many Mensheviks regarded the right deviation as a kind of undeveloped menshevism'; while Petunin invented a letter from Dan and Abramovitch, allegedly written in 1929, which expressed the hope that the right deviationists in the Central Committee of the Bolshevik party would shortly adopt an essentially Social Democratic (that is Menshevik) position.

The most striking fact about this trial was that, after many months of effort, the GPU managed to produce only one real Menshevik. It is known that during the preparation of the trial dozens of Mensheviks were assembled in the Inner Prison of the GPU, yet neither Sergei Ezhov nor Cherevanin nor Ber nor Kuchin — all members of the Central Committee and of the real Bureau — appeared in the dock. Nor did Eva Broido, a member of the Menshevik Delegation Abroad, or Michael Braunstein, both of whom had secretly re-entered Russia and on whose movements the imaginary journey of Abramovitch was obviously based. Eva Broido was not mentioned at all, though Vassilii Sher, in the past a close and trusted friend of the Broido family, must have met her. Braunstein was mentioned repeatedly during the trial but was never produced. Clearly only one of the real Mensheviks could be broken by torture.

The trial ran its lurid course. In the streets thousands of people demonstrated with banners saying: 'Death to counter-revolutionaries!' and 'No mercy to the servants of capital!' Inside the court room the packed audience interrupted the accused with howls of abuse.* Counsel for the defence entered a plea for indulgence in view of the sincere repentence of 'these far from ordinary and highly qualified people' and in view of the fact that their confessions had 'dealt a death blow to Russian menshevism and world menshevism'. In the event none of the accused was sentenced to death; nor was anyone pardoned. All of them were sentenced to many years' imprisonment, and most of them served their terms in the politisolator of Verkhne Uralsk — where, in 1936, the leading right deviationist Bolsheviks Zinoviev and Kamenev also found themselves.

*A booklet issued to coincide with the trial, entitled 'Mensheviks-Interventionists', showed Bolshevik propaganda at its crudest. Contributions from Zinoviev, Radek, Iaroslavskii, poems by Demian Bednyi, hideous caricatures reprinted from *Pravda*, *Komsomolskaiia Pravda* and *Izvestiia* combined in defaming and vilifying the Menshevik party.

Bibliographical Notes

Abbreviations: The letters BNC stand for the Boris I. Nicolaevsky Collection, Hoover Institution Archives, Stanford, California; and the letters IISH for the International Institute of Social History, Amsterdam, Holland.

Preface

1 Schapiro, L. (2),* *The Origin of the Communist Autocracy*, pp. 190–209.
2 Haimson, L.H. (ed.), *The Mensheviks: From the Revolution of 1917 to the Second World War*, p. xiii.

Chapter 1: Bolshevism versus Menshevism

1 Martov, Iu. (1), *Zapiski sotsial demokrata* (Journal of a Social Democrat), pp. 129–160, 213–238, 255–298.
2 Ibid, p. 138.
3 Quoted in Ascher, A. (1), *Pavel Axelrod and the Development of Menshevism*, p. 57.
4 Steinberg, I. (1), *In the Workshop of the Revolution*, p. 9.
5 Dan, F. (1), pp. 171, 172, 172 (footnote).
6 Ibid, *Proiskhozhdenie bolshevisma* (Origins of Bolshevism), pp. 173, 175, 185.
7 Martov (1), pp. 105, 233.
8 Ibid, pp. 269–288.
9 Ibid, pp. 289, 298. (See also Pipes, R. (1), *Social Democracy and the St Petersburg Labor movement, 1885*–97.)
10 Ibid, pp. 314–395.
11 Martov, L., Maslov, P., Potresov, A. (eds), *Obshchestvennoe*

*The numbers following some authors' names in the Bibliographical Notes refer to numbering in the Bibliography.

dvizhenie v Rossii v nachale XX veka (Social Movements in Russia at the Beginning of the Twentieth Century), l. vol. i, p. 377.
12 Ibid, pp. 399–400; Martov (1), p. 412; Dan (1), pp. 259 sq.
13 Dan (1), pp. 266–280.
14 Ibid, pp. 280–295. (See also Axelrod, Pavel, in *Iskra*, no. 55, 15 December 1903 and no. 57, 15 January 1904.)
15 Quoted in Ascher (1), pp. 382–383. (See also Sapir, B., in Haimson, p. 355, on Pavel Axelrod's personal influence.)
16 Leggett, G., *The Cheka: Lenin's political police*, p. xxxii, quoting from an article in *Novaia Zhisn* (New Life), Petrograd, no. 11 (24), January 1918.
17 Bunyan, J., *The Origin of Forced Labor in the Soviet State, 1917–1921*, pp. 259–261, quoting from *Desiatyi sezd RKP(b), 1921* (The Tenth Congress of the RCP, 1921), pp. 585–587.
18 Dan (1), p. 376, quoting from *Proletarii* (The Proletarian), Geneva, no. 11, 27 July 1905.
19 Sapir (2), p. 354, quoting from Trotsky, L., *V zastchitu partii* (In Defence of the Party), St Petersburg, 1907, p. xvii.
20 *Vospominaniia o V.I. Lenine* (Recollections of V.I. Lenin), vol. i, pp. 365–392.
21 Schapiro (4), 'Minority Men', in *The Russian Revolution*, p. 63.
22 Denicke, Iu., in Haimson, p. 186, quoting from a letter by Martov to Alexander Stein in Berlin, dated 25 October 1918 (in the BNC).
23 Krupskaia, N. (2), *Vospominaniia o V.I. Lenine*, p. 289.
24 *Vospominaniia o V.I. Lenine*, vol. i, pp. 244–261.
25 Wolfe, B. (1), *The Three who Made the Revolution*, p. 528.
26 In the Soviet Union an overwhelming amount has been written about Lenin, but most of it obscures rather than illuminates his true character. In the West there is no shortage of biographies of Lenin and of these I have mainly used those of his contemporaries.
27 Ascher (1), p. 119.
28 Martov (1), p. 268.
29 *Sotsialisticheskii Vestnik* (Socialist Courier), no. 9(79),* 17 April 1924, pp. 7–8.
30 Serge, Victor, *Memoirs of a Revolutionary 1901–1931*, p. 102.
31 Balabanova, A. (3), *Lenin*, p. 117.
32 Fischer, L., *Zhisn Lenina* (Life of Lenin), p. 71.
33 Valentinov, N. (2), '*Rannie gody Lenina*' (Lenin's early years), in *Novyi Zhurnal* (The New Review), vol. 36, p. 188.

*Where two numbers are given against an issue of the *Socialist Courier*, the first refers to its number in the year of issue, the second to its number in the whole series from first publication of the journal.

34 Balabanova (3), p. 19.
35 Fischer, p. 762.
36 Ibid, p. 250.
37 Russell, B., *The Practice and Theory of Bolshevism*, pp. 36–38.
38 Fischer, p. 71. On Lenin's relations with Inessa Armand and his views on free love, see Wolfe, B. (2), *Revolution and Reality*, pp. 91–93.
39 Getzler, I. (1), *Martov: A Political Biography of a Russian Social Democrat*, p. 90.
40 Balabanova (3), p. 58.
41 Dan (1), pp. 389–390, 400.

Chapter 2: The February Revolution and the October Coup

1 'Troops fire on St Petersburg crowd', in *The Times*, 24 January 1905 (reprinted in *The Times*, 24 January 1985).
2 Dan (1), pp. 395–396.
3 Chamberlin, W.H., *The Russian Revolution 1917–1921*, vol. ii, p. 452.
4 Lenin, V., *Sochineniia* (Works), 4th edition, vol. xxiii, p. 246.
5 Abramovitch, R. (1), *The Soviet Revolution 1917–1939*, pp. 12–14; Chamberlin, vol. i, pp. 75–85; Sukhanov, N. (1), *The Russian Revolution 1917*, pp. 6–42.
6 Sukhanov (1), p. 15.
7 Chamberlin, vol. i, p. 112; Abramovitch (1), p. 22.
8 Trotsky, L. (1), *Sochineniia* (Works), vol. iii, part 1, p. 64.
9 Chamberlin, vol. i, p. 88.
10 Fischer, p. 611, quoting from Lenin, 2nd edition, vol. xxv, p. 368.
11 Lande, L., in Haimson, p. 17, quoting from *Rabochaia Gazeta* (Workers' Journal), Petrograd, no. 139, 22 August 1917.
12 Sapir (2), p. 364.
13 Dan (1), p. 404.
14 Lande, pp. 9–10 and 405, note 11.
15 Ibid, p. 28, quoting from *Rabochaia Gazeta*, no. 161, 15 September 1917.
16 Lenin, 4th edition, vol. ix, pp. 92–93.
17 Axelrod, P., Speech at the International Conference at Bern (1919), reprinted in Ascher, A. (ed.) (2), *The Mensheviks in the Russian Revolution*, p. 128.
18 Lande, p. 44, quoting from Abramovitch, R., *In tsvey revolutsies* (In two revolutions), part 2, New York, 1944, p. 160.
19 Sukhanov (1), pp. 283, 287.
20 Abramovitch (1), p. 62; Lande, p. 21.

21 Chamberlin, vol. i, p. 300.
22 Chamberlin, vol. i, p. 307.
23 Chamberlin, vol. i, p. 319; Lande, p. 39.
24 Lande, pp. 3, 45.
25 Sukhanov (2), vol. i, pp. 636–640; Lande, p. 45; Rabinovitch, A., *The Bolsheviks come to power: The revolution of 1917 in Petrograd*, pp. 292–296.
26 Fischer, p. 312, quoting from Lenin's article in *Pravda*, 21 February 1918, entitled 'About the Revolutionary Phrase'.

Chapter 3: The Mensheviks After the October Coup

1 The Menshevik party programme of July 1919, 'What's to be Done?', is reprinted in Ascher (2), pp. 111–117; also see Dallin, D. (2), in Haimson, pp. 212–213; and Sapir (2), p. 373.
2 Lande, pp. 35–36, quoting from *Vpered* (Forward), Moscow, no. 200, 4 November (O.S.) 1917.
3 Ibid, pp. 47–53.
4 Dallin (2), pp. 202, 206, 220, 222; Sapir (2), p. 372.
5 Ibid, p. 103, quoting from a letter from Martov to Axelrod of 19 November 1917.
6 Lande, p. 4, quoting from the Moscow Mensheviks' declaration of 7 November 1917.
7 Abramovitch (1), pp. 104–119; Lande, pp. 61 sq.
8 Lande, p. 67; Abramovitch (1), pp. 110–111.
9 Lande, p. 68, quoting from *Krasnyi Arkhiv* (Red Archive), Moscow, no. 9, p. 169.
10 Lenin, 5th edition, vol. xxxv, p. 550.
11 Lande, p. 77; Chamberlin, vol. i, p. 352.
12 Lande, pp. 42, 44, quoting from Popov, A., *Oktiabrskii perevorot* (The October Coup), Petrograd, 1918, pp. 174–175, and from *Revolutsiia 1917 goda (Khronika sobytii)* (The Revolution of 1917 (Chronicle of Events)), Moscow, Leningrad, 1926, part 5, p. 270.
13 Ibid, p. 55, quoting from *Den* (The Day), no. 205, 11 November 1917.
14 Ibid, p. 56.
15 Ibid, pp. 7–8; Dallin (2), p. 101.
16 Doctorow, G., in Haimson, p. 94: iv.
17 Sapir (2), p. 381.
18 Dallin (2), p. 102.
19 Wolfe (1), pp. 435–436; *Vospominaniia o V.I. Lenine*, vol. i, pp. 365–392.
20 Sukhanov (1), p. 354.

21 Getzler (1), p. 180, quoting from Paustovskii, K., *Sobranie sochinenii* (Collected Works), Moscow, 1957, vol. 3, pp. 628–631.
22 Ibid, p. 224, quoting from Martov, Iu., *Protiv voiny* (Against War), Moscow, 1917, p.x.
23 Wolfe (1), p. 528.
24 Sapir (2), p. 372.
25 Dallin (2), p. 184, quoting from Martov's theses adopted by the Menshevik Central Committee in October 1918; Denicke (2), pp. 110–111, quoting from *Tretii vserossiiskii sezd sovetov* (The Third All-Russian Congress of Soviets), Petrograd, 1918, p. 59.
26 *Martov i ego blizkie* (Martov and his Family), pp. 48–49.
27 Dallin (2), p. 96, and Lande, p. 389; Lenin, 5th edition, vol. xxxiv, p. 313; Doctorow, p. 94: iii.
28 Abramovitch (1), p. 68; Denicke (2), p. 115. The funeral was described in *Novyi Luch* (The New Ray), Moscow, 12 January 1918. See also Schapiro (1), *The Communist Party of the Soviet Union*, 2nd edition, pp. 181–183.
29 Lande, p. 91, quoting from *Novyi Luch*, no. 1, 1 December 1917.
30 Dvinov, B. (1), *Ot legalnosti k podpoliu (1921–22)* (From Legality to the Underground (1921–22)), p. 55; Dallin (2), p. 184. Martov gave an interview with reference to Radek's joke to *Utro Moskvy* (Moscow Morning), no. 19, 21 October 1918.
31 Martov, Iu. (2), *Doloi smertnuiu kazn!* (Away with the Death Penalty!). It appeared in Moscow in August 1918 and was later reprinted by the Menshevik Delegation Abroad (see Dallin (2), pp. 156–157.)
32 Getzler (1), p. 178.
33 Ibid, p. 179.

Chapter 4: The Terror

1 Lenin, The third 'Letter from Afar', in Lenin, 5th edition, vol. xxxi, pp. 40–42; ibid, *Gosudarstvo i revolutsiia* (State and Revolution), in vol. xxxiii, p. 91.
2 Leggett, p. 17, quoting from *Lenin i VChK* (Lenin and the Vecheka), Moscow, 1975, pp. 36–37.
3 Ibid, p. xxv, quoting from Browder, R. and Kerensky, A. (eds), *The Russian Provisional Government, 1917: Documents*, Stanford, 1961, vol. i, p. 135.
4 Grossman, V., *Vse techet* (Everything Flows), pp. 173–183, 179.
5 Leggett, p. 17, quoting from Bonch-Bruevich, V., *Na boevykh postakh fevralskoi i oktiabrskoi revolutsii* (On Battle Stations in the February and the October Revolutions), Moscow, 1930, p. 199.

6 Ibid, pp. 17, 371 (note 159).
7 Ibid, p. 22, quoting from Bukharin, N., 'Proletarskii Iakobinets' (A Proletarian Jacobin), in *Feliks Dzerzhinskii*, Moscow, 1931, p. 141; and from Bonch-Bruevich, p. 197.
8 Getzler (1), p. 176, quoting from Trotsky's speech to the Executive Committee of Soviets on 3 December 1917, reprinted in *Delo naroda* (People's Cause), Petrograd, no. 223, 3 December 1917.
9 Blum, C., 'Rousseau's Concept of "Virtue" and the French Revolution', in *Enlightment Studies in Honour of Lester G. Crocker*, p. 44, quoting from Rousseau, J.J., *Oeuvres complètes* (edited by B. Gagnebin and M. Raymond), Paris, 1959, vol. x, p. 357.
10 Morley, J., *Rousseau*, vol. ii, pp. 132–133.
11 Gul, R., *Dzerzhinskii*, p. 75.
12 Ibid, p. 80.
13 Melgunov, S. (1), *The Red Terror in Russia*, p. 245.
14 Leggett, p. 158, quoting from *Protokoly IX sezda RKP (b)* (The Protocols of the Ninth Congress of the RCP), p. 398.
15 Conquest, R. (2), *The Great Terror*, pp. 724, 812.
16 Gerson, L., *The Secret Police in Lenin's Russia*, p. 134, quoting from Lenin, 5th edition, vol. xxvi, pp. 404–415.
17 *Dictionary of the Russian Language*, compiled by S.I. Ozhegov, 3rd edition, pp. 305–306.
18 Ascher (1), p. 280.
19 Russell, pp. 100, 101, 102.
20 Medvedev, R. (1), *The October Revolution*, p. 150, quoting from Ustrialov, N., *Pod znakom revolutsii* (Under the Sign of the Revolution), Harbin, 1925, p. 80.
21 Leggett, pp. 250–254.
22 Ibid, pp. 162, 396 (note 36), 187, quoting from Tikunov, V., in *Sovetskoie gosudarstvo i pravo* (Soviet State and Law), no. 8, 1959, p. 22.
23 Gerson, p. 39, quoting from Sofinov, P., *Ocherki istorii vserossiiskoi chrezvychainoi kommissii, 1917–1922 g.* (Essays on the History of the Extraordinary Commission in the Years 1917 to 1922), Moscow, 1960, p. 40.
24 Lenin, 5th edition, vol. xli, p. 383.
25 Ibid, *State and Revolution*, in vol. xxxiii, pp. 1–120.
26 Leggett, p. 320, quoting from *Sedmoi vserossiiskii sezd sovetov* (The Seventh All-Russian Congress of Soviets), pp. 60–63, 75.
27 Gerson, pp. 193–194, quoting from *Pravda*, 8 October 1918, p. 1; and from *Vechernie Izvestiia* (Evening Izvestiia), no. 161, 3 February 1919.
28 Steinberg (1), p. 145.

29 Ibid, p. 152; Melgunov (1), pp. 39–40, quoting from Latsis, M. (1), *Krassnyi terror* (Red Terror).
30 Steinberg, (1), pp. 149–150.
31 Leggett, p. 111, quoting from *Izvestiia*, 3 and 7 September 1918; Chamberlin, vol. ii, pp. 66–67.
32 Leggett, p. 111, quoting from *Collection of Reports on Bolshevism in Russia*, an abridged edition of parliamentary papers on Russia, no. 1 (1919), p. 26.
33 Ibid, pp. 109–110.
34 Ibid, p. 109.
35 Ibid, p. 108, quoting from a Vecheka proclamation published in *Izvestiia*, 3 September 1918.
36 Ibid, p. 112.
37 *Vecheka Weekly*, Moscow, 22 September 1918.
38 Dallin (2), p. 158, quoting from *Krasnaia Gazeta* (Red Journal), Petrograd, 21 August 1918.
39 Bunyan, p. 251, quoting from *The Tenth Congress of the Russian Communist Party*, 1921, pp. 353–355.

Chapter 5: Anti-Bolshevik Revolts and the Civil War

1 Dallin (2), pp. 168–174.
2 Ibid, pp. 166–169; Nicolaevsky, B. (3), *RSDRP (Mensheviki) za vremie s dekabria 1917 po iul 1918* – predvaritelnaia spravka (RSDRP (Mensheviks) During the Period December 1917 to July 1918 — Preliminary Note), pp. 33–38.
3 Leggett, pp. 104, 280; Nicolaevsky, B. (1), *Power and the Soviet Elite*, p. 231.
4 Footman, D., *Civil War in Russia*, pp. 85–93; Schapiro (2), pp. 155–156.
5 Denicke (2), p. 152.
6 Chamberlin, vol. ii, pp. 14–23; Footman, pp. 93–113; Chernov, V. (1), *Mes tribulations en Russie soviétique* (My Tribulations in Soviet Russia), pp. 7–20.
7 Dallin (2), pp. 170–172.
8 Ibid, p. 173; Footman, p. 127.
9 Footman, pp. 232–242.
10 Dallin (2), p. 174.
11 Ibid, pp. 171–174.
12 Chamberlin, vol. ii, p. 112; Leggett, p. 205.
13 Dallin (2), pp. 177–178.
14 Leggett, pp. 290–292; Abramovitch (1), pp. 203–208.
15 Leggett, p. 292, quoting from Duranty, W., *I Write as I Please*,

London, 1935, p. 127; and from Weissman, B., *Herbert Hoover and Famine Relief to Soviet Russia, 1921–1923*, Stanford, 1974, p. 182.

16 Abramovitch (1), p. 190, quoting from data given in Kritsman, L., *The Heroic Period of the Russian Revolution*, 2nd edition, Moscow, 1926, p. 187.

17 Ibid, p. 205; Leggett, p. 246, quoting from Sofinov, p. 215; and from Tsvigun, S., *et al.* (eds), *F.E.Dzerzhinskii: Biografia*, Moscow, 1977, p. 281, which gives the figure of five million.

18 Tsereteli, I., *Vospominaniia o fevralskoi revolutsii* (Recollections of the February Revolution), vol. ii, pp. 76, 133–158; Abramovitch (1), p. 60.

19 Denikin, A., *Ocherki russkoi smuty* (Essays on Russia's Troubles), vol. v, p. 137.

20 Ibid.

21 Ibid, vol. v, p. 122.

22 Ibid, vol. v, p. 223.

23 Ibid, vol. iv, p. 223.

24 Abramovitch (1), pp. 174, 182, quoting from Trotsky, L., *My Life*, London, 1930, pp. 180–181.

25 Volin, V., *The Unknown Revolution: The struggle in the Ukraine*, 1918–1921, part 2, pp. 83 sq.

26 Ibid, pp. 85–87.

27 Abramovitch (1), p. 185.

28 Footman, pp. 232–242.

29 Abramovitch (1), p. 189.

30 Dallin (2), pp. 204–205. The letter, written by Martov, is preserved at the BNC.

31 Leggett, pp. 319–320, quoting from *Izvestiia*, 9 July 1919.

32 Ibid, p. 320, quoting from *The Seventh Congress of Soviets*, pp. 60–63, 79, 80.

33 Dallin (2), p. 223, quoting from 'Tezisy Tsk RSDRP k avgustovskoi konferentsii 1920g.' (Theses of the Central Committee of the RSDRP for the conference of August 1920) (in the BNC).

34 Leggett, pp. 204, 464–465.

35 Zhordania, N., *Moia zhisn* (My Life), pp. 73–120.

36 Chamberlin, vol. ii, p. 415.

37 Pipes, R. (2), *The Formation of the Soviet Union 1917–1923*, p. 237.

38 Ibid, p. 238 (footnote).

Chapter 6: The Harassment of Socialists

1 Dan (2), pp. 59, 136.
2 Schapiro (2), p. 208, quoting from Lenin, 3rd edition, vol. xxvii, pp. 525–526.
3 Ibid, p. 170.
4 Ibid, p. 127, quoting from the Left SR publication *Kreml za reshetkoi: Podpolnaia Rossiia* (Kremlin Behind Bars: Underground Russia), Berlin, 1922, pp. 205–208, 214–216.
5 Chamberlin, vol. i, p. 423; Leggett, p. 35, quoting from *Izvestiia*, 13, 16 and 27 April 1918.
6 Leggett, p. 35, quoting from *Izvestiia*, 27 April 1918.
7 Ibid, pp. 310–311, quoting from *Goneniia na anarkhism v sovetskoi Rossii* (Persecution of Anarchism in Soviet Russia), Berlin, 1922, pp. 27–63; Schapiro (2), p. 184.
8 Leggett, p. 306, quoting from *Doneseniia Komissarov Petrogradskogo VRK* (Reports by the Commissars of the Petrograd VRK), p. 227.
9 Lande, p. 80.
10 Leggett, pp. 306–308.
11 Dallin (2), pp. 158–159, quoting from *Rabochii Internatsional* (Workers' International), Petrograd, no. 11, 14 August 1918.
12 Bunyan, pp. 56–57, quoting from Trotsky's speech of 29 June 1918, in Trotsky (1), vol. xvii, part 1, p. 293.
13 Chamberlin, vol. ii, p. 28.
14 Dallin (2), p. 158, quoting from *Utro Moskvy*, no. 21, 4 November 1918.
15 Leggett, p. 323, quoting from Belov, G. *et al.* (eds), *Iz istorii V Ch K 1917–1921 gg. Sbornik dokumentov* (From the History of the Vecheka in the Years 1917 to 1921. A collection of documents), Moscow, 1958, p. 146.

Chapter 7: The Bolshevik Government Against Workers and Peasants

1 Dan (1), p. 461.
2 Bunyan, pp. 1, 2, 3, quoting from Lenin, 3rd edition, vol. xxi, pp. 399, 402–403, 147–148, 259.
3 Ibid, pp. 6–7, quoting from the Sovnarkom decree of November 1917 and from *Trudy I Vserossiiskogo sezda sovetov narodnogo khosiastva* (The Proceedings of the First All-Russian Congress of Councils of National Economy), Moscow, 1918, p. 104.
4 Ibid, p. 8, quoting from Bunyan, J. and Fisher, H., *The Bolshevik*

Revolution, 1917–1918, Stanford, 1961, p. 279.

5 Ibid, p. 18, quoting from *Izvestiia*, 27 March 1918.

6 Ibid, p. 25, quoting from *Novaia Zhisn*, no. 95, 21 May 1918.

7 Ibid, p. 4.

8 Ibid, pp. 20–21, quoting from a statement made by Shliapnikov to the Central Executive Committee, 20 March 1918.

9 Ibid, p. 21, quoting from an article by Tomskii in *Professionalnyi Vestnik* (Trade Union News), Moscow, nos 7–8, 25 May 1918, p. 7.

10 Ibid, p. 83, quoting from Rykov's speech at the All-Russian Congress of *Guberniia* Departments of the Committee of State Construction, 20–26 June 1919, published in *Narodnoe khosiastvo* (National Economy), Moscow, no. 8, 1919, p. 76.

11 Ibid, pp. 21–22, quoting from a statement made by Gastev at the First All-Russian Congress of Councils of National Economy, 30 May 1918, published in *The Proceedings of the First All-Russian Congress of Councils of National Economy*, p. 380.

12 Ibid, p. 16, quoting from Lenin, 3rd edition, vol. xxii, p. 216.

13 Ibid, p. 48, quoting from Lenin's speech at the Eighth Party Congress, 18 March 1919, in the shorthand report of the Congress, pp. 16–18.

14 Ibid, p. 41, quoting from Lenin's speech at the Second All-Russian Congress of Trade Unions, 20 January 1919, in *Vtoroi Vserossiiskii sezd professionalnykh soiuzov* (Second All-Russian Congress of Trade Unions), p. 54.

15 Ibid, p. 39, quoting from Lenin's speech at the Sixth All-Russian Congress of Soviets, 6 November 1918, in Lenin, 3rd edition, vol. xxiii, pp. 250–251.

16 Ibid, p. 32.

17 Ibid, pp. 48–49, quoting from Lenin's speech at the Eighth Party Congress, 18 March 1919, in the shorthand report of the Congress, pp. 16–18.

18 Dan (2), pp. 55–57; Schwarz, S., *Labor in the Soviet Union*, pp. 188–199; Godson, J., in Schapiro, L. and Godson, J. (eds), *The Soviet Worker: Illusions and Realities*, pp. 115, 123–124.

19 Bunyan, pp. 262–265, referring to the Sovnarkom decree of 5 April 1921, in *Sobranie uzakonenii i rasporiazhenii rabochego i krestianskogo pravitelstva* (Collection of Government Decrees and Regulations), 1921, no. 23/24, article 142.

20 Ibid, page v, quoting from Anikst, A., *Organisatsia rabochei sily v 1920 godu* (Organisation of Manpower in 1920), Moscow, 1920, p. 63.

21 Ibid, p. 121, quoting from Trotsky's speech at the Ninth Party Congress, 30 March 1920, in *The Ninth Congress of the Russian*

Communist Party, pp. 79–81.

22 Ibid, pp. 54–56, quoting from Trotsky's speech at the Fourth Trade Union Conference, in Bunyan, J., *Intervention, Civil War, and Communism in Russia*, Baltimore, 1936, p.268.

23 Ibid, p. 121, quoting from Trotsky's speech at the Ninth Party Congress, 30 March 1920, in *The Ninth Congress of the Russian Communist Party*, pp. 79–81.

24 Lenin, 5th edition, vol. xxxv, pp. 156–158.

25 Bunyan, pp. 109–114.

26 Ibid, p. 103, quoting from Trotsky (1), vol. xv, p. 71.

27 Ibid, p. 119, quoting from *The Ninth Congress of the Russian Communist Party*, p. 16.

28 Ibid, p. 187 (footnote 12), quoting from *Vestnik putei soobshcheniia* (Transport News), Moscow, 1919, no. 12, p. 18.

29 Ibid, pp. 181–188.

30 Ibid, p. 190, quoting from *The Tenth Congress of the Russian Communist Party*, p. 871.

31 Ibid, p. 261.

32 Chamberlin, vol. i, p. 426, quoting from *Znamie Truda* (Banner of Labour), 16 May 1918.

33 Leggett, p. 63, quoting from the *Collection of Government Decrees and Regulations*, 9 May 1918, no. 35, p. 468.

34 Ibid, p. 64, quoting from the *Collection of Government Decrees and Regulations*, 27 May 1918, no. 38, p. 498.

35 Chamberlin, vol. ii, p. 45; Schapiro (2), p. 191.

36 Dallin (2), p. 156.

37 Abramovitch (1), p. 192.

38 Steinberg (1), p. 154.

39 Leggett, p. 64, quoting from *Vestnik Narodnogo Kommissariata vnutrennikh del* (Journal of the People's Commissariat of Home Affairs), Moscow, 1918, nos 21–23, p. 2.

40 Latsis, M. (2), *Dva goda borby na vnutrennom fronte* (Two years of Struggle on the Home Front), p. 75.

41 Leggett, p. 330, quoting from Meijer, J.M. (ed.), *The Trotsky Papers 1920–1922*, The Hague, London, Paris, 1971, vol. ii, p. 481.

42 Melgunov (1), p. 18.

43 Leggett, p. 333, quoting from Meijer, p. 497.

44 Ibid, p. 329, quoting from Belov, pp. 417–421; Dan (2), pp. 170–171; Major, J., *The Western World: Renaissance to the Present*, p. 472.

Chapter 8: The Destruction of Trade Unions, Cooperatives and Soviets

1 Lenin, 5th edition, vol. xli, p. 38.
2 Godson, in Schapiro and Godson (eds), p. 107.
3 Ibid, pp. 109–110.
4 Schapiro (2), p. 202, quoting from *Tretii vserossiiskii sezd professionalnykh soiuzov* (The Third All-Russian Congress of Trade Unions), 6–15 April 1920, pp. 43, 110.
5 Abramovitch (1), p. 122.
6 Dallin (2), pp. 225–228; Schapiro (2), pp. 206–207; Berkman, A., *The Bolshevik Myth*, pp. 133–141.
7 Dan (2), pp. 7–15; Chernov (1), pp. 53–60.
8 Snowden, Mrs Philip, *Through Bolshevik Russia*.
9 Schapiro (2), p. 207.
10 Alexandrova, V., *Perezhitoe (1917–1921)* (Past Life), paper no. 12, Inter-University Project on the History of the Menshevik Movement, pp. 69–82.
11 Schapiro (2), pp. 306, 327–328; Dvinov (1), pp. 89–90.
12 *Socialist Courier*, no. 4, 23 February 1922, pp. 2–4.
13 Ibid, no. 6, 21 March 1922, pp. 5–6; no. 9, 2 May 1922, p. 10.
14 Lenin, 3rd edition, vol. xxvi, p. 87.
15 Bunyan, pp. 245–248, quoting from Kolontai, Alexandra, *Rabochaia opozitsiia* (The Workers' Opposition), Moscow, 1921, pp. 25–29.
16 Ibid, pp. 230–237, quoting from *The Tenth Congress of the Russian Communist Party*, pp. 716–725.
17 Ibid, pp. 221–229, quoting from *The Tenth Congress of the Russian Communist Party*, pp. 703 sq.
18 Ibid, pp. 258–261, quoting from the 'Unity of the party' resolution, in *The Tenth Congress of the Russian Communist Party*, pp. 585–587.
19 Shagin, N., *Sudba kooperatsii* (The Fate of the Cooperative Movement), in *Pamiat* (Memory), no. 5, p. 436.
20 Ibid, pp. 435–437.
21 Ibid, p. 442.
22 Ibid, pp. 447–449.
23 Alexandrova, pp. 53–55.
24 Ibid, p. 56.
25 *Socialist Courier*, no. 5, 5 April 1921, p. 14.
26 Alexandrova, pp. 55–56; Sapir, B. (1), *Memorandum Prepared for the Socialist International, 1927*, pp. 7–8.
27 Denicke (2), pp. 114–123, 150–152, and in *Socialist Courier*, February/March, 1960; Abramovitch (1), pp. 156–165; Aronson,

G. (4), *Dvizhenie upolnomochenykh fabrik i zavodov v 1918 godu* (The Movement of Factory Representatives in 1918), Inter-University Project on the History of the Menshevik Movement, pp. 12–17.

28 *Martov i ego blizkie*, p. 64.
29 Aronson (4), p. 16, quoting from *Iskra*, Moscow, 17 June 1918.
30 Ibid, p. 17, quoting from *Vecher Moskvy* (Moscow Evening), 30 June 1918.
31 Abramovitch (1), pp. 161–163; Denicke (2), pp. 150–152.
32 Abramovitch (1), p. 157.
33 Denicke (2), p. 151
34 Aronson (4), p. 26.
35 Godson, in Schapiro and Godson (eds), pp. 125–128.
36 Denicke (2), p. 118, quoting from Martov, Iu., '*Rabochaia i gosudarstvennaia vlast* (Government by the Workers and by the State), in *Novaia Zhisn*, no. 1, 22 April 1918, p. 15.
37 Lande, pp. 78–79.
38 Nicolaevsky (3), p. 23 (footnote).
39 Aronson (4), p. 23.
40 Denicke (2), pp. 166–169; Nicolaevsky (3), pp. 36–41.
41 Dallin (2), pp. 159–163.
42 Drabkina, E., *Chernyie sukhari. Povest o nenapisannoi knige* (Black rusks. The Story of the Book that was not Written), pp. 148–151.
43 Dallin (2), p. 209.
44 Ibid, p. 210.
45 Dan, in Martov (4), *Geschichte der russischen Sozialdemokratie* (The History of the Russian Social Democracy), p. 318.
46 Dallin (2), p. 236.
47 Ibid.
48 Ibid, p. 237; Dan (2), pp. 87–93.
49 Dallin (2), p. 237.
50 Dan (2), p. 94.
51 Dvinov (1), pp. 57–58.
52 Ibid, p. 46; Wolin, S. (2), in Haimson, p. 262.
53 Dan (2), p. 176; Dvinov (1), pp. 46–47.
54 Dvinov (1), p. 48.
55 Wolin (2), p. 263, quoting from the leaflet issued by the Bureau of the Central Committee, *Vybory v Sovety* (Elections to the Soviets), September 1922 (in the BNC).

Chapter 9: Prisons, Camps, Exile

1 *Socialist Courier*, no. 7(29), 1 April 1922, pp. 8–9.

2 Ibid, no. 11(33), 3 June 1922, pp. 15–16.
3 Lenin, 5th edition, vol. xxxvii, p. 245.
4 Ibid, vol. xli, p. 383.
5 Leggett, pp. 171–172, quoting from Lenin, 2nd edition, vol. xxvi, p. 339.
6 Melgunov (1), pp. 54–55.
7 Sutuzhenko, N., 'La guillotine sèche' (The Dry Guillotine), in *Tche-ka*, p. 62; Abramovitch, R. (2), *Die politischen Gefangenen in der Soviet-Union* (Political Prisoners in the Soviet Union).
8 Leggett, pp. 179–180.
9 *Martov i ego blizkie*, p. 41.
10 Sutuzhenko, in *Tche-ka*, p. 69.
11 Dan (2), p. 59.
12 *Socialist Courier*, no. 2(48), 17 January 1923, p. 17.
13 Dan (2), pp. 131–132; Bezsonov, Iu., *Mes vingt-six prisons et mon évasion de Solovki* (My Twenty-Six prisons and my escape from the Solovki), p. 27.
14 Dallin, D. and Nicolaevsky, B., *Forced Labor in Soviet Russia*, part II, p. 161.
15 Ibid, pp. 206–207.
16 Dan (2), p. 150; Nadezhdin, 'A Year's Detention in Butyrki', in *Tche-ka*, p. 151.
17 *Socialist Courier*, no. 13/14 (35/36), 20 July 1922, p. 8, quoting from the official report by the People's Commissariat of Justice to the Ninth All-Russian Congress of Soviets (printed as a booklet: *Tiuremnoe delo v 1921 g.* (Prison Affairs in 1921) in Moscow by the Taganka prison printers), 32 pp.
18 *Socialist Courier*, no. 13/14 (35/36), 20 July 1922, p. 8.
19 Leggett, p. 193, quoting from *Interim Report of the Committee to Collect Information on Russia*, 1920, pp. 8–10.
20 Aronson (3), p. 70; Nadezhdin, in *Tche-ka*, pp. 175–177.
21 Dan (2), pp. 202–203.
22 *Socialist Courier*, no. 5(27), 5 March 1922, p. 18; Lusmarin, G., 'Le Tcheka de Kuban' (The Cheka of Kuban), in *Tche-ka*, p. 259.
23 Dan (2), pp. 200–201; Aronson (3), p. 76.
24 Dan (2), pp. 191–192.
25 Chumakov, A., 'Le Vaisseau de la Mort' (The Ship of Death), in *Tche-ka*, pp. 28 sq.
26 Dan (2), pp. 118–119.
27 Aronson (3), p. 86; Sutuzhenko, in *Tche-ka*, pp. 71–72.
28 Bezsonov, pp. 146, 204.
29 *Socialist Courier*, no. 21(43), 2 November 1922, p. 15; no. 3(217), 8 February 1930, p. 15.
30 Ibid, no. 23/24 (117/118), 21 December 1925.

31 Aronson (3), pp. 64, 88–92.
32 Dan (2), pp. 160–165.
33 *Socialist Courier*, no. 14(84), 6 July 1924, p. 15.
34 Ibid, no. 9, 5 June 1921, p. 15.
35 *Revolutsionnaia Rossiia* (Revolutionary Russia), no. 2, January 1921, pp. 29–30; Volodin, S., 'Le transport des socialistes au bagne de Iaroslavl, 12 août 1920' (The Transfer of Socialists to the Strict Prison of Iaroslavl, 12 August 1920), in *Tche-ka*, pp. 109–111.
36 Olitskaia, E., *Moii vospominaniia* (My Memories), vol. ii, pp. 190–191.
37 Aronson (3), pp. 109–111.
38 Gernet, M., *Istoriia tsarskoi tiurmy* (The History of the Tsarist Prison), 3rd edition, vol. iv, p. 19.
39 Ibid, vol. i, pp. 217–218; vol. ii, pp. 458–462.
40 Dallin and Nicolaevsky, p. 169.
41 Ibid, pp. 168–170.
42 Sapir, B. (3), 'The Journey to the Northern Camps', in Dallin and Nicolaevsky, p. 173.
43 Dallin and Nicolaevsky, p. 190.
44 Bezsonov, pp. 217–218.
45 Sapir (3), p. 185.
46 Ibid, pp. 185–187; Bezsonov, pp. 189–208.
47 Solzhenitsin, A., *Arkhipelag Gulag* (The Gulag Archipelago), vol. iii, pp. 28–29.
48 Dallin and Nicolaevsky, p. 235.
49 Sapir (3), pp. 174–176, 182–183; *Socialist Courier*, no. 3(73), 11 February 1924, p. 11; no. 21(91), 10 November 1924, p. 13.
50 Sapir (3), p. 177.
51 Sapir (1), p. 3; *Socialist Courier*, no. 22/23 (188/189), 5 December 1928, p. 14.
52 Sapir (3), p. 172.
53 Gernet, vol. i, pp. 232–236; vol. ii, pp. 467–468.
54 Olitskaiia, vol. ii, pp. 133–137, 148.
55 *Socialist Courier*, no. 24(94), 20 December 1924, pp. 13–14; no. 1 (71), 10 January 1924, p. 9.
56 Olitskaiia, vol. ii, p. 157.
57 Sapir (1), pp. 1–2; *Socialist Courier*, no. 1(71), 10 January 1924, pp. 9–10; no. 6(172), 21 March 1928, p. 15; no. 12(178), 23 June 1928, p. 13.
58 *Socialist Courier*, no. 19(185), 13 October 1928, p. 16; unpublished letters from Eva Broido (in the Broido family archive).
59 Unpublished letter from an unidentified Menshevik exiled in

Tashkent, dated 16 May 1922 (in the BNC, no.25, box 4); unpublished letter from Konkordia Zakharova from Saratov, dated 27 April 1928 (in the BNC).

60 Unpublished letter from B. (unidentified Menshevik) exiled to a small place near Uralsk, undated but probably written in 1922–1924 ('Letters from Exile', in the BNC).

61 Three unpublished letters from P.A. (unidentified Menshevik), addressed to Sofia Garvi, dated 10 October 1928, 1 March 1929 and 9 April 1930 (in the BNC).

62 Unpublished letter from Konkordia Zakharova from Saratov, dated 9 September 1929 (in the BNC).

63 Unpublished letter from Konkordia Zakharova from Saratov, dated 29 October 1928 (in the BNC).

64 Unpublished letters from Eva Broido: from Tashkent, dated 19 September 1931 and to the end of 1933, and from Oirot Tura, dated 12 April 1936 (in the Broido family archive).

65 Unpublished letter from Boris Ber (Gurevich) from Vizinga, dated 13 March 1929 (in the Gurevich family archive).

66 *Martov i ego blizkie*, pp. 41–42.

67 Ibid, p. 45.

68 Ibid, pp. 146–147; on the pre- and post- censorship see unpublished letter from Konkordia Zakharova, dated ·20 December 1926, (in the BNC); according to Till, T., 'Sotsial-demokraticheskoe dvizhenie molodezhy 1920-kh godov' (Social Democratic Youth Movement of the 1920s), in *Pamiat*, no. 3, p. 193, Andrei's manuscript was lost.

69 Unpublished letter from Sergei Ezhov, dated 10 October 1924 (in the BNC).

70 Sapir (1), pp. 10–11.

71 Ibid, p. 10; *Martov i ego blizkie*, pp. 138–147; unpublished letter from Konkordia Zakharova, dated 28 February 1927 (in the BNC).

72 *Socialist Courier*, no. 9(79), 17 April 1924, p. 15; *Letters from Russian Prisoners*, p. 20.

73 Unpublished letter from Sergei Ezhov, dated 30 November 1926 (in the BNC).

74 Sapir (1), pp. 8–9; *Martov i ego blizkie*, pp. 39–42.

75 Sapir (1), p. 10.

76 Ibid, pp. 9–10; Alexandrova, p. 60; unpublished biographical notes on Boris Ber (Gurevich) and his wife (in the Gurevich family archive).

77 Unpublished biographical notes on Eva Broido (in the Broido family archive).

78 Unpublished letter from Konkordia Zakharova from Minussinsk,

dated 5 May 1927 (in the BNC); unpublished letters from Eva Broido from Oirot Tura, dated 18 and 26 March 1936 (in the Broido family archive); *Socialist Courier*, no. 2/3(164/165), 5 February, 1927, p. 22.
79 Sapir (1), pp. 5–6.
80 Unpublished letter from an unidentified person, dated 22 July 1963 (in the BNC, no. 25, box 4).
81 Zenzinov, V., a book review in *Novaiia Rossiia* (New Russia), London, no. 3, 5 April 1936 (in the BNC).
82 Sapir (3), pp. 170–171.
83 *Socialist Courier*, no. 8, 20 May 1921, pp. 14–15.
84 Ibid, no. 1(71), 10 January 1924, p. 9; no. 9 (79), 17 April 1924, p. 15.
85 Conquest, R. (1), *The Great Terror*, book 2, The Ezhov Years, pp. 151 sq.
86 Akhmatova, Anna, *Rekviem* (Requiem), p. 8.
87 Chukovskaia, L., *Zapiski ob Anne Akhmatovoi* (Notes on Anna Akhmatova), vol. i, pp. 7–8.
88 Unpublished letter from Jacob (unidentified), dated 17 July 1928 ('Letters from Exile', in the BNC).
89 Alexandrova, pp. 65–69.
90 *Socialist Courier*, no. 14(84), 6 July 1924, p. 14.
91 Ibid, no. 24(94), 20 December 1924, p. 14.
92 Unpublished letter from Eva Broido's daughter Alexandra, dated July 1929 (in the Broido family archive).
93 Broido, V., *Apostles into Terrorists*, pp. 76–77.
94 Martov (1), pp. 133–135.
95 Solzhenitsin, vol. i, p. 53; Berberova, N., *The Italics are Mine*, p. 314; verbal communication from Sofia Erlich-Dubnova.

Chapter 10: A Chronicle of Persecutions and Resistance

1 Denicke (2), pp. 392–393; Nicolaevsky (2), pp. 15, 18, 20, 28, 31; Nicolaevsky (3), pp. 4, 6, 28; Nicolaevsky (5), pp. 15, 39.
2 Wolfe (1), pp. 526–528.
3 Dallin (2), pp. 159–160.
4 Ibid, p. 193.
5 Ibid, pp. 196–197.
6 Ibid, p. 198.
7 Ibid, p. 199.
8 Ibid, p. 197.
9 Ibid, pp. 199–200.
10 Ibid, p. 211.

11 Wolin, S. (1), *Mensheviki na Ukraine, 1917–1921* (The Mensheviks in the Ukraine, 1917–1921), paper no. 11, Inter-University Project on the History of the Menshevik Movement, pp. 121–129; Chizhevskii, D., *Vospominaniia o menshevikakh na Ukraine, 1919–1920* (Recollections of Mensheviks in the Ukraine, 1919–1920) (typrescript, item no. 25, in the BNC).
12 *Socialist Courier*, no. 1, 1 February 1921, p. 15.
13 Ibid, no. 9, 5 June 1921, p. 14.
14 Wolin (2), pp. 264–265; Till, pp. 190, 218–219; Dvinov (1), pp. 27–28.
15 Till, pp. 193–194.
16 Ibid, pp. 187, 205.
17 Ibid, pp. 207, 247.
18 *Socialist Courier*, no. 1, 1 February 1921, p. 15.
19 Ibid.
20 Ibid.
21 Ibid.
22 Ibid.
23 Ibid.
24 Ibid, pp. 15–16.
25 *Martov i ego blizkie*, p. 83; Dallin (2), p. 224; Wolin (2), p. 250.
26 *Socialist Courier*, no. 1, 1 February 1921, p. 16.
27 Ibid, no. 2, 16 February 1921, p. 14.
28 Ibid, no. 1, 1 February 1921, p. 14.
29 Ibid, no. 2, 16 February 1921, p.14.
30 Dvinov (1), pp. 28–32; *Socialist Courier*, no. 5, 5 April 1921, p. 15; no. 6, 20 April 1921, pp. 15–16.
31 *Socialist Courier*, no. 7(29), 1 April 1922, pp. 8–9.
32 Dvinov (1), pp. 33, 37–39; Wolin (2), pp. 250, 289, 308; Sapir (2), p. 375; Broido, Eva, 'Na zare Sotsialisticheskogo Vestnika' (At the Dawn of the Socialist Courier), in *Socialist Courier*, no. 6 (100), 4 April 1925, pp. 21–22.
33 Dvinov (1), pp. 32, 33.
34 Ibid, p. 38.
35 Ibid, pp. 74–75, 127.
36 Getzler, I. (2), *Kronstadt 1917–1921*, pp. 213 sq.; Wolin (2), pp. 244–245.
37 Wolin (2), p. 260; Lenin, 4th edition, vol. xxxiii, p. 253.
38 Till, pp. 167–169, quoting from Lenin, 5th edition, vol. liv, pp. 130–131.
39 *Socialist Courier*, no. 11(33), 3 June 1922, pp. 15–16.
40 Wolin (2), p. 262.
41 *Socialist Courier*, no. 7(29), 30 April 1922, pp. 8–9; Aronson (3), *Na zare krasnogo terrora* (At the Dawn of the Red Terror), pp.

100–105.
42 Volodin, in *Tche-ka*, pp. 220–226; *Revolutsionnaia Rossiia*, no. 2, January 1921, pp. 29–30.
43 *Socialist Courier*, no. 9, 5 June 1921, pp. 7–8.
44 Sutuzhenko, in *Tche-ka*, pp. 77–82.
45 Aronson (3), p. 105.
46 Dvinov (1), p. 45.
47 *Socialist Courier*, no. 9, 5 June 1921, p. 9.
48 Dvinov (1), p. 46.
49 *Social Courier*, no. 9, 5 June 1921, p. 8.
50 Ibid, p. 9.
51 Unpublished letter from Anna Drozdova, dated 4 August 1921 (item 26, no. 6, box 2, in the BNC).
52 Dvinov (1), p. 46.
53 *Socialist Courier*, no. 9, 5 June 1921, p. 11; no. 11 (33), 3 June 1922, p. 12, quoting from a letter by Vladimir Korolenko to Maxim Gorky, dated 29 June 1921: 'History will one day note that the Bolshevik revolution destroyed sincere revolutionaries and socialists by the same methods as the tsarist regime.'
54 Dvinov (1), p. 50.
55 *Socialist Courier*, no. 9, 5 June 1921, p. 11.
56 Dvinov (1), p. 60.
57 Ibid, p. 57; *Socialist Courier*, no. 17, 1 October 1921, pp. 11–12.
58 *Socialist Courier*, no. 10, 19 June 1921, p. 10.
59 Dvinov (1), pp. 50–51; *Socialist Courier*, no. 14/15, 1 September 1921, p. 14.
60 Wolin (2), p. 262.
61 *Socialist Courier*, no. 12, 22 July 1921, pp. 14–15.
62 Ibid, no. 14/15, 1 September 1921, p. 14.
63 Dvinov (1), pp. 57–58; *Socialist Courier*, no. 14/15, 1 September 1921, pp. 8–10.
64 Dvinov (1), p. 61.
65 Ibid, p. 68.
66 Ibid, p. 70.
67 Ibid, p. 71.
68 Ibid, pp. 70–71.
69 Ibid, p. 72.
70 Ibid, p. 76.
71 *Socialist Courier*, no. 16, 16 September 1921, pp. 1–2.
72 Dvinov (1), p. 127.
73 *Socialist Courier*, no. 7(53), 1 April 1923, p. 10.
74 Dan (2), pp. 238–251.
75 Dvinov (1), pp. 82–83. (Boris Sapir informs me that the telegram sent by Lev Lande to Berlin was meant for Grigorii Bienstock.)

76 Ibid, pp. 84–85. (The date of 28 January is a mistake as can be seen from Dan's account: Dan (2), p. 267.)
77 Ibid, pp. 86–88.
78 Ibid, p. 92.
79 *Socialist Courier*, no. 4 (26), 23 February 1922, pp. 9–10.
80 Dvinov (1), p. 93.
81 Leggett, pp. 344–350.
82 Dvinov (1), pp. 96–97; Wolin (2), p. 256.
83 *Socialist Courier*, no. 7(29), 30 April 1922, p. 11.
84 Dan (2), pp. 179–180, 122–123.
85 *Socialist Courier*, no. 11(33), 3 June 1922, pp. 15–16.
86 Ibid, no. 8(30), 20 April 1922, p. 10; Dvinov (1), p. 106.
87 Dvinov (1), pp. 116–117.
88 *Socialist Courier*, no. 13/14, 20 July 1922, pp. 15–16.
89 Dvinov (1), pp. 106, 108.
90 *Socialist Courier*, no. 15(37), 2 August 1922, p. 11.
91 Ibid, no. 17(39), 8 September 1922, p. 11.
92 Ibid, no. 8(30), 20 April 1922, pp. 8–9; Dvinov (1), p. 107.
93 *Socialist Courier*, no. 9(31), 2 May 1922, p. 2.
94 Ibid, no. 10(32), 16 May 1922, p. 11.
95 Ibid, no. 9(31), 2 May 1922, p. 15.
96 Ibid, no. 17(39), 8 September 1922, p. 11.
97 Ibid, no. 11(33), 3 June 1922, p. 15.
98 Dvinov (1), pp. 141–145.
99 *Socialist Courier*, no. 13/14(35/36), 20 July 1922, p. 15; no. 16(38), 16 August 1922, pp. 2–3.
100 Ibid, no. 13/14(35/36), 20 July 1922, p. 18.
101 Ibid, no. 17(39), 8 September 1922, p. 8.
102 Ibid, no. 18(40), 21 September 1922, pp. 1–2, 10.
103 Dvinov (1), p. 152.
104 *Socialist Courier*, no. 21(43), 2 November 1922, p. 15.
105 Ibid, no. 19(41), 4 October 1922, p. 8.
106 Ibid, no. 21(43), 2 November 1922, pp. 14, 15.
107 Ibid, pp. 10–13; unpublished letter from Georgii Kuchin, dated 16/17 October 1922 ('Letters from Russia', file no. 1, in the BNC).
108 Dvinov (1), p. 144.
109 Ibid, pp. 155–156.
110 Sapir (2), pp. 377–388.
111 Dvinov (1), pp. 152, 153, 155; Kuchin, G., 'Notes', in Dvinov (1), pp. 167, 168–169, 173, 184.
112 *Socialist Courier*, no. 7(53), 1 April 1923, p. 1; no. 10 (56), 12 May 1923, p. 18.
113 Ibid, no. 5/6(51/52), 16 March 1923, pp. 16–17; no. 11(57), 12

June 1923, pp. 15–16; no. 12(58), 1 July 1923, pp. 15–16.
114 Ibid, no. 17/18(63/64), 1 October 1923, p. 19.
115 Kuchin, p. 174.
116 Ibid, p. 179.
117 *Socialist Courier*, no.7(53), 1 April 1923, p. 18; no. 8/9(54/55), 24 April 1923, p. 19.
118 Kuchin, pp. 176–181, 190–194; Wolin (2), p. 302.
119 *Socialist Courier*, no. 7(53), 1 April 1923, p. 18; no. 5/6(51/52), 16 March 1923, p. 17; no. 10(56), 12 May 1923, p. 8; no. 12(58), 1 July 1923, p. 8; no. 13(59), 26 July 1923, pp. 7,12; no. 19(65), 18 October 1923, p. 14; no. 21/22(67/68), 27 November 1923, pp. 19–20; Wolin (2), p. 301.
120 Podbolotov, P., 'Borba RKP(b) s menshevismom i krakh partii rossiiskikh menshevikov' (The Struggle of the RCP(b) against Menshevism and the Collapse of the Party of Russian Mensheviks), in Smyshliaev, V. *et al.* (eds), p. 31.
121 *Socialist Courier*, no. 14(60), 16 August 1923, p. 7.
122 Ibid, no. 13(59), 26 July 1923, p. 12.
123 Krupskaia (1), p. 99.
124 *Socialist Courier*, no.10(56), 12 May 1923, p. 18.
125 Ibid, no. 16(62), 16 September 1923, p. 13.
126 Ibid, no. 11(57), 12 June 1923, pp. 1, 8, 11, 14.
127 Ibid, p. 15; Kuchin, p. 182.
128 *Socialist Courier*, no. 11(57), 12 June 1923, pp. 15–16.
129 Kuchin, pp. 173–174.
130 Ibid, pp. 183, 184–186.
131 *Socialist Courier*, no. 17/18(63/64), 1 October 1923, pp. 1, 15, 17.
132 Ibid, no. 14(60), 16 August 1923, p. 11.
133 Ibid, no. 17/18(63/64), 1 October 1923, p. 17.
134 Ibid, no. 13(59), 26 July 1923, p. 12.
135 Ibid, no. 14(60), 16 August 1923, p. 15.
136 Ibid, no. 12(58), 1 July 1923, pp. 10–11.
137 Sapir (2), p. 384; Kuchin, pp. 187–188.
138 *Socialist Courier*, no. 1(71), 10 January 1924, p. 14.
139 Unpublished letter from Georgii Kuchin to the Menshevik Delegation Abroad, dated 14 September 1923 (in the BNC).
140 *Socialist Courier*, no. 17/18(63/64), 1 October 1923, p. 11.
141 Ibid, no. 23/24(69/70), 17 December 1923, p. 10.
142 Ibid, pp. 16, 19; no. 24(94), 20 December 1924, pp. 13–14.
143 Ibid, no. 21/22(67/68), 27 November 1923, p. 19.
144 Ibid.
145 Ibid, p. 20.
146 Ibid, no. 1(71), 10 January 1924, p. 13.
147 Ibid, no. 23/24(69/70), 17 December 1923, p. 9.

148 Ibid, pp. 12–13.
149 Ibid, no. 4(74), 25 February 1924, p. 1; no. 20(90), 22 October 1924, p. 1.
150 Ibid, no. 6(76), 24 March 1924, p. 14.
151 Ibid, no. 2(72), 25 January 1924, p. 12.
152 Ibid, no. 6(76), 24 March 1924, p. 10.
153 Ibid, no. 4(74), 15 February 1924, p. 16.
154 Fischer, pp. 951, 961, quoting from *Pravda*, 15 January and 2 March 1923.
155 Ibid, p. 909, quoting Lenin's personal doctor, Dr Rozanov, in *Vospominaniia o V.I. Lenine,* vol. ii, p. 346; Ulam, A., *The Bolsheviks: The intellectual and political history of the triumph of communism in Russia*, p. 578, quoting from Semashko, N. *et al.*, *What was the Disease from which Lenin Died?*, Leningrad, 1924, p. 35.
156 *Socialist Courier*, no. 2(72), 25 January 1924, p.1.
157 Ibid, no. 7/8(77/78), 4 April 1924, p.24.
158 Ibid, no. 9(79), 17 April 1924, pp. 7–8.
159 Ibid, p. 12.
160 Ibid, no. 11(81), 28 May 1924, p. 15.
161 Ibid, no. 14(84), 6 July 1924, p. 16.
162 Ibid, no. 10(80), 10 May 1924, p. 14.
163 Ibid, no. 12/13(82/83), 20 June 1924, p. 9; no. 15(85), 24 July 1924, p. 13; no. 17(87), 1 September 1924, p. 15.
164 Ibid, no. 15(85), 24 July 1924, p. 14.
165 Wolin (2), pp. 310–319.
166 *Socialist Courier*, no. 3(97), 18 February 1925, pp. 13–14; no. 4(98), 5 March 1925, p. 14.
167 Ibid, no. 12/13(82/83) 20 June 1924, p. 16.
168 Ibid, no. 16(86), 16 August 1924, p. 13.
169 Ibid, no. 17(87), 1 September 1924, pp. 13–14.
170 Ibid, no. 19(89), 8 October 1924, p. 8.
171 Ibid, pp. 8, 15.
172 Ibid, no. 22/23(93/94), 1 December 1924, p. 17.
173 Ibid, no. 18(88), 20 September 1924, pp. 1, 2, 3, 4–5; no. 23/24(117/118), 21 December 1925, p. 11.
174 Ibid, no. 1(95), 17 January 1925, p. 13.
175 Ibid, no. 20(90), 22 October 1924, p. 13; no. 1(95), 17 January 1925, p.13.
176 Ibid, no. 1(95), 17 January 1925, p. 15.
177 Ibid, no. 3(97), 18 February 1925, p. 13.
178 Ibid, pp. 14–15.
179 Ibid, no.4(98), 5 March 1925, p.12.
180 Ibid, pp. 12, 14.

181 Ibid, no. 7/8(101/102), 25 April 1925, p. 14.
182 Ibid, no. 11/12(105/106), 20 June 1925, p. 22.
183 Ibid, no. 13(107), 10 July 1925, p.1; no. 15/16(109/110), 18 August 1925, p. 40; no. 17/18(111/112), 28 September 1925, p. 23; no. 19(113), 15 October 1925, p. 15.
184 Ibid, no. 22(116), 30 November 1925, p.2.
185 Sapir (2), p. 384.
186 Wolin (2), p. 307.
187 Ibid, p. 305.
188 Ibid, p. 317; unpublished letter from the Delegation Abroad to the Bureau in Russia, dated 5 January 1926 (in the BNC).
189 Unpublished letter from the Bureau in Russia to the Delegation Abroad, dated 8 March 1926 (in the BNC).
190 Unpublished letter from the Bureau in Russia to the Delegation Abroad, dated 6 July 1927 and signed Zoë, whose identity remains uncertain (in the BNC).
191 Unpublished letter from the Bureau in Russia to the Delegation Abroad, dated 21 August 1927 and signed Z (in the BNC).
192 Unpublished and unsigned letter from Russia to the Delegation Abroad, dated 22 December 1927 (in the BNC).
193 Unpublished letter from Kharkov, dated 29 December 1928 and signed Sergei (in the BNC).
194 Unpublished letter to the Delegation Abroad, dated March 1928 and signed Victor and Zoë (in the BNC).
195 Unpublished letter to the Delegation Abroad, dated 23 December 1928 and signed Zoë (in the BNC).
196 *Socialist Courier*, no. 1/2(262/263), 23 January 1932.
197 Till, p. 247.

Appendix I: The Trial of the Right SRs

1 Woitinskii, V., *Dvenatsat smertnikov* (The Twelve who are to Die); *Protsess partii SR. K sotsialisticheskim partiiam vsego mira* (An Appeal to the Socialist Parties of the World); Jansen, M., 'A Show Trial under Lenin'; *Socialist Courier* for 1922, starting with no. 7.
2 *Socialist Courier*, no. 8(30), 20 April 1922, p. 10.
3 Martov, Iu., 'Krovavyi fars' (A Bloody Farce), in *Socialist Courier*, no. 12(34), 18 June 1922, pp. 3–7.
4 *Socialist Courier*, no. 15(37), 2 August 1922, pp. 5–6.
5 Ibid, pp. 5–8.
6 Ibid, p. 8.
7 Schapiro (2), p. 167, quoting from *Pravda*, 24 June 1922, p. 3.
8 *Socialist Courier*, no. 17(39), 8 September 1922, p. 9; no. 18(40),

21 September 1922, p. 10; no. 21(43), 2 November 1922, p. 14.

9 Ibid, no. 2(72), 25 January 1924, p. 2.

10 Ibid.

Appendix II: The 'Menshevik' Trial of March 1931

1 *Protsess kontrrevolutsionnoi organisatsii menshevikov, 1 marta–9 marta 1931 g. Stenogramma sudebnogo protsessa, obvinitelnoe zakluchenie i prigovor* (The shorthand record of the court proceedings, indictment and verdict of the trial of the counter-revolutionary organisation of the Mensheviks, 1–9 March 1931); Wolin (2), pp. 394–402; *Socialist Courier*, from February 1931 to the end of the year.

2 *Sovetskie dokumenty* (Soviet documents): M. Iakubovich's letter to the Procurator General of the USSR and biographical notes on M. Iakubovich, reprinted from the Samizdat journal *Khronika tekushchikh sobytii* (Chronicle of Current Events), no. 10, in *Novoe Russkoe Slovo* (The New Russian Word), 11 October 1969 and 10 January 1970.

3 Yasnyi, N., 'A Soviet planner — V. Groman', in *The Russian Review* of January 1954.

Bibliography

Abramovitch, R. (1),* *The Soviet Revolution 1917–1939*, New York, 1962.

——— (2), *Die politischen Gefangenen in der Sowjet-Union* (Political Prisoners in the Soviet Union), published by the Commission for the Study of the Situation of Political Prisoners, Berlin, 1930.

Akhmatova, Anna, *Rekviem* (Requiem), published by the Association of Writers Abroad, Munich, 1963.

Alexandrova, Vera, *Perezhitoe, 1917–1921* (Past Life, 1917–1921), paper no. 12, Inter-University Project on the History of the Menshevik Movement, New York, 1962.

Anon, *Pravda o Kronshtate* (The Truth about Kronstadt), Prague, 1921.

Aronson, G. (1), *Bolshevistskaia revolutsiia i mensheviki* (The Bolshevik Revolution and the Mensheviks), New York, 1955.

——— (2), *Rossiia nakanune revolutsii* (Russia on the Eve of the Revolution), New York, 1962.

——— (3), *Na zare krasnogo terrora* (At the Dawn of the Red Terror), Berlin, 1929.

——— (4), *Dvizhenie upolnomochenykh ot rabochikh fabrik i zavodov v 1918 godu* (The Movement of Factory Representatives in 1918), Inter-University Project on the History of the Menshevik Movement, New York, 1960.

Ascher, A. (1), *Pavel Axelrod and the Development of Menshevism*, Cambridge (Mass.), 1972.

——— (2), *The Mensheviks in the Russian Revolution*, Documents of Revolution series, general editor, Heinz Lubasz, London, 1976.

Avrich, P., *Kronstadt 1921*, Princeton, 1970.

———, *The Russian Anarchists*, Princeton, 1967.

——— (ed.), *The Anarchists in the Russian Revolution*, Documents

*These numbers indicate different works by the same author referred to in the Bibliographical Notes.

of Revolution series, general editor, Heinz Lubasz, London, 1973.
Axelrod, P., articles in *Iskra*, no. 55, 15 December 1903, and no. 57, 15 January 1904.
Balabanova, Angelica (1), *My Life as a Rebel*, New York, 1938.
——— (2), *Impressions of Lenin*, translated by Isotta Cesari from the original Italian *Lenin visto de vicino*, Ann Arbor, 1964.
——— (3), *Lenin* (German translation), Hanover, 1961.
Ber, B. (Gurevich), Letters from exile, 1924–1934, and biographical notes on Boris Ber and his wife Lidia Abramovich (in the Gurevich family archive).
Berberova, Nina, *The Italics are Mine*, translated from the Russian by Philppe Radley, London, 1969.
Berger, J., *Shipwreck of a Generation: Memoirs*, London, 1971.
Berkman, A., *The Bolshevik Myth (Diary 1920–1922)*, New York, 1925.
Bernshtam, M. (ed.), *Nezavissimoe rabocheie dvizhenie v 1918 g.* (Independent workers' movement in 1918), no. 2 of the Studies in Modern Russian History, Documents and Materials, general editor A. Solzhenitsin.
Bezsonov, Iu., *Mes vingt-six prisons et mon évasion de Solovki* (My Twenty-Six Prisons and my Escape from the Solovki), translated from the Russian *Dvatsat shest tiurem i pobeg s Solovkov* by E. Semenov, Paris, 1928. Also exists in English translation.
Blanqui, A., *Textes choisis* (Selected Texts), Paris, 1955.
Blum, Carol K., 'Rousseau's concept of "virtue" and the French Revolution' in *Enlightment studies in honour of Lester G. Crocker*, Oxford: Voltaire Foundation, 1980.
Boni, A. and Boni, Ch. (eds), *Letters from Russian Prisoners*, published for the International Committee for Political Prisoners, New York, 1925.
Bourguina, Anna, *Russian Social Democracy, the Menshevik Movement: A Bibliography*, Stanford, 1968.
Broido, Eva, Letters from prison and exile, 1928–1937 (in the Broido family archive).
——— Letters to Pavel Axelrod, April–October 1920 (in the Broido family archive).
Broido, Vera, *Apostles into Terrorists*, New York, 1977.
Bunyan, J., *The Origin of Forced Labor in the Soviet State, 1917–1921*, Documents and Materials, Baltimore, 1967.
Carr, E.H., *The Bolshevik Revolution 1917–1923*, 3 vols, London, 1950–1953.
Chamberlin, W.H., *The Russian Revolution 1917–1921*, 2 vols, New York, 1935.
Cheka — see *Tche-ka*.

Cherniavin, V., *I speak for the Silent Prisoners of the Soviets*, London, 1935.

Cherniavina, Tatiana, *Escape from the Soviets*, London. 1933.

Chernov, V. (1), *Mes tribulations en Russie soviëtique* (My Tribulations in Soviet Russia), Paris 1921.

——— (2), *The Great Russian Revolution*, New Haven, 1936.

———(3), *Pered burei. Vospominaniia* (Before the Storm: Memoirs), paperback, New York, 1953.

Chizhevskii, D., *Vospominaniia o menshevikakh na Ukraine, 1919–1920* (Recollections of Mensheviks in the Ukraine, 1919–1920) (typescript in the BNC, no. 25, item 2).

Chukovskaia, Lidia, *Zapiski ob Anne Akhmatovoi* (Notes on Anna Akhmatova), Paris, 1976.

Chumakov, A., 'Le Vaisseau de la Mort' (The Ship of Death), in *Tche-ka*, pp. 23–55.

Ciliga, A., *The Russian Enigma*, London, 1940.

Conquest, R.(1), *The Great Terror: Stalin's Purge of the Thirties*, London and Melbourne, 1968.

——— (2), *The Great Terror*, paperback, Harmondsworth, 1971.

Dallin, D. (1), *Posle voin i revolutsii* (After Wars and Revolutions), Berlin, 1922.

——— (2), 'Introduction to the Period of War Communism and the Civil War', 'The Outbreak of the Civil War', 'Between the World War and the NEP', in Haimson, pp. 95–106, 156–190, 191–240.

Dallin, D. and Nicolaevsky, B., *Forced labor in Soviet Russia*, London, 1948.

Dan, F. (1), *Proizkhozhdenie bolshevisma* (Origins of Bolshevism), New York, 1946.

——— (2), *Dva goda skitanii, 1919–1921* (Two Years of Roaming, 1919–1921), Berlin, 1922.

——— (3), 'Die Sozialdemokratie Russlands nach dem Jahre 1908', in Martov (4).

Denicke, G. (1), *Erinnerungen und Aufzätze eines Menscheviken und Sozialdemokraten*, published by the Friedrich Ebert Stiftung, Bonn, 1980.

——— (2), 'From the Dissolution of the Constituent Assembly to the Outbreak of the Civil War' and 'The Social-Democratic Press of 1918', in Haimson, pp. 107–155, 392–393.

Denikin, A., *Ocherki russkoi smuty* (Essays on Russia's Troubles), Berlin, 1925–1926.

Doctorow, G., 'Chronology of Events', in Haimson, pp. 94: i-vi.

Drabkina, Elisaveta, *Chernye sukhari. Povest o nenapisannoi knige* (Black rusks: The Story of a Book that was not Written), Moscow, 1963.

Dvinov, B. (1), *Ot legalnosti k podpoliu (1921–1922)* (From Legality to the Underground), with a Preface by L. Haimson and an Introduction by Boris Sapir, Stanford, 1968.

——— (2), *Moskovskii sovet rabochikh deputatov, 1917–1922. Vospominaniia* (The Moscow Soviet of Workers' Deputies, 1917–1922: Memoirs), paper no. 1, Inter-University Project on the History of the Menshevik Movement, New York, 1961.

Fischer, L., *Zhisn Lenina* (The Life of Lenin), translated into Russian by Omri Renan, London, 1970 (originally published in English, New York and London, 1964).

Garvi, P., *Vospominaniia sotsialdemokrata* (Memoirs of a Social Democrat), New York, 1946.

——— *Revolutsionnye siluety* (Revolutionary Silhouettes), Inter-University Project on the History of the Menshevik Movement, New York, 1962.

———, *The Trade Unions in Russia*, New York, 1958.

Geller, M., *Kontsentrationnyi mir i sovetskaia literatura* (The World of Concentration Camps and Soviet Literature), London, 1974.

Gernet, M., *Istoriia tsarskoi tiurmy* (The History of the Tsarist Prison), 3rd edition, 5 vols, Moscow, 1960–1963.

Gerson, L., *The Secret Police in Lenin's Russia*, Philadelphia, 1976.

Getzler, I. (1), *Martov: A Political Biography of a Russian Social Democrat*, Cambridge and Melbourne, 1967.

——— (2), *Kronstadt 1917–1921*, Cambridge, 1983.

——— (3), 'Martov e i menscevichi primo e dope la revoluzione' (Martov and the Mensheviks Before and After the Revolution), in Hobsbawm, E. *et al.* (eds), *Storia del marxismo*, Turin, 1980, vol. iii/1, pp. 169–192.

Goldman, Emma, *My Disillusionment in Russia*, London, 1925.

———, *Living my Life*, paperback, 2 vols, New York, 1970.

Gorky, M., *Untimely Thoughts: Essays on Revolution, Culture and the Bolsheviks*, 1917–1918, translated by N. Ermolaev, London, 1970.

———, in *Novaia Zhisn (New Life)*, Petrograd, no. 11(24), January 1918.

Government and Opposition, a journal of comparative politics, London.

Grossman, V., *Vse techet* (Everything Flows), Frankfurt on Main, 1970.

Gul, R., *Dzerzhinskii* (Russian edition), New York, 1974.

Haimson, L. (ed.), *The Mensheviks: From the revolution of 1917 to the Second World War*, with contributions by D. Dallin, Iu. Denicke, L. Lande, B. Sapir, S. Wolin and G. Doctorow, translated by Gertrude Vakar, Chicago and London, 1974.

Hingley, R., *The Russian Secret Police: Moscovite, Imperial Russian and Soviet Political Security Operations 1565–1970*, London, 1970.

Hudson, G., *50 Years of Communism, 1917–1967*, London, 1968.

Iskra, Munich, London, Geneva, Vienna, 1900–1904.

Ivanov-Razumnik, R., *Memoirs*, translated by P. Squire, London, New York, Toronto, 1965.

Jansen, M., *A Show Trial under Lenin: The Trial of the Socialist-Revolutionaries in Moscow in 1922*, The Hague, Boston, London, 1982.

Joll, J., *The Anarchists*, London, 1964.

Katkov, G., *Russia 1917: The February Revolution*, London, 1967.

Keep, J., *The Russian Revolution: A study in Mass Mobilization*, London, 1976.

Kochan, L., *Russia in Revolution, 1890–1918*, New York, 1966.

Krupskaia, Nadezhda (1), *Vospominaniia o V.I. Lenine* (Recollections of V.I. Lenin), Moscow, 1959.

——— (2), 2nd edition, Moscow, 1968.

Krylenko, N., *Sudebnye rechi, 1922–1930* (Court Speeches, 1922–1930), Moscow, 1931.

——— *Obvinitelnyie rechi po naiboleie krupnym politicheskim protsessam* (Speeches for the Prosecution at the Most Important Political Trials), Moscow, 1937.

Kuchin, G. (Oranskii), 'Zapiski' (Notes), in Dvinov (1), pp. 167–196.

Kuklin, G., *Severnyi soiuz Russkikh Rabochikh i Stepan Khalturin (1878–1882)* (The Northern Union of Russian Workers and Stepan Khalturin), Geneva, 1904.

Kumar, K., (ed.), *Revolution: The Theory and Practice of a European Idea*, with an introduction by the editor, London, 1971.

Lande, L., 'The Mensheviks in 1917' and 'Some Statistics of the Unification Congress, August 1917', in Haimson, pp. 1–91 and 389–391.

Latsis, M. (1), *Krasnyi terror* (Red Terror), Moscow, 1918.

——— (2), *Dva goda borby na vnutrennom fronte* (Two Years of Struggle on the Home Front), Moscow, 1920.

——— (3), *Chrezvychainyie kommissii po borbe s kontrrevolutsiei* (Extraordinary Commissions for the Struggle Against the Counter-Revolution), Moscow, 1921.

Leggett, G., *The Cheka: Lenin's Political Police*, Oxford, 1981.

Lenin, V., *Sochineniia* (Works), 3rd edition, Moscow, 1935–1937; 4th edition, Moscow, 1946–1950; 5th edition, Moscow, 1958–1966.

Lenin i Stalin. Sbornik (Lenin and Stalin: An Anthology), Moscow, 1936.

'Letters from exile' (in the BNC).

'Letters from Russia' (in the BNC).

Letters from Russia to the Menshevik Delegation Abroad, 1921–1929 (in the BNC).

Letters from the Delegation Abroad to the Bureau of the Central Committee in Russia, 1927–1928 (in the BNC).

Liebich, A., 'I menscevichi di fronte alla construzione dell 'Urss' (The Mensheviks and the Construction of the Soviet Union), in Hobsbawm, E. *et al.* (eds), *Storia del marxismo*, Turin, 1980, vol. iii/2, pp. 131–162.

——— *Les Mensheviks en exil face à l'Union sovietique* (The Mensheviks in exile and the Soviet Union), Research report no. 4, Interuniversity Centre for European Studies, Montreal, 1982.

Lunacharskii, A., *Revolutionary Silhouettes*, translated from the Russian and edited by Michael Glenny, with an Introduction by Isaac Deutscher, London, 1967.

Lusmarin, G., 'Le Tcheka de Kuban' (The Cheka of Kuban), in *Tche-ka*, pp. 250–289.

Major, J., *The Western World: Renaissance to the Present*, London, 1967.

Makintsian (ed.), *Krasnaia kniga VCHK* (The Red Book of the Vecheka), vol. i, Moscow, 1920.

Maksimov, G., *The Guillotine at Work*, Chicago, 1940.

Malitskii, A., *Cheka i GPU* (The Cheka and the GPU), Kharkov, 1923.

Martov, Iu. (1), *Zapiski sotsial-demokrata* (The Journal of a Social Democrat), Berlin, 1922.

——— (2), *Doloi smertnuiu kazn*! (Down with the Death Penalty!), Moscow, 1918.

——— (3), *Bolshevism v Rossii i v Internatsionale* (Bolshevism in Russia and in the International), speech given at the Congress of the German Independent Socialist party at Halle, 15 October 1920, published by the *Socialist Courier*, Berlin, 1923.

——— (4), *Geschichte der russischen Sozialdemokratie*, mit einem Nachtrag von Th. Dan: Die sozialdemokratie Russlands nach dem Jahre 1908 (History of the Russian Social Democracy, with a postscript by F. Dan: Russian social democracy after 1908), Berlin, 1926.

——— (5), 'Kravavyi fars' (A Bloody Farce), in *Socialist Courier*, no. 12(34), 18 June 1922, pp. 3–7.

Martov, L., Maslov, P. and Potresov, A. (eds), *Obshchestvennoe dvizhenie v Rossii v nachale XX veka* (Social Movements in Russia at the Beginning of the Twentieth Century), 4 vols, St Petersburg, 1909–1914.

Martov i ego blizkie (Martov and his Family), New York, 1959.

Materials (on conditions in Russia) prepared by Russian Mensheviks for the British Labour Delegation, 1920 (in the BNC, no. 6, box I, document 16(2)).

Medvedev, R. (1), *The October Revolution*, translated by George Saunders, with a foreword by Harrison E. Salisbury, London, 1979.

——— (2), *On Socialist Democracy*, translated and edited by Ellen de Kadt, paperback, New York, 1977.

Melgunov, S.(1), *The Red Terror in Russia*, London, 1926. Originally published in Russian as *Krasnyi terror v Rossii 1918–1923*, Berlin, 1924.

——— (2), *Kak bolsheviki zakhvatili vlast* (How the Bolsheviks Seized Power), Paris, 1939.

Melgunova-Stepanova, P., *Gde ne slyshno smekha* (Where Nobody Laughs), Paris, 1928.

Mett, Ida, *La Commune de Cronstadt: Crépuscule sanglant des Soviets* (The Commune of Kronstadt: the Bloody Twilight of the Soviets), Paris, 1949.

Meyer, J., *Leninism*, Cambridge (Mass.), 1957.

Miller, J., 'Kalinin and the Jews: a Possible Explanation', in *Soviet Jewish Affairs*, vol. 4, no. 1, 1974, pp. 61–65.

Molnar, Th., *Utopia: The Perennial Heresy*, New York, 1967.

Morley, J., *Rousseau*, London, 1915.

Nadezhdin, 'A year's detention in Butyrki', translated by S. Danilov, in *Tche-ka*, pp. 151–187.

Nicolaevsky, B. (1), *Power and the Soviet Elite*, edited by Janet Zagoria, New York, Washington, London, 1965.

——— (2), *Mensheviki v dni oktiabrskogo perevorota* (The Mensheviks in the Days of the October Coup), paper no. 8, Inter-University Project on the History of the Menshevik Movement, New York, 1962.

——— (3), *RSDRP (mensh.) za vremie s dekobria 1917 po iul 1918 (predvoritelnaia spravka)* (RSDRP (Mensh.) During the Period December 1917 to July 1918: a Preliminary Note), no date (typescript in my possession).

——— (4), *RSDRP (Mensheviki) v pervyie gody revolutsii – 1917–1918* (RSDRP (Mensheviks) in the First Years of the Revolution), no date (typescript in my possession).

——— (5), *Menshevism v period voennogo kommunisma, 1918–1921* (Menshevism During the Period of War Communism, 1918–1921), no date (typescript in my possession).

——— (6), *Grupa 'sibirskikh zimmerwaldistov'* (The Group of 'Siberian Zimmerwaldists'), no date (typescript in my possession).

Novoe Russkoe Slovo (The New Russian Word), New York.

Nomad, N., *Apostles of Revolution*, London, 1939.

Olitskaia, E., *Moi vospominaniia* (My Memoirs), 2 vols, Frankfurt on

Main, 1973. First appeared in Samizdat.

Pamiat (Memory), a historical journal, Paris.

Peters, Ia., 'Vospominaniia o rabote v VCHK v pervyi god revolutsii' (Recollections of my Work in the Vecheka in the First Year of the Revolution), in Burtsev, V. (ed.), *Byloe* (The Past), vol. 47, Paris, 1933.

Pethybridge, R. (ed.), *Witnesses of the Russian Revolution*, New York, 1967.

Pipes, R. (1), *Social Democracy and the St Petersburg Labour Movement, 1885–1897*, Cambridge (Mass.), 1963.

——— (2), *The Formation of the Soviet Union 1917–1923*, Cambridge (Mass.), 1964.

——— (3), *Russia Under the Old Regime*, paperback, Harmondsworth, 1977.

Platforma RSDRP (The Platform of the RSDRP), published by the *Socialist Courier*, Berlin, 1924.

Podbolotov, P., 'Borba RKP(b) s *menschevizmom* i krakh partii rossiiskikh menshevikov' (The Struggle of the RCP(b) against Menshevism and the Collapse of the Party of Russian Mensheviks), in Smyshliaev, V. *et al.* (eds), pp. 23–57.

Protsess kontrrevolutsionnoi organisatii menshevikov (1 marta–9 marta). Stenogramma sudebnogo protsessa, obvinitelnoe zakluchenie i prigovor (The shorthand record of the court proceedings, indictment and verdict of the trial of the counter-revolutionary organisation of the Mensheviks, 1–9 March), Moscow, 1931; English edition, London 1931.

Protsess partii SR. Rechi gosudarstvennykh obvinitelei: Lunacharskogo, Pokrovskogo, Krylenko; predstavitelei Kominterna: K. Zetkin, Moon, Bokani (The trial of the party of the SRs, the speeches of the state prosecutors: Lunacharskii, Pokrovskii, Krylenko; the representatives of the Comintern, Klara Zetkin, Moon and Bokani), printed from the shorthand report of the trial in *Krasnaia Nov* (Red Virgin Soil), Moscow, 1922.

Protsess partii SR. K sotsialisticheskim partiiam vsego mira (The Trial of the SRs: An appeal to the socialist parties of the world), signed by the members of the SR Delegation Abroad: V. Zenzinov, I. Rubanovich, N. Russanov, V. Sukhamlin, V. Chernov, Berlin, 9 March 1922 (in the BNC, no. 17, box I, document 19).

Rabinovitch, A., *The Bolsheviks Come to Power: The Revolution of 1917 in Petrograd*, New York, 1976.

Radkey, O., *The Sickle and the Hammer: The Russian Socialist Revolutionaries in the Early Months of Soviet Rule*, New York and London, 1963.

——— *The Agrarian Foes of Bolshevism: Promise and Defeat of the*

Russian Socialist Revolutionaries, February to October 1917, New York, 1958.

Revolutsionnaia Rossiia (Revolutionary Russia), newspaper of the SR party, Tallin.

Rigby, T., Brown, A. and Reddaway, P. (eds), *Authority, Power and Policy in the USSR*, Essays dedicated to Leonard Schapiro, London, 1983.

Russell, B., *The Practice and Theory of Bolshevism*, London, 1920.

Sapir, B. (1), *Memorandum Prepared for the Socialist International, 1927* (unpublished typescript in the Boris Axelrod papers at the IISH).

——— (2), 'Notes and Reflections on the History of Menshevism', in Haimson, pp. 349–388.

——— (3), 'The Journey to the Northern Camps', in Dallin and Nicolaevsky, pp. 170–188.

Schapiro, L. (1), *The Communist Party of the Soviet Union*, 2nd edition, London, 1970.

——— (2), *The Origin of the Communist Autocracy*, 2nd edition, London, 1977.

——— (3), *1917: The Russian Revolutions and the Origins of Present-Day Communism*, London, 1984.

——— (4), 'Russia's "Minority Men"', in *The Russian Revolution*, pp. 51–66.

——— *Totalitarianism*, London, 1972.

——— 'Trotsky "wie er eigentlich gewesen"', in *Government and Opposition*, vol. 17, no. 3, 1982, pp. 259–267.

——— 'Reflections after Kerensky: On the Passing of a Myth', in *Encounter*, vol. xxxv, no. 4, October, 1970, pp. 42–45.

Schapiro, L. and Godson, J. (eds), *The Soviet Worker: Illusions and Realities*, 2nd edition, London, 1982.

Schapiro, L. and Reddaway, P. (eds), *Lenin the Man, the Theorist, the Leader: A Reappraisal*, London, 1967.

Schwarz, S., *Labor in the Soviet Union*, New York, 1951.

——— *The Russian Revolution of 1905*, translated by Gertrude Vakar, Chicago and London, 1967.

Serge, Victor (Kibalchich), *Memoirs of a Revolutionary, 1901–1941*, translated and edited by Peter Sedgwick, paperback, London, Oxford, New York, 1967.

——— *Conquered City*, translated and introduced by Richard Greeman, paperback, London, 1978.

Shagin, N., 'Sudba kooperatsii' (The Fate of the Cooperative Movement), in *Pamiat* (Memory), no. 5, 1982, pp. 435–458.

Shalamov, V., *Raskazy o lageriakh* (Stories from the Camps), Samizdat.

Shub, D., *Lenin: A Biography*, paperback, Harmondsworth, 1966.

Smyshliaev, V. *et al.* (eds), *Borba kommunisticheskoi partii protiv neproletarskikh partii, grup i techenii* (The Struggle of the Communist Party against Nonproletarian Parties, Groups and Currents), (published by Leningrad University for the use of university teachers and others), Leningrad, 1982.

Snowden, Mrs Philip, *Through Bolshevik Russia*, London, 1920.

Solzhenitsin, A., *Arkhipelag Gulag* (The Gulag Archipelago), 4 vols, Paris, 1973–1974.

Sotsialisticheskii Vestnik (Socialist Courier), Berlin, Paris, New York, 1921–1965.

Sovetskie dokumenty: M. Iakubovich's letter to the Procurator General of the USSR and biographical notes on M. Iakubovich, reprinted from the Samizdat journal *Khronika tekushchikh sobytii* (Chronicle of Current Events), in *Novoe Russkoe Slovo* (The New Russian Word) of 11 October 1969 and 10 January 1970.

Soviet Jewish Affairs, London.

Steinberg, I. (1), *In the Workshop of the Revolution*, London, 1955.

——— (2), *Spiridonova*, London, 1935.

Sukhanov, N. (1), *The Russian Revolution 1917*, edited, abridged and translated by Joel Carmichael, London, New York, Toronto, 1955.

——— (2), *Zapiski o revolutsii* (Notes on the Revolution), 7 vols, Berlin, Petrograd, Moscow, 1922–1923.

Sutuzhenko, N., 'La guillotine sèche' (The Dry Guillotine), in *Tche-ka*, pp. 56–84.

Szamuely, T., *The Russian Tradition*, edited and introduced by Robert Conquest, London, 1974.

Tche-ka. Matériaux et documents sur la terreur bolcheviste recueillis par le bureau central du parti socialiste-révolutionnaire russe (The Cheka: Materials and documents on Bolshevik terror collected by the central bureau of the Russian SR party), translated into French by E. Pierremont, Paris, 1922.

The Russian Revolution, a CBC Legacy book, New York, 1967.

Till, T., 'Sotsial-demokraticheskoe dvizhenie molodezhy 1920-kh godov' (The Social-Democratic Youth Movement of the 1920s), in *Pamiat*, no. 3, 1980, pp. 165–283. (Originally appeared in Samizdat in Moscow, in 1978).

Trotsky, L. (1), *Sochineniia* (Works), Moscow, Leningrad, 1927.

——— (2), *The History of the Russian Revolution*, translated by Max Eastman, London, 1936.

Tsereteli, I., *Vospominaniia o fevralskoi revolutsii* (Recollections of the February Revolution), 2 vols, The Hague, 1963.

Ulam, A., *The Bolsheviks: The Intellectual and Political History of the Triumph of Communism in Russia*, New York, 1965.

Upovalov, I., 'Vospominaniia rabochego sotsial-demokrata. Kak my poteriali svobodu' (The Memoirs of a Social-Democratic Worker: How we Lost Freedom), in *Zaria* (The Dawn), Berlin, 1922.

Valentinov, N. (1), *Vstrechi s Leninom* (Meetings with Lenin), New York, 1953.

——— (2), 'Rannie gody Lenina' (Lenin's Early Years), in *Novyi Zhurnal* (The New Journal), New York, no. 36, pp. 220–237; no. 37, pp. 211–235; no. 38, pp. 176–196.

Vishinskii, A., *Revolutsionnaia zakonnost na sovremennom etape, 1917–1933* (Revolutionary Legality at the Present Stage), Moscow, 1933.

Volin, V. (Eikhenbaum), *The Unknown Revolution: Kronstadt, 1921/Ukraine, 1918–1921*, translated by Holley Cantine, London, 1955.

Volodin, S., 'Le transport des socialistes au bagne de Iaroslavl, 12 août 1920' (The Transfer of Socialists to the Strict Prison of Iaroslavl, 12 August 1920), in *Tche-ka*, pp. 219–239.

Vospominaniia o V.I. Lenine (Recollections of V.I. Lenin), (a collection of articles), vol. i, Moscow, 1956.

Weeks, A., *The First Bolshevik: A Political Biography of Peter Tkachev*, New York, London, 1968.

Wildman, A., *The Making of a Workers' Revolution*, Chicago, London, 1967.

Woitinskii, V., *Dvenatsat smertnikov* (The Twelve who are to Die), Berlin, 1922.

Wolfe, B. (1), *Three who Made a Revolution*, paperback, Harmondsworth, 1966.

——— (2), *Revolution and Reality*, North Carolina, 1981.

——— (3), *The Bridge and the Abyss: The Troubled Friendship of Maxim Gorky and V.I. Lenin*, London, 1967.

Wolin, S. (1), *Mensheviki na Ukraine, 1917–1921* (Mensheviks in the Ukraine, 1917–1921), paper no. 11, the Inter-University Project on the History of the Menshevik Movement, New York, 1962.

——— (2), 'The Mensheviks under the NEP and in Emigration' and 'The "Menshevik" Trial of 1931', in Haimson, pp. 241–348 and 394–402.

Yasnyi, N., 'A Soviet planner–V. Groman', in *The Russian Review*, of January, 1954.

Zenzinov, V., Book review in *Novaiia Rossiia*, London, no. 3, 5 April 1936 (in the BNC).

Zhordania, N., *Moiia zhisn* (My Life), translated from the Georgian into Russian by Ina Zhordania, with an Introduction, in English, by L. H. Haimson, Stanford, 1968.

Index